# The Span... Coaching Bible

## Volume Two
## High School & College

**Laureano Ruiz**

**Library of Congress
Cataloging - in - Publication Data**

by Laureano Ruiz
    Spanish Soccer Coaching Bible
    Volume Two - High School & College

ISBN No. 1-59164-022-9
Lib. of Congress Catalog No. 2002107646
© 2002

*Translated at Bray's English
Centre, Santander by*
Jimmy Basterrechea and
Alan Bray

*Editor*
Bryan R. Beaver

*Printed by*
DATA REPRODUCTIONS
Auburn, Michigan

Reedswain Publishing
612 Pughtown Road
Spring City, PA 19475
800.331.5191
www.reedswain.com
info@reedswain.com

# Table of Contents

iv

# *F* *oreword:*
## *The Early Days to the Glory Days*

Life is wonderful now that I am playing for the best club in the world, Real Madrid. I am trying to think of a way to describe the feeling of winning the European Cup but the sensations are so overwhelming it is difficult to put it into words. I have come a long way since my debut in a Real Madrid shirt in 1998 and I have won the league and the Supercup and I have the chance of playing in the World Cup.

But it is a mistake to take success for granted. The only way to reach the top is by suffering, working hard and above all learning as much as possible on the field of play.

When I was a boy all I ever wanted to do was to play soccer 24 hours a day, every day. Me and my brother Luis (who plays for Udinense in Italy) were called Zipy and Zape (two mischievous brothers - comic characters) because we used to break everything with the ball. Whilst our friends were experiencing the new sensations of adolescence you could always find me and my brother on the local soccer yard dreaming of scoring goals in The Santiago Bernabeu. When I think about these days now the hair on the back of my neck stands up because it has all come true, even the goals in the Charmartín stadium. I have to thank three people for where I am today. First and foremost my parents Luis and Josefina to whom I shall be eternally grateful. They recognized my potential and have made every sacrifice to do everything possible for their two sons. The third person who has had the greatest influence on my professional development is Laureano. I have never had a coach with more knowledge of the game. He is a true scholar of the sport and he knows soccer inside out.

He made us study the game. Yes, I remember that every week we had a theoretical test. It was just like being in school. Everything I learned, I learned thanks to him. It is true that every coach you come into contact with teaches you something, but I learned the most important aspects of the game with Laureano. He always used to say to me:

"Ivan you have great quality but above all TALENT which is hard to find, make full use of it." If you are reading this book you will see what I am referring to.

I spent my early childhood years under his tutorship at the Municipal Soccer School in Santander and later when I was playing for Racing. Laureano was no longer the coach at the club when I was 17 years old but he advised the technical team to promote me to the first team. Everybody thought he was mad. Not only did they ignore his recommendation but they forced me to leave the club, saying that I was not good enough. Laureano shrugged his shoulders and sat down calmly to speak with my father. He said that the best thing for me to do was to go elsewhere and play, even if this meant dropping down in class. The most important thing at this stage was to be playing and everything would turn out just fine.

This is exactly what happened. After playing for Manchego, Albacete, Roma and Español I made it to Real Madrid, the best club in the world. This year, I am also proud to say that I have been selected as a potential candidate to win the 'Golden Ball'.

But I am not the only one. It is incredible, but thanks to Laureano a great many players of my generation made it to the top: Iván de la Peña, my brother Luis, Munitis, Ismael…

I can guarantee you that a great coach will get you to the top in the game. Laureano is the best and this book will show you how to become a 'star' either as a player or as a coach.

Iván Helguera

Ivan Helguera, after winning the
Champions Cup with Real Madrid.

# The Laureano Ruiz Method

Soccer began in England in 1863, which means it is still in it's infancy. Moreover, until 1925 what was then called soccer was more similar to the game of rugby. The game involved very little passing and the best players were always the strongest and the most powerful. This is because the rules were very different in those days and the most valuable players were those who could:
-challenge well and even knock an opponent over
-kick the ball a long way
-run quickly

Soccer has only become more technical and skilful in the last 50 years. But this is a relatively short time to study and develop such a complex and varied sport, which is full of creativity and improvisation. There is still so much to discover and learn about the game, including appropriate training methods with the right quality and quantity of the exercises. There is so much to learn about the best form of defense and the best form of attack both on an individual and especially on a collective basis.

Well-respected coaches such as Capello, Valdano, Trapattoni, Clemente etc. all maintain that the defense can be properly drilled and prepared but the attack is up to the individual inspiration of the players. What is really incredible is the fact that people actually listen to this nonsense (can you imagine a basketball coach saying that it is impossible to organize and prepare the attack?). In any case, if this was true (which it isn't) there would be no need for coaches in the game!

I have spent 50 years as a coach (at one stage I played and coached at the same time) and I have really studied the game and come up with my own method.

These are the guiding principles:

1. Players should start playing the game when they are 6-8 years old, even though the learning curve becomes a lot steeper from the age of 10-11. This is the age (normally) when the nervous system develops the necessary links to allow the child to perform complicated motor skills. If this natural development does not take place during puberty then it is very unlikely to be improved unlike other physical attributes that are best worked on when the players are adults.

2. Nobody needs extra special physical characteristics in order to play soccer, unlike in some other sports (height for basketball, white fibers for sprinters, long arms for boxing etc). Anyone can take up soccer and become one of the 'greats', even if they are short, fat, one footed and cannot head a ball as demonstrated by Puskas, Kopa, Sívori and Maradona.

3. The only way to master the sport and become a top player is to spend 10 years practicing 3-4 hours per day. The practice could involve: playing a match, performing ball-juggling skills, practicing crossing the ball to a friend and vice versa, watching and studying videos of the 'Greats' in the game etc. The best way to learn is to observe a top player and then practice the technique under the guidance of a knowledgeable coach.

4. It is important for players of different ages to train differently. Players should never train in the same way as professionals. Even 10 and 13 year old players should train differently. Of course the older the player the better the standard. Unfortunately, lots of coaches at grass roots level go to watch the professionals train in the morning and then get their own players to train in the same way in the afternoon.

5. The quality and technique is learned by practicing ball-juggling skills, familiarization of soccer-related movements, playing 'rounds', 'small-sided' games and matches. The player should start practicing ball-juggling skills from day one. These constant movements with the feet require great balance and coor-

dination that over time allow the player to develop a tremendous 'touch' and control of the ball (especially in the danger areas of the pitch) and a very high skill level. Players also practice by playing soccer-tennis, by doing exercises at the 'suspended ball' or against a wall.

6. The soccer-related movements are: twists and turns, speed off the mark, stopping suddenly, changing direction etc. These attributes allow the player to exploit the space and create chances. 'The method' uses a variety of different games and exercises to develop these qualities: relays in a cone obstacle course, playing in a restricted area, practicing with more space, running in a zigzag, playing in triangular-shaped and square-shaped areas etc.

7. As far as the ball-juggling skills and the soccer-related movements are concerned (all 'the method' really) the overriding principle is 'Step by Step Achievements'. In other words, master one step before attempting the next. The players are given skills to learn that, although difficult, with practice are achievable and within their capabilities. This keeps the player motivated, makes him work that little bit harder and keeps him interested.

8. The player gains a real understanding of the logic of the game and how it works. The stages are as follows:

    a) Learn to play with a light-weight rubber ball (not a full-sized leather ball). Learn to control the ball, run with it and dribble. At first the practice is on an individual basis.

    b) Learn to play with teammates (playing with a number 4 ball). The player still concentrates on individual play but learns to form part of a team and the 'magical' world of passing is experienced for the first time.

    c) Learn to play against and overcome the opposition (playing with a regulation size ball). Many players do very well in the first two stages only to fail in this one as they are unable to compete against players of similar ability but who have more determination and bravery.

**9.** In order to achieve the objectives in the above three stages 'the method' uses the 'less is more' approach. Start off small and with fewer players:

- *Fewer players.* The players have more opportunity to practice and get involved in the game as there are fewer players. This makes the games more intense and encourages the players to learn the tactical and technical side of the game quickly and it also helps improve physical fitness.

- *Smaller pitch.* This makes the activity an aerobic one and thus helps to improve physical fitness levels. The small playing area also helps the players to understand the game a lot better.

- *Smaller goals.* If the beginners play in a regulation size goal they can do little more than look on helplessly as the ball bounces over their head or flies past them. They are too small to do anything about it even if they jump and dive. The outfield players also learn bad habits and shoot from anywhere, knowing that there is a good chance of scoring in the 'huge' goal. As these players get older suddenly their 'great' shot from distance will not be effective and they will lack the necessary quality technique because they never practiced it.

- *Smaller ball.* A lighter ball is used in order to avoid injury and to allow the players to control the ball and manipulate it more easily.

**10.** A series of 'Golden rules' are used throughout the training sessions involving the 'small-sided' games, games and 'rounds':

**a)** *Evenly matched teams.* The two teams should always be evenly matched both in ability and as far as physical fitness is concerned. This type of competition has both a physiological and psychological effect on the players as they build up reserves to confront the opposition. If the teams are not evenly matched and no effort is involved, the body is not prepared for a 'real' match against a stiff opposition.

4

**b)** *Play the 'offside' rule.* It is not possible to fully understand the game unless this rule is fully understood. The very young only play 'offside' near the goals. Once the players reach 11-13 the 'offside' rule is played in the 18-yard box. The rule is used as normal once the players reach the age of 14.

**c)** *Playing 'one-touch and not playing 'one-touch.* Playing the ball 'first-time' is a very difficult thing to do, so the beginners do not even attempt to do it. Nor do I ask them to 'look up' as it is difficult enough for them to keep the ball under control when they totally focus on it. However, the player should start playing 'one-touch' once he has achieved a good technique and 'feel' for the game. From this moment on the player should try to master this skill by practicing it over and over again.

**d)** *Marking.* Beginners are not expected to mark as they have enough trouble trying to learn how to play with the ball first on an individual basis and then with teammates. However, once these early skills are mastered the main objective during the training sessions is to practice beating an opponent in order to attack and score goals. From this moment on tight marking is imperative.

**5**

**e)** *Playing a system.* This is defined as the following: each player is given a defined role in the team and an area on the pitch where he will primarily play, all in accordance with a predetermined match plan.

The learning process is based on progressive development that starts with '5-a-side' games and progresses to '11-a-side' games.

**'5-a-side' (players 9-10 years old)**

| Line Up | 1-2-1 |
|---------|-------|
| Pitch | 40 x 28 m |
| Goals | 4 x 2 m |
| Ball | Small Rubber |

This line up is flexible and varies depending on the circumstances of the game and the individual creativity of the players. At this stage, none of the players (including the goalkeepers) play in a certain position as they continually swap in order to experience playing in each position.

**'7-a-side' (players 11-12 years old)**

| Line Up | 3-1-2 |
|---------|-------|
| Pitch | 68 x 50 m |
| Goals | 6 x 2.10 m |
| Ball | Size 4 |

The 3 players at the back defend in zones and join the attack whenever possible (there should always be 2 players at the back). The player in midfield has to have plenty of stamina because he has to continually run from one end of the pitch to the other, always ready to defend, start attacking moves and finish them off with a shot at goal. The 2 players up front play very wide, almost like conventional wingers, in order to use the whole width of the pitch to create more space for the attacks.

**'9-a-side' (players 13-14 years old)**

| Line Up | 3-2-1-2 |
|---------|---------|
| Pitch | 18 to 18, Full Width |
| Goals | 6 x 2.10 m |
| Ball | Size 4 |

One of the 3 players at the back acts as a 'sweeper' and the other 2 act as markers. The 'sweeper' has to 'read' the game and use his anticipation skills in order to cover and support his 2 teammates. The 2 midfield players perform the dual role of defender and attacker which requires plenty of stamina, sacrifice and above all, creativity. One of the players plays between the midfield and the attack and acts as the 'link' between the two. At the start the forwards are positioned very wide like conventional wingers. But these players are the goal-scorers in the team and to do this they move into the center-forward's position when appropriate.

**'11-a-side' (players from 15 years old)**

| Line Up | 4-3-3 |
|---------|-------|
| Pitch | Regulation Size |
| Goals | Regulation Size |
| Ball | Size 5 |

One of the 4 players at the back acts as a 'sweeper' and the other 3 are markers. The 3 midfield players need plenty of stamina as they play both in defense and in attack, but above all they need creativity. There are 3 attackers, 1 plays in the middle and the other 2 play very wide and act as 'beacons'. They stay up front and should always be available to receive the ball. The '11-a-side' game is very similar to, but is the natural progression from the '9-a-side' game.

The 'small-sided' games and games played during training also focus on playing a certain system or formation. The players are given a certain role and position on the pitch where they learn to position themselves correctly, use the space effectively and support each other. This means that a certain harmony evolves whereby the player supports the team and the team supports the player.

**f)** Not many coaches get their teams to play with a system and those who do believe that this can only be learned in theory at the blackboard and not in practice on the training pitch. Unfortunately, once the team plays against an opposition the talks and advice serve no purpose and the team usually has no idea how to put the theory into practice. The players forget all they were told and chaos prevails as all the players have different ideas and play their own way. However, if after the theory the players go and practice the positions and movements repeatedly on the training pitch they are able to remember and play the system during official matches. The movements and system of play becomes automatic and the players do it without thinking because they have done it over and over on the training ground.

**11.** There are certain movements and ways of playing both in defense and in attack.

**In defense**: covering, dropping back, swapping positions and playing as a unit. The different types of marking: Zonal, man-marking, mixture (a 'dangerous' player is being man-marked or the midfield play zonal and the defenders man-mark), combination (e.g. a defender man-marks a player in his zone while an attack takes place and follows him wherever he goes throughout the move, but when it finishes, he moves back to his position) and 'pressing' etc.

**In attack**: supporting runs, support and run, give and support, hold your position and then make a run, dispersion. All of these can involve the 'doblada', the inside pass (exploiting the space in the middle in front of goal), the 'overlap', the 'one-two', rotation, changing direction etc.

12. 'The method' also uses a series of useful phrases in order to help facilitate and speed up the learning process:

"Give and go."
"Give and support."
"Look before passing."
"Pass the ball into the 'light'."
"Soccer players are made, not born."
"Close down space in order to create space."
"Dribble or pass?"
"Pass and dribble!"
"Does making yourself available mean running away?"
"Stop and come closer."
"Running a lot does not mean you are playing well, but in order to play well you have to run a lot."
"You can be in great shape and have a perfect technique but be a poor soccer player."
"The closer you get to the goal the further you are away from scoring."
"A truly 'Great' soccer player is one who plays well against a good opposition game after game, season after season."

# *Towards Perfection: 17-18 years old*

Once a player has reached this stage he has achieved the fundamental objective of knowing how to 'play' soccer.

Any player will have reached this stage with little difficulty if he has followed my method, dedicated many hours to training and had a good coach to help and guide him along the way. I make the point that a good coach is essential because too often it is the coach who causes the player to fail. This is especially true of coaches who have never played soccer themselves. How are they going to develop good skills and impart knowledge to the players?

I would urge coaches at the grass roots level of the game to be honest with themselves and reflect on the players they have branded as 'no hopers' due to lack of pace, lack of technique, lack of anticipation or because of a strong personality. But the coaches are to blame because they lack the necessary knowledge and 'know-how' and are unable to help the players overcome these defects that would allow some of them to play at the highest level.

*Helenio Herrera, Sep Herberger and Benito Diaz, three 'Great' coaches in the game. Unfortunately they are not with us today.*

Here are the three main principles that anybody who has reached this level must have followed and understood, keeping in mind that their work is not complete and they will need to double their effort in the next few years in order to achieve an even higher standard:

1. "The only way to learn how to play soccer is by playing soccer". Benito Diaz, Helenio Herrera and the very knowledgeable German coach Sep Herberger who won The World Cup in 1954 all espoused this idea 50 years ago. Strangely enough, these three 'Great' coaches all shared the same philosophy on the game although they never actually met or spoke to each other.

2. Every player should play a game of soccer at least once a week during the learning process with his team or with a group of friends if he is not picked to play in the side. It is impossible to keep sharp and 'match fit' without playing matches. The learning process is more effective and has more relevance when the players take part in competitive matches. This is where he learns his craft.

3. Expanding on the previous point, the best form of training is playing the game and the best type of game is a competitive one.

At this level the idea is basically to get the players to improve strengths, correct weaknesses and become comfortable playing as part of a team.

The players concentrate on general technical and tactical play with the emphasis on trying to improve and 'grow' as a player. Perfection is achieved by improving execution speed as much as possible but this depends on individual dedication and hard work. If a player has a great deal of technical ability, the only way to keep it at this level is to perform the skills at 'match' speed.

One of the best ways to achieve this speed of execution is by performing difficult ball juggling skills as early as possible. These skills should continue to be worked on throughout a player's career.

In order to encourage the players and keep them interested when they practice these skills over and over again, incorporate a number of games and competitions involving technical skills (always appropriate to the level). These competitions provoke intense rivalry among the players and produce excellent results because they simulate situations and activities that happen in a game and they are performed at 'match' speed.

## Technical Skills Competition

The following is an example of a competition for players between 17-18 years old.

**1.** 'Bicycle kick' and diving header

*1st* The player stands between the penalty spot and the edge of the 18-yard box with his back to goal. The coach throws the ball to him at a suitable height to allow him to attempt the 'bicycle kick'.

*2nd* Next, the player has to control a lofted ball on his chest or head before attempting the 'bicycle kick'.

*3rd* Next, the player stands side-on to the goal as the ball is crossed and he shoots using his stronger foot. The cross is either delivered from the left or right depending on which foot the player wants to use.

*4th* The next step is the diving header. The player is in the same location but this time he is facing the goal. As the player runs towards the goal the ball is thrown slightly in front of him at a suitable height so that he can try a diving header.

*5th* Finally the ball is delivered from the other side and the player tries the diving header again.

The player has two goes at each exercise and so has ten attempts on goal in total. Each player has to indicate where he wants the ball and if the delivery is not as requested or is poor then it is taken again.

**2.** Good control and shot

The player has to keep the ball up in the air as he runs. As he heads towards the goal he has to go round an obstacle (this is in a zigzag formation with each obstacle 2.5m apart). Once the player gets beyond the last obstacle (20 m from goal) he kicks the ball forward 3-4 yards up in the air and not letting the ball drop to the ground, he runs to control it on his chest or thigh. Then the ball is allowed to bounce once and the player, still running, has a shot on the volley.

Each player gets two attempts at this. The coach looks for speed, precision and good control when awarding points.

**3.** Execution speed

The player has to run as fast as he can zigzagging in and out of eight cones either 1 or 2 yards apart. Before the player goes around the last cone the coach blows his whistle to indicate a change of direction. After the whistle is blown four or five times, the player completes the course and shoots at goal as quickly as he can. The most important thing during this exercise is speed and it does not matter if the player touches the cones. The gap between each cone is different to help the player get used to judging distances and changing pace. Each player has two attempts.

**4.** Putting swerve on the ball

The ball is positioned 3yds from the touchline and 1yd from the goal and the idea is to put swerve on the ball. The player has two attempts to score a goal (it is better if the ball does not bounce before entering the goal) by putting swerve on the ball using the outside of the foot and two attempts using the inside of the foot. This can be done in any order. The important thing to look out for here is plenty of curl on the ball involving either an in-swinging or out-swinging trajectory.

**5.** Playing in goal

- The coach has the ball in his hands on the edge of the 18-yard box and the goalkeeper is positioned on the near post with his back to him. The coach calls out before throwing the ball towards the goal. On hearing the signal the goalkeeper turns, runs backwards and stretches to save the ball. There are two attempts at the near post and two at the far post.

- The coach has the ball in his hands on the edge of the 18-yard box and the goalkeeper stands in the center of the goal with his back to him. Two or three players act as attackers and are positioned near the penalty spot. The coach calls out and throws the ball high up in the air towards the attackers. On hearing the signal the goalkeeper turns, runs out and tries to punch the ball away as the attackers try to make life difficult for him. There are two attempts from each side of the pitch.

13

- The coach is opposite the goal on the edge of the 18-yard box. The goalkeeper is on the goal line in the center of the goal with his back to him. The coach calls out and throws the ball short at medium height. On hearing the signal the goalkeeper turns, runs out and tries to catch the ball, stretching forwards. He gets two attempts at this exercise.

- The coach is on the penalty spot. The goalkeeper is on the goal line in the center of the goal with his back to him. The coach calls out and shoots at goal. On hearing the signal the goalkeeper turns and tries to save the shot. There are two shots to each side of the goal and the coach tells the goalkeeper where the ball is heading each time.

**6.** Running with the ball and shooting (using the weaker foot)

The player zigzags in and out of cones positioned 1.5 yards apart and then takes the ball slightly further on before shooting using his weaker foot. The player chooses which part of the foot makes contact with the ball. The coach looks for speed, accuracy and a good shot. The ball should not touch any of the cones as they act as the 'dummy' opposition. Each player has two attempts.

**7.** Ball juggling skills

At first the players do their favorite two or three ball juggling skills and then they do the following:

*1st* Keeping the ball up with the outside and then the inside of the foot.

*2nd* Keeping the ball up and then 'killing' the ball and balancing it on the foot. This is done five or six times.

*3rd.* Keeping the ball up touching it once with the right foot and then once with the left foot, twice with the right foot and twice with the left foot up to ten. Once this has been achieved the player sits down (keeps the ball up a few times) and then stands up again, always keeping the ball under control. There is a maximum of three attempts at this exercise. If the player has completed the other parts successfully but fails to complete the sitting down and standing up part then he only concentrates on trying to master this skill during his remaining attempts.

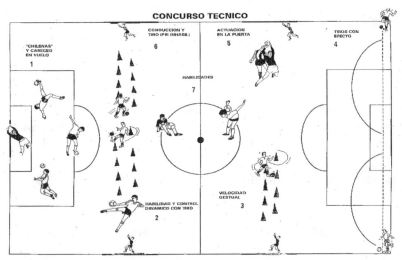

CONCURSO TECNICO

## A Difficult Age

At this stage the players are taught to position themselves purposefully and use the space effectively on the pitch, no matter what they are trying to achieve.

The main objective is to continue the progression by developing a passing game that ends with a shot on goal. This challenges the player to:

- Try difficult techniques: the long ball game, heading and volleys.

- Change and vary the pace of the game in order to improve execution speed.

It is important that the players know how to play without the ball by the end of this stage, but in order to achieve this they need a wide repertoire of skills and excellent tactical awareness. They need the presence of mind to know when best to switch to the long ball game, when to react immediately and play the ball first time on the volley and they need to be able to time runs to perfection. Basically, they need to acquire a 'feel' for the game, almost a sixth sense.

In order to develop and perfect these movements and skills the players practice under less than perfect conditions. They have to get used to being harassed constantly by an adversary, making a variety of different runs in different directions and receiving the ball at all speeds and from difficult angles.

At the same time they need to correct any bad habits or minor flaws in order to constantly improve and produce better performances on the field of play. I am thinking of things such as poor technique in certain areas, wasting time, poor concentration, keeping hold of the ball too long, not using the wings or passing back too often.

By this stage the players have usually overcome the traumas

and uncertainties of puberty. In general their bodies are developed and their personalities formed. The nervous system is also well developed by this age. The players demonstrate an improved mental attitude and physical maturity.

Having said this, experience has shown that this age is often a crucial period for the players as far as soccer is concerned. This is especially true for the talented early developers who have been used to success and praise over the years. Of course, ability is always desirable when trying to make it in the game, but there are players who although not overflowing with talent do well in the game thanks to their hard work and determination. On the other hand, the more naturally gifted players are often so confident in their own ability that they make less effort and are therefore inconsistent performers. This type of player often has a poor temperament, lacks self-discipline and as a consequence sooner or later leaves the game. This type of player needs to understand that a good professional requires more than just ability. Talent is just one of the many important qualities needed. Others are willpower, fighting spirit, determination and hard work.

At this age some players have a good knowledge of the game and tremendous technical ability. Nevertheless, there are gaps in skill and technique at this age and it is very common for players to be exceptionally gifted at one particular skill or part of the game: breath-taking acceleration, silky skills or a 'nose' for goal etc. Irrespective of the type of player, at this stage they should all be playing with the professionals, making sure that they combine individual, group and team training sessions effectively. This does not put too much strain on the players but usually has the opposite effect, motivating them and accelerating the learning curve.

Earlier I spoke about correcting technical faults. This might sound easy in theory but in practice it is an extremely difficult problem to resolve. I recommend that all coaches and players have a look at the following information that offers some ideas and guidance on the subject:

   - Every player makes technical errors at every level of the
     game, but it is up to the coach to be able to differentiate

between real faults that a player should not make at this stage or techniques that have not been fully developed because of the level and are beyond the player for the time being. The former is a more serious problem having to do with poor body positioning, execution and understanding during the learning process. In other words, the technique has never been learned correctly. The latter is more a question of a minor problem with a technique where the execution and movements have been learned properly and fully understood but are not fully developed. *Example: a player might know that that the higher the back-lift the more power he will generate when he shoots the ball. However, when a player reaches this level he is expected to understand that taking a high back-lift takes too much time and should therefore only be used when the circumstances are right. In other words it is one thing to learn and understand a technique but it takes further development to be able to apply the technique correctly according to the numerous and ever-changing circumstances a player will face in a game.*

**17**

- If time is limited, the power in the execution should be generated from the knee. This will generate less power but it is quicker and will not give the opposition time to respond. This is a tremendous advantage anywhere on the pitch but especially in the final third, where speed and effectiveness are particularly important. Over the years players such as Best, Pele, Muller, Quini, Zico, Papin, Kluivert, Raul etc. have got the better of defenders by using a very short back lift and hardly any noticeable set up play.

- This technique is also very useful where challenging for the ball. If one of the players takes a long back lift the other has time to get the ball. The player who wins the ball runs the risk of experiencing all the power generated by the other player who was too slow to get to the ball but quick enough to give him an involuntary kick.

All the above is explained to the players at this level and they are expected to use their 'soccer brain' and make decisions according to the circumstances. At first this is difficult for the players to put into practice, but they soon get the hang of it. Once they get used to the idea that the last movement they make before touching the ball has to be short, they soon realize that under normal circumstances there is no time for an extravagant back lift.

It is very important that the players are not allowed to develop 'bad habits' during the previous levels of learning. It is no good repeating a skill over and over if it is not being executed correctly.

If a player reaches this age with serious flaws in his game it is a real problem for him and his coach because he has to unlearn the 'bad habits' and start to do things properly during this stage.

The first thing the coach needs to discover is how and why the gaps in the player's learning and understanding have arisen. Once he establishes this he can structure a training program so that the player starts to learn in the correct way. Here is a list of the most common faults a coach is likely to come across as the player:

- Misinterprets the motor skill signal e.g. perhaps thinking that his leg is fully stretched or generating as much power as it can.

- Performs one skill badly because it is similar to another one that he is not very confident or good at executing. (Negative transfer).

- Lacks physical fitness, coordination etc.

- Worries about the opposition, getting injured or falling and so is tense when trying to produce the skill.

- Learns the techniques as a 'simple' exercise out of context and does not play the game in a competitive manner during training. The player soon finds it is not the same trying to reproduce the technique in a real match.

- Lacks concentration due to fatigue.

- Is affected by the psychological pressure and shirks responsibility.

Apart from the problem of poor physical fitness, all the others
should be worked on in a relaxed and calm atmosphere. If this is
not the case and the atmosphere is tense and pressurized then
the player will make little progress and will quickly revert to his
old habits. I recommend that if we are talking about a real
prospect for the future, instead of playing competitive games and
matches he should take a break and concentrate on perfecting
his own game.

The coach should also be aware that it is very problematic
trying to correct technique at this level. The psychological influence is significant and can trigger additional and unwanted movements in unrelated muscles that cause errors and provoke injury.

The player himself has to have a good understanding of what
his problems are if he is to have any chance of correcting them.
He also needs total dedication and strong will power to achieve
his objectives. From experience I know that this is very challenging and asks an awful lot of players at this age and unfortunately
many become disillusioned with the game.

There are other types of players who show a good attitude
and are very keen and anxious to do well and improve their
game. In this case there needs to be a good understanding and
rapport between the player and the coach and above all plenty of
encouragement and support. A typical example of how this might
work is as follows: *The coach needs to set out his objectives
clearly and spell out how he hopes to achieve them. Next he
gives instructions to the player and demonstrates the technique.
The player usually asks questions or seeks clarification, tries the
exercise and gives feedback. The coach looks on intently, listen-
ing and observing even the smallest detail. He changes things
and relays the instructions to the player. The player makes com-
ments and does the exercise again.*

When the coach explains a particular technique he tells the
player what, how, when and why to do things so he is able to go

through this advice in his mind as he is doing the exercise. For example, when executing a volley a player might say to himself: "Drop the shoulder!", "Raise the hips!", "Flex the leg!". Over time these instructions (although already short) become very brief, ending up as a series of sounds as the different parts of the routine are executed. Constant repetition and hard work, along with what has just been said, nearly always eliminates the mistakes and reprograms the psychomotor impulses correctly.

Correcting or learning a difficult skill such as controlling a high ball on the turn or volleying is a lot more mentally demanding on a player than learning a relatively straightforward skill such as kicking the ball with the inside of the foot or running with the ball. The coach should bear this in mind at all times. This is particularly true at this stage where the skills reach a very high degree of difficulty.

Another significant point is how players react to antibiotics. It is a proven medical fact that antibiotics have a brief but negative effect on the function of the memory. So, if a player has been ill and on antibiotics, once he returns to training he should not be expected to learn new and complicated technical skills and in fact the physical side of the training should also be kept to a minimum for a brief period.

## Perfecting Ball Control

Up to this stage the players have learned how to control the ball in a 'text-book' fashion. The technique and movements are learned in the classic and orthodox style. From now on the players are expected to learn how to control the ball quickly and effectively. A player needs to think about what he is trying to do, listen to the advice from his coach and teammates in order to develop and perfect his ball control. Here are some useful ideas for coaches that can be developed further, about teaching ball control:

- Every type of control requires great balance and coordination.

- Every player must use his peripheral vision to observe what is going on around him but must be looking at the ball when the execution is made.

- There is an infinite number of ways to control a ball but there are only four classic and conventional areas used: foot, thigh, chest and head.

- There is no set way to control a ball, as this always depends on the particular circumstances at the time the control is being made and the unexpected always occurs.

One of the failings of modern-day soccer is that it is played at such a pace, it is full of too many monotonous and non-penetrative passes and ball control and positioning leave a lot to be desired. But I can never envisage a day when being able to control a ball well will not be an important aspect of the game. What we should all be striving for in the game is the ability to control the ball quickly and effectively and then play it with imagination. 'Great' players do not 'telegraph' their intentions and pass the ball from 'A' to 'B' They might feint playing the ball to the left only to quickly change direction and pass to an unmarked player on the right, thus wrong-footing the opposition.

Feints and dummies are essential when trying to play with speed and creativity. A player runs to the ball, positions himself correctly and is well-balanced. He pretends he is merely going to put his foot on the ball and control it, but suddenly turns and moves off with the ball as he decides on the best action to take next (run with the ball, pass or shoot). This feint has three advantages over playing the ball conventionally and predictably: it fools and beats any close rival, it makes time and it wrong-foots the opposition in general.

The consequence of a feint is not always a run or dribble. Sometimes it might involve a player pretending to shoot only to control the ball and watch the defender make a lunge in a vain attempt to block the shot. A player can also feint to use the inside of the right foot to move the ball left only to use the outside of the right foot to move right and beat his man.

When trying to control a ball traveling at speed it is more effective to 'kill' the ball using the thigh or chest. The quickest way to control a ball in the air is by using the head, but if for any reason this is impossible then the next best option is the chest. If it is impossible to control the ball on these areas then it is always preferable to use the thigh before the foot. Of course if there is no pace on the ball and it falls to the ground then it is best played with feet.

Any player who wants to control the ball and execute a skill as quickly as possible should take note of the following advice, bearing in mind that this is just one of various options he could use to achieve the same objective. The player should control the ball with his weaker foot, setting it up nicely for a shot using the stronger foot. In other words, if a player wants to shoot with his left foot then he should first control the ball with his right and vice versa. In this way the player is ready to shoot immediately by putting his weight on the foot he has just finished controlling the ball with. If a player controls and shoots with the same foot, it

takes longer and gives him less chance of success. It is less likely for a shot to be executed with power and precision if the player has to take an extra step or touch, or is too static and off balance.

Any player controlling the ball using his head, chest or thigh should never put his weight on the shooting foot. Instead, his weight should be on both or on the opposite leg.

In my experience a common fault is that passes are either poor, played behind players or straight to them

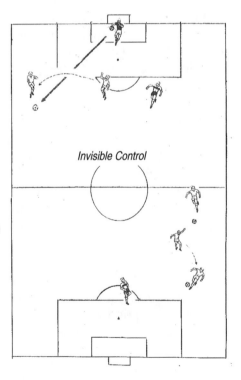

*Invisible Control*

when they should be played near them into space. Here are a few examples of what I mean:

1. The right-winger sees his goalkeeper has the ball and so sets off to make space down the wing. The goalkeeper tries to get the ball to him, but it is a bit short as the player has moved on and as a consequence it ends up behind him. The winger immediately runs back to collect the ball and then sets off with it to confront the opposition. By this time the surprise attack has been wasted.

2. An attacker makes a diagonal run into space and receives the ball from a teammate. If the ball is passed slightly ahead of the player making the run, he can take it in his stride and advance on goal.

3. Playing into space and thus saving time is even more of an advantage in the penalty area. It does not matter if the ball is passed in the air or along the ground.

If in any one of these three examples the player receiving the ball touches the ball and has to control it, he loses time and position as he may find himself with his back to goal. Of course it is a different matter if the player is unmarked and in plenty of space. In this case he has time to control the ball and look-up before playing it.

This skill that I call 'invisible control', where players move their body and let the ball do the work, was performed perfectly by Best, Pele and Cruyff. Today, few players have this ability.

## Perfecting Feints and Dummies

I strongly believe that players should learn to dribble and perform feints and dummies. This ability is both a spectacular and practical skill. The game of soccer would be a much better spectacle if players (from any position) had the confidence and the ability to take the ball and head for goal, beating their opponents by dribbling and playing feints and dummies. Furthermore, this ability is invaluable when confronted by a '1 v 1' situation and the knowledge helps give the player the extra awareness, appreciation and anticipation needed to be able to intercept passes.

Nevertheless, unfortunately the game will never be full of players with this ability until or unless coaches, directors, family and fans fully support the idea that dribbling and playing feints and dummies should be practiced at length and not criticized as is the case at the moment. The criticism stems from the fact that the skill does not always come off and when it fails it can look silly and put the team in a difficult situation. But I say it is always worth having a go as long as the circumstances are right.

Here are some useful guidelines to help perfect dribbling, feints and dummies:

1. In theory, to be a good dribbler you need explosive speed and acceleration off the mark. But any player who does not have this ability can make up for it (totally or in part) by playing at a fast pace and by thinking and producing the skills and techniques as quickly as possible. Usually players have the ability to produce the first feint at speed but the second (which is the most important) is done more slowly. It is far better to do this the other way round i.e. the first more slowly and the second feint and dummy a lot quicker. The first feint does not need to be quick as the opponent should have enough time to see it and hopefully move in the same direction. Once the opponent is committed, the second feint needs to be performed as quickly as possible so that by the time he reacts the ball is beyond him. So, half the battle is to commit your opponent with the first feint and once this has been achieved the speed of the second should wrong foot him and beat him.

2. Some players have flair and tremendous ability to dribble. By using their imagination and silky skills they are able to beat their rival with relative ease. However, a common problem is that once this happens they seem to wait in order to beat their man a second and sometimes a third time until they eventually lose the ball. They are very pleased with themselves if they manage to keep possession after all this, but in reality all they

do is give the opposition enough time to get back and regroup, making it a lot more difficult for any of their teammates to continue the attack.

3. It is far better to start dribbling on the run. If a player starts from a standing position it is far more difficult to generate enough speed and momentum. The ball should be taken directly towards the opposition, which is another difficulty for some players. I know players who have tremendous dribbling ability but tend to shy away from their opponents and instead run towards the wings. This is easier for the opposition to deal with as they can run alongside and make a challenge at the appropriate time or just shepherd the ball out of play or at least from a potentially dangerous position. If a player runs directly at his opponent then the latter has to make (perhaps in desperation) a challenge or else he will be beaten. The great advantage in this case is that the player dribbling dictates the play. You choose when the challenge is made.

4. The state of the pitch can be a deciding factor when thinking about dribbling and using feints and dummies. Defenders have difficulty keeping their feet and balance when playing on a slippery surface. So it is especially advisable to dribble as much as possible under these circumstances. However, it is a completely different story if the pitch is heavy and muddy. Under these circumstances it is advisable to dribble as little as possible. This is because the mud sticks to the ball and makes it difficult to produce the technique at speed which often allows the opponent to either win the ball or at the very least gives him enough time to successfully continue marking and hold up the attack.

5. Another extremely useful and effective technique for dribbling is to use a change of pace. The player on the ball slows down in order to get the defender to do the same. Once this happens the player on the ball immediately accelerates again, leaving the defender still 'braking'. If this is done correctly the defender will not be able to react quickly enough to the change of pace and will be beaten. This technique is especially effective if there is no covering defender beyond the beaten player.

Players such as Best, Di Stefano and Cruyff played this move with tremendous success. This move is best played down the wings as these areas are less congested and the attacker can exploit the space once he beats his man. However these great players often used this technique when playing down the center because they were able to change pace in an instant thanks to their incredible acceleration. These days Ronaldo stands out as the player who can change pace instantly and attack down the middle.

6. Another player who was great at attacking down the middle, but for different reasons, was Maradona. In this situation the defender is committed to stopping the attacker any way he can even if this means producing some heavy (often illegal) tackles. Maradona was an expert at avoiding and parrying these lunges from defenders. Not only did he have fantastic ball control but he also used every part of his body (arms, shoulders, hips and buttocks) to shield the ball and 'ride' the challenges. He had tremendous balance that allowed him to bounce off defenders and still remain on his feet and keep possession. Of course he had the great advantage of being short and strong with a low center of gravity.

7. Another area of the pitch that is ideal for dribbling is in the opposition's penalty area. The reason for this is that the threat on goal is imminent and the defenders often make desperate attempts to stop the danger. But unfortunately too few players these days have the confidence or the ability to use feints and dummies in the box. Dribbling in the penalty area may not end with the player scoring a goal but may leave a teammate in the clear to exploit the space, and 'goal'! Defenders often panic in the box because they do not want to commit a foul and give away a penalty, so they may even let you pass without actually making a challenge. I recommend that you try to perfect dribbling techniques such as feints and dummies time after time during training and that you use this exciting and dangerous move during games as often as you can. Do not be overly concerned about giving the ball away or losing possession. Sometimes it comes off and sometimes it does not but when it does it is not only a joy to watch but also

a very penetrative and dangerous move that can lead to goals. The more you try the more chance there is that you will perfect the skills and play it more effectively.

8. It is imperative to play feints and dummies when dribbling with the ball. A player might control the ball with one foot and look as if he is going to play the ball with the same foot only to dummy and move away in the other direction using the other foot. This type of move is a good way to fool an opponent and gain an advantage, which is greater or lesser depending on where on the pitch it occurs. Van Basten had a very effective technique to fool an opponent. He ran towards a defender and as he got closer he looked as if he was going to play the ball with the outside of his right foot running to the right. Then he moved his foot over the ball and immediately touched the ball with his left foot and moved to the left. Any player who hopes to achieve success when playing this type of move has to have total self-confidence in his own ability to be able to feint one way and then move in the other direction with tremendous acceleration and conviction. If a player lacks this self-confidence and plays a few dummies to try to wrong-foot an opponent but then fails to change pace and move away, all he does is demonstrate his intentions to his opponent and gives the rest of the opposition more time to get back and cover. However, if a player finds himself surrounded by various opponents then this type of 'stalling' tactic is a good way to keep possession in the hope that a teammate will soon arrive on the scene to support. Also, this type of feint and dummy without changing pace or trying to beat a man is useful when a player spots a teammate making a run and needs to buy time to release the ball at the perfect moment. The last two examples are ways to use feints and dummies to keep possession while waiting for support.

9. In soccer it is always best to make an opponent receive the ball with his back to goal. This makes sense because from this position it is difficult for him to see how the play is developing. Nevertheless, in my experience having your back to a defender can be a positive advantage when it comes to dribbling. This is because the defender's view of the ball is restricted and

so he is greatly influenced by the movements of the player on the ball. This is the beauty of this particular situation. If the player on the ball is aware of this he can use it to his advantage by feinting to go one way and instantly moving off in the other direction with the defender still trying to recover from the dummy. I have asked many players to do this over the years (even professionals) and they usually perform the feint very well but at first fail to move away in the other direction, which defeats the object of the exercise as the defender has time to regain his composure and position. If you videotape the exercise and show the players the video of both the movements (their's and the defender's), they usually get the

*Van Basten, another soccer genius. Despite being tall few people in the history of the game can compete with his ability to dribble using feints and dummies.*

idea and learn to move away at pace in the opposite direction after making a feint, leaving the defender chasing shadows.

10. The possibilities of a successful dribble are greatly enhanced if the player has his body positioned correctly and shields the ball. The player should position himself between the ball and his opponent, though not too close to the ball and use his elbows, arms and legs to keep the defender at bay. He should not have his back to the defender (unless as in the earlier example) and should be sideways on to the defender. This will create the most space between the defender and the ball. At this level all of the above ideas should be practiced time after time.

# Perfecting Heading Technique

Dribbling is therefore one of the most effective ways to unlock any defense, but many goals are scored indirectly or directly with headers. This is why clubs are willing to pay a small fortune to secure the services of someone who is good in the air, especially as these are few and far between.

Heading technique is one of the most difficult executions to perform correctly in the game of soccer. This is particularly true when jumping against an opponent. Despite the technical demands of the discipline, it is not always the most skillful players who perform this technique the best. In fact, good headers of the ball can often look quite clumsy with the ball at their feet. Players such as Kubala, Puskas, Kopa, Gento, Cruyff, Maradona, Butrageño, Laudrup, Bebeto, Romario, Suker and present-day players such as Iván de la Peña and Raul, all have incredible touch and skill on the ball but lack good heading ability.

This is also an interesting point: the Latin American players are recognized as the most technically gifted players in the world, far superior to the Europeans. When referring to heading ability the reverse is true as the Europeans (especially the English) are much better than the Latin American players.

I have asked coaches from all around the world to give me their views on this situation. The majority are of the opinion that technical ability is cerebral, cold and calculated, whereas heading ability involves such things as fighting spirit, enthusiasm and bravery. At a young age the bravest and most determined players risk getting hurt and subsequently master the technique.

Iv·n and Raul, two great players but not as far as heading is concerned.

I agree with this theory up to a point but I also believe that poor coaching is also to blame. Right through from beginners to the professional game very little time is spent on heading exercises during training. Furthermore, the training that does take place is unrealistic and of little use to the player as it does not usually involve competing in the air with an opponent, so when it comes to a 'real' game the player is not properly prepared.

I have coached many technically gifted players over the years who have had very poor heading ability. However, once they follow the ideas in this book consistently and persistently over the long term, all of the players reach at least an acceptable level. If a player is frightened of getting hurt when competing for the ball in the air he should continue to practice and slowly but surely he will realize that it is not such a big deal and will begin to jump freely for the ball. This confidence particularly helps those players who are technically gifted with their feet overcome the initial anxiety of getting a knock in the face. However, if at this stage a player refuses to attempt to compete for the ball in the air, the likelihood is that he will shy away from heading altogether, even at goal. In other words if a player does not practice how is he ever going to gain confidence and improve.

Let me clear one thing up before I go on. Iván de la Peña left The Soccer School when he was 15 years old and by this stage he had spent a relatively short time practicing heading on a serious basis. Nevertheless he still managed to improve his heading technique significantly although his other ball skills were far more impressive. I am convinced that if he had stayed at The School until he was 18 years old his heading ability would have reached a very good standard. I am not suggesting that he would ever have been a natural header of the ball like Kocsis or Santillana, but his technique would have been more than acceptable.
These are the qualities needed in order to become a good header of the ball:

1. *Height*. It is only logical that under normal circumstances a tall player has more chance of winning the high ball than a shorter player.

**2.** *Bravery.* Competing for a ball in the air against an opponent requires a fair degree of bravery and courage. Sometimes short players are able to beat tall players with a good jump because the latter have a fear of getting hurt in the challenge.

**3.** *Powerful legs.* The legs need to be strong enough to generate enough explosive power to execute the leap and compete with opponents doing their best to impede any progress.

**4.** *Timing.* On the face of it some players have all the necessary attributes to be good in the air; they are tall, brave and have a good leap but they rarely win a ball. This is because they lack timing. They do not judge the distance, speed and trajectory of the ball and jump accordingly. Sometimes they jump too soon before the ball has arrived and sometimes they jump too late and an opponent gets to the ball first.

Uwe Seeler (1'69), Pele (1'70), Zico (1'71), Di Stefano (1'74), Kocsis (1'77) and Santillana (1,75) have all demonstrated over the years that there is more to heading than just height and bravery. All these players had a wonderful instinct for goal and used a combination of perfect positioning and an extraordinary ability to get their body at the correct angle to score lots of headed goals. They also managed to get the better of much taller players by always being in the right place at the right time (knowing where to be and when to jump). They timed their jump perfectly and then used their body and elbows to prevent the defender from getting to the ball.

Years ago the exact time to head the ball was a topic of contention for many people. Nowadays it seems most people agree that it is not a good

*Iv·n Helguera is a very gifted player on the ball and he is also very dominant in the air. He is a 'natural' at heading a ball but nevertheless spent hour after hour practicing the technique at The Soccer School.*

idea to head the ball when descending as the body is passive and the header will lack power. Also, this type of header slows the game down considerably.

If a player wants to head the ball a long way (perhaps a clearance) then he should meet the ball on the ascending phase of the jump. Defenders tend to meet the ball this way when they are surrounded by attackers and want to clear the danger. However, this is not a good technique for trying to score a goal as the ball will generally be directed high over the cross bar.

When trying to score or pass using headers, the ball should be struck at the highest point of the jump. The player should take full advantage of the fact that at this point the body is under perfect control and is momentarily still before the descent. It is also true to say that the opposition has less chance of getting to the ball at this point. Goals are often scored thanks to wonderful improvisation and anticipation and for this the player should use the 'diving header'.

## The Great Secret of the Great Headers

All great headers of the ball have a secret technique which allows them to win apparently unreachable and impossible balls in the air. I will explain: the jump involves two antagonistic forces: gravity and propulsion. The latter allows the player to leap and the former brings the player back down. All the great headers of the ball have an inate ability to get the very best out of these forces, which allows them to almost 'hang' in the air for a split second.

At this precise moment the player quickly drops an arm at the perfect angle, allowing him to stretch up another couple of centi-yards and reach balls that other people cannot touch. This ability to 'hang' in the air for a split second allows them to jump earlier than other players and stops defenders from getting to the ball. In the final of the 1970 World Cup Pele (1'70) out-jumped Burgnich (1'86) to score a goal. This is what the Italian player had to say after the game: "We both jumped together but as I landed back on my feet, Pele was still up in the air".

The ability to jump well depends on such qualities as explosive power, agility, reaction speed, balance and coordination. Nevertheless, soccer players should not try to improve their jump by strengthening the relevant muscles. This improvement involves performing and repeating technical heading exercises. Good heading ability relies on all the following factors:

- Anticipating the trajectory of the ball.

- Heading the ball at the highest point of the jump (timing).

- Getting the body in the best possible position to affect the header on goal or pass (the ability to twist the body as appropriate)

- Striking the ball correctly using the forehead.

In summary, the best way to train to improve the jump, technique and timing is to use the traditional heading exercises (the use of the 'suspended ball', ball juggling skills and small-sided games) plus realistic competition that simulates the situation that the player is up against an enthusiastic and committed opponent.

Finally, I must get back to the most important theme running through this book: the small-sided games. These games form the basis of the training exercises and involve games for 4-6 players, regulation size balls and a pitch size of 25 x 25yds. The pitch size needs to be increased if the objective is to work the physical side as well as the heading technique. In any case I strongly recommend that the heading technique take precedence over any physical conditioning activity.

This level continues and adds to the methods taught in the previous levels which are always worth reinforcing so the players do not lose sight of the continuity and progression. At this stage two vitally important new disciplines are introduced:

**1.** The teams play a committed 'man-to-man' marking system. The players should be of similar ability as far as heading technique is concerned.

**2.** All the players need to anticipate and jump for the ball anywhere on the pitch. In other words, even if a player is unmarked he has to pretend he is marked and jump for the ball accordingly, no matter where he is on the pitch. If the ball comes at medium height or slightly out of reach, the player has to produce a 'diving' header to try to get to the ball.

If a player forgets to mark then a free kick is awarded. After three similar infringements a penalty kick is awarded. Anyone who fails to execute the 'diving' header is sent to practice at the 'suspended ball' and can only return to the game once he has satisfactorily mastered the technique.

It is important to mention that these games should be competitive and played at a very high intensity and this sometimes results in the occasional clash resulting in a knock to the face or head. For this reason, these small-sided games should never be played any closer than 48 hours before a match. If a player picks up an injury the day before a game he may miss the match or play well within himself to avoid getting hit near the affected area.

*Three different periods of history and three great headers of a ball: Zarra, Kocsis and Santillana.*

# Perfecting Passing

The 'Great' players usually demonstrate their talent, creativity and genius by producing wonderful passes. When a ball is passed well soccer transforms into a 'work of art'. Alsua, Kubala, Kopa, Pele, Cruyff, Zico, Maradona, Laudrup and Ivan de la Peña all have one thing in common: the ability to play an unthinkable pass to a teammate that takes the opposition and even the crowd by total surprise. This ability is pure artistry.

The great advantage of passing is that the ball travels a lot faster than any player. Also, players get tired but the ball is incessant and always obeys what is asked of it. The secret is to know how to manipulate it effectively.

All 'Great' teams such as the Hungarian team of '54 with Puskas, the Madrid team with Di Stefano, the Brazilian team of '70 with Pele, the '82 team with Zico and the Barcelona teams with Koeman, Laudrup, Stoichkov, Bakero and Guardiola have all been extraordinarily good passing teams. This is what Sacchi the ex-Italian coach had to say on the subject: "A team that does not pass the ball does not know how to play the game".

This is why I put so much emphasis on good passing and any player who has reached this level perfects his technique by constantly repeating difficult and complex passes.

Here are some guidelines to help you improve your tactical passing awareness:

1. Anyone who wants to be a top passer of the ball needs to be able to concentrate on the ball and the field of play at the same time in order to spot what both teammates and the opposition are doing. This is a very difficult skill to perfect but with hard work and effort it is achievable.

2. Players need to have a good touch to ensure that passes reach the desired destination. But how does a player know where best to play a pass? Well, it is simple really, as the best

place to play a ball is near the opposition's goal. In other words it is often decisive in a game to play a long pass to threaten the opponent's goal. But these passes require great technique, precision and power and unfortunately there are too few players in the game able to produce this type of quality. A pass over 8 yards may miss the desired target by some 50 inches but the teammate will still receive the ball. However, if the pass is over 40 yards then the ball may deviate so much that it has no possibility of reaching its destination.

3. A quality passing game requires an intelligent combination of short, medium and long passes. This creates a positive and free-flowing game. Perhaps three short and medium passes to one long pass is the ideal. Without doubt, a series of short passes is usually less effective without a long one and the latter usually culminates in a short pass.

4. A long pass is able to travel from one area to the next at incredible speed. This can catch any opponent by surprise and leave them desperately running back to try to regain their defensive formation. So, long passing is a way of making the game a lot faster and it is a tactic used often these days in the modern game. But I am not referring to a 'long ball' game (which unfortunately is the usual end-result when a team erroneously misinterprets the concept) where the ball is passed (or hoofed) up field monotonously without any real thought or imagination. These passes should be used wisely and should demonstrate the quality, skill, technique, intelligence, vision and creativity of a player.

5. It is always best to conceal the intentions of a pass from the opposition. A player should never look in the direction of the pass nor should he run towards where his teammate is positioned. Ten years ago I wrote in my first book 'De la base a la cúspide': "The crowd would marvel at the breath-taking precision and elegant passing of Schuster. There is no questioning his technique but he had flaws as far as tactics were concerned because he did not conceal his passes. For example, when approaching the opposition's area down the left he would turn and play the ball with his right to change the

direction of play and in this way would make his intentions clear to the other team. A great passer of the ball would use his left foot or the outside of his right in order to conceal his intention. Schuster's movement meant that he was almost 'telegraphing' his pass. Thanks to the accuracy, technique and the power of the pass, the other team were usually powerless to intercept the ball but they were able to position themselves in such a way that the move often had no positive results for the attacking team". For this reason I offer the following advice: the best pass is one that takes the opposition by surprise and is played into space so that a teammate can run onto it.

6. Passes should not be made just to move the ball from one place to another. Passes should be made for a reason. They should be played to change the direction or rhythm of the game or to create a totally new move that leaves the opposition struggling. If a team is content playing meaningless sideways passes, they are indeed keeping possession but they cause no real threat as the opposition has time to organize themselves and control the situation. Furthermore, if the ball is intercepted there is a greater possibility that a goal will be scored on the counterattack (as happened in the '82 World Cup when Rossi got the ball off the fabulous Brazilian team and scored a decisive goal).

Try to hide your intention when playing a pass and try to play the ball across defenders. Do not 'telegraph' passes as this alerts the opposition and gives them time to organize themselves. Also, do not forget that your work is not complete once you have released the ball instead you should keep or start running to support and possibly get the ball back. What started off as 'give and go' develops into 'give and support', which implies a stage further, whereby a player is already moving as he approaches an opponent then gives a disguised pass to a colleague and runs into a space in support.

## **C**rossing Machines

**7.** Years ago wingers were called 'crossing machines'. They ran
down the flanks, received a pass from a teammate, got to the
'dead ball line' and crossed. If possible they ran right up to the
goal post and passed the ball back, in what became known as
a 'killer pass'. No matter what the particular move, these
wingers always posed a threat as they were able to deliver the
ball in front of teammates who from this position (running onto
the ball and facing the goal) found it easier to shoot and score.
The defenders on the other hand had to run back as quickly as
they could and found it very difficult to clear the ball because
they were usually facing their own goal as well. Occasionally
this panic in defense caused own-goals to be scored. This
type of move is not out of date and is still an important factor
in the modern game. Unfortunately, it is not as common.
Today, players are usually happy to cross the ball as soon as
they approach the opposition's penalty area. I recommend that
you run the extra 15 yards and cross from the 'dead ball line'
because: it overcomes the problem of 'offside' as the ball is not
being passed forwards, attackers receive the ball in front of
them which makes it easier to score and the defenders are
facing their own goal and so may score themselves, give away
a corner or at the very least find it difficult to clear the ball upfield. However, this is not a 'golden rule'. It is up to the player to use his judgment depending on the circumstances of the
game. If he is confronted by a disciplined and well-organized
defense then he should try to get to the 'dead ball line', but if
he has possibilities of approaching the goal instead then of
course he should take this option.

**8.** Even though this seems like a logical move and is anticipated
and expected, it still proves very effective and difficult to stop.
Matthews, Gainza, Garincha, Gento and even Michel used this
move time after time with great success. The vast majority of
goals scored in games come from this type of move, where the
ball is crossed for a teammate to shoot or head a goal. It is
also interesting to know that over the last 10 years this type of
move has resulted in an average of 42 own goals being scored

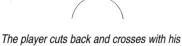

Gento crosses on the run for Puskas (or the defender) to score.

The player cuts back and crosses with his other foot. (This is fatal as his teammate is now caught offside).

every season in the Spanish First Division. As I say, players do not often get to the 'dead ball line' in the modern game, so just imagine what this total would be if they did. Some players even manage to get to the 'dead ball line' and lose any advantage gained by checking back and crossing with the other foot.

The crowd applauds when this happens, especially if the defender ends up flat on his backside. But tactically the attacker has made the wrong decision. If he had crossed on the run, the attackers were in a perfect position to receive the ball in front, producing a wonderful goal-scoring opportunity. Once he 'checks' and 'cuts back' facing the other way, the situation changes totally. Now the attackers have to adjust and move backwards or sideways, losing both momentum and any advantage they had over the struggling defenders. The latter now have time to organize themselves and may catch the strikers 'offside'.

9. The best place to dribble with the ball is in the opposition's half and this is also true as far as passing is concerned. If a player has the ability to analyze the situation coolly and calmly before producing an intelligent pass, he has the potential to totally unsettle and unlock any defense. Of course, the move does not just depend on the player passing the ball. A teammate needs to make a run, find some space or be willing to chase the ball. It is very difficult for players to lose their markers in the box and so getting a clear view of goal is always problematic. The great skill of all the top goal scorers over the years is

*Laudrup and Stoichkov*

the ability to be in the right place at the right time. Look at the picture that shows how Stoichkov scored a goal in The European Cup. He received the ball and passed it to Laudrup on the left wing. Then he immediately made a run to the far post behind the two defenders whilst the only other defender available went to challenge Laudrup. Stoichkov was in a good position to be able to receive a high ball from Laudrup. However, Laudrup 'took on' and beat his man and ran towards the goal. The nearest defender went across to challenge Laudrup and now Stoichkov was not in such a good position. If Laudrup crossed, the ball was sure to go beyond Stoichkov and if he played it along the ground the defenders or the goal keeper would surely intercept it. But Stoichkov made an intelligent move and got himself between the two defenders allowing enough 'light' for the pass. Laudrup feinted to shoot and then passed back to Stoichkov who shot and scored.

10. The fact that Stoichkov was able to get into a good position and make space for himself makes me reflect that it seems unfair for the player who makes the pass to receive all the plaudits from the crowd. Of course the wonderful pass should be applauded but it is only possible if a teammate is able to receive it and this is down to his ability to anticipate, use his 'soccer brain', make space and get into position.

The player on the ball has to be aware of how the play develops all around him and needs the ability to be able to play a perfect pass to the right person at the right time. But the player hoping to receive the ball is faced with other difficulties: he has to keep an eye on the ball, monitor what is happening all around him (especially behind him), the position of the opposition, the position of teammates and he has avoid being caught 'offside'. All this information has to be assimilated as quickly as possible so that he is able to take advantage of any space if it becomes (or he anticipates it will become) available. Nevertheless, when he does make his move it is only of any real value if the player on the ball has the necessary vision and technical ability to be able to get the ball to him. If this is not the case then the striker wastes valuable energy as his run achieved no positive benefits. The striker may even provoke an injury in his attempt to sprint, twist and turn to find space. As you can appreciate, the circumstances need to be just right for a move (the run and the pass) to work perfectly.

*Stoichkov, a real 'goal-machine.*

11. In summary, a soccer player should be judged on what he does with the ball and what he does off the ball. If a player has good acceleration, the ability to change direction, pace, suddenly stop and set off again in an instant then he is a very difficult player to mark (assuming he uses all these virtues wisely). The other objectives when making space are as follows:

   - The movement makes it easier for the player on the ball to make the pass.

   - The run may 'drag' defenders out of position and thus open up space for teammates.

12. There are other types of passes (that could even be described as dribbling) that are extremely difficult to perform. I am thinking of the 'auto-pass' and the other 'wall' pass played by Pele. The former is when a player kicks the ball on into space and has every intention of chasing after the ball and

collecting it himself. This is a very direct and spectacular move that is normally played down the flanks. When a player is faced by an opponent he kicks the ball past him on one side and he runs around the other and chases after the ball. It is possible to play this move anywhere on the pitch but it is particularly effective against a team playing 'offside'. As a player sees the defenders all coming out as a unit in a line he kicks the ball forward (it often needs to be kicked over their heads) and chases after it. The defenders are at a disadvantage as they have to stop and turn to catch the attacker. As far as the other 'wall' pass is concerned, Pele often used this move in and around the opposition's penalty box with total mastery.

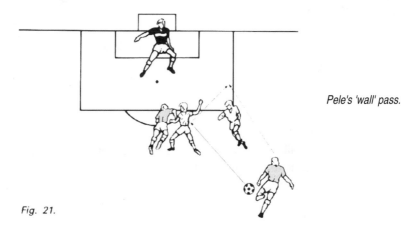

*Pele's 'wall' pass.*

*Fig. 21.*

This is how it works:

**a)** Pele receives the ball near an opponent. He stops. Taking the defender by surprise, Pele kicks the ball against him and at the same time runs to collect the rebound. He gets to the ball and shoots at goal.

**b)** Sometimes Pele does not kick the ball against the nearest defender but chooses instead to use the covering defender as the 'wall'. Just as before, Pele runs to collect the rebound and shoots before anyone has a chance to react to the audacious move.

**13.** The Hungarians Bozsik and Puskas played the ball near the opponent's weaker foot. A player usually has all his weight on this side. It is difficult for the player to control the ball because he first has to change his weight to the other side. If he tries to use his stronger foot and bring it across, he usually ends up tying himself in knots and looking a bit clumsy. It is an ingenious move. Try it and you will see what I mean.

## The One-Two, the Doblada, and the Overlap

If a player repeats a skill on a regular basis it soon becomes part of the team system. The system I teach at The School principally involves three offensive strategies: the 'one-two', the 'doblada' and the 'overlap'. These moves are rehearsed time after time until they become 'second nature' to the players. This type of attacking play is practical, direct and penetrative.

Here are the movements needed to play and perfect the 'one-two':

**1.** *Run with the ball and conceal intentions.*

Sometimes the 'one-two' is played from a stationary position such as when playing 'one-touch' but usually it is played on the run. This should be at medium pace and never directly towards the player you want to play the move with or else your intentions become too obvious. Nor should you look at your teammate for the same reasons. It is best to feint a pass in a different direction before making your move.

**2.** *Change pace and direction.*

Just before the pass is made the player on the ball should start to sprint, but never in the direction of his teammate. In earlier stages I called this the 'give and go' but now I refer to it as the 'give and support'.

If the ball goes to the right of the opponent then the player makes his run to the left and vice versa. This is very disconcerting for the defender who realizes he has been beaten and that the attacker is behind him.

**3.** *Release the ball at the right time.*

If an attacker releases the ball when the defender is a long way away then the latter has time to turn and may get to the ball first. On the other hand, if the attacker gets too close then the defender has a greater chance of intercepting the ball. The attacker should tempt the defender closer and when he is approximately 3 yards away he should release the ball. It is only natural for the defender to stick out a leg to try to intercept the ball (usually in vain) as he has no chance of getting to the ball.

**4.** *Pass with accuracy and put pace on the ball.*

As I have just explained, the player starts to sprint just as he is about to make the pass. The pass needs to be precise as the player is trying to hit an imaginary wall and he hopes to collect the rebound. If the player fails to hit the target he has no possibility of getting the ball returned to him. The pass also needs to be hit with pace.

If the pass is weak and takes too long to reach its destination then the opponent takes advantage of this situation as the defender might anticipate and get into position. Moreover, a pass with little pace on it can leave the attacker in an 'offside' position.

**5.** *Contact area.*

The 'one-two' can be played with various surface areas such as the toe, heel, chest and head etc. It is normally played with the inside of the instep and on occasion with the outside of the instep. It does make a difference which surface area is used. If the teammate is on the right then the player hoping to play the 'one-two' should use the inside of the left instep or the outside of the right instep. If the teammate is on the left then the ball should be passed using the inside of the right foot or the outside of the left foot. If the player tries to pass with the inside of the left foot to a teammate on his left then he has to turn slightly and this will slow the game down and make his intentions clear to the opposition. Here is some advice about passing.

This is what the teammate has to do if he is acting as the 'wall':

**1.** *Position yourself sideways.*

This is a very important principle for attackers to follow. The player stands sideways on as the danger always comes from behind, especially from his marker but also from any other opponent. In this way he is able to monitor the situation and he is also ready to turn in any direction.

**2.** *Conceal intentions.*

Just as I said that the player on the ball should conceal his intentions, the same is also true of the player acting as the 'wall'. The player should remain still almost admitting he is being marked out of the game, and then suddenly make a sprint towards his teammate on the ball. Another option is for him to casually trot off in another direction and suddenly turn and sprint to support his teammate.

**3.** *Get close, but only when the time is right.*

The sprint towards his teammate should be timed to perfection. If the player on the ball is not being impeded by an opponent then the teammate waiting to support should remain still and only make quick feints unsettle his marker. Once the ball is approximately 4 yards away, the player makes his run to get closer to his teammate and act as the 'wall. If he makes his run too soon, his opponent will be alerted to his intentions and will be able to anticipate the move. But it is even easier for an opponent if the player makes his run too late.

**4.** *Contact area.*

The same principles are true for the player playing the 'one-two' and the teammate who acts as the 'wall' when it comes to which part of the foot to use. If the player uses the outside of the foot then the execution is a lot faster and is usually kept well under control. However, if the player tries to play a ball to the right using the inside of the right foot then the following happens:

**a)** He 'telegraphs' his intentions.

**b)** He takes longer to execute the move and so may give his opponent the time he needs to anticipate and deal with the situation.

**c)** He runs the risk of producing a poor technique because he is not properly balanced.

**5.** *Pass with accuracy.*

The return pass should always be precise and should be played into space to allow his teammate to take it in his stride. If the pass is poor then the move breaks down. The strength of the pass depends on the particular circumstances at the time, such as the position and distance of the players involved. The return pass therefore can be hard, medium or soft, depending on the circumstances.

**6.** *The possibility of the double 'one-two' or other possibilities.*

I have already mentioned that the player acting as the 'wall' needs to be standing sideways on and he also needs to be alert. He should also be aware that his marker usually only has three possible things he can do under these circumstances and so he should observe and be ready to anticipate each one:

**a)** The marker tries to anticipate (the attacker moves forward, plays the 'one-two' and continues to support in case he is required to play another 'one-two' or can help out in any other way).

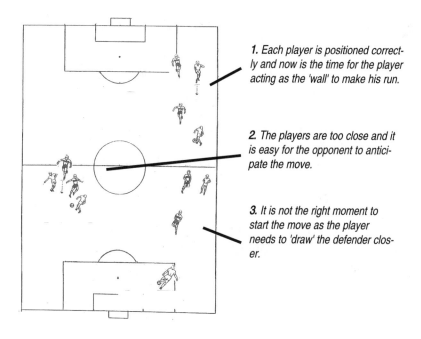

*1. Each player is positioned correctly and now is the time for the player acting as the 'wall' to make his run.*

*2. The players are too close and it is easy for the opponent to anticipate the move.*

*3. It is not the right moment to start the move as the player needs to 'draw' the defender closer.*

**b)** The marker tries to intercept the 'one-two' that has been 'telegraphed'. (The attacker has only feinted the move and plays something totally different. Perhaps he plays the 'overlap' by playing the ball behind the defender, or if he is near the goal he runs with the ball himself and shoots).

**c)** Sometimes the marker does not react at all and stays where he is (Under these circumstances, the attacker can do pretty much what he wants to do. He is not facing any resistance).

# The Overlap and the Inside Pass

The 'overlap' is just as direct as the 'one-two' but even easier to perform. It is possible to play the 'inside' pass with other team-mates as a direct result of the 'one-two' and the 'overlap' but these are far more common and likely as a result of the 'doblada'.

These are the main points to follow for the player on the ball:

**1.** *Conceal intentions.*

Just as with the 'one-two', it is vital for the player to hide his intentions so that the defender is not able to anticipate the move.

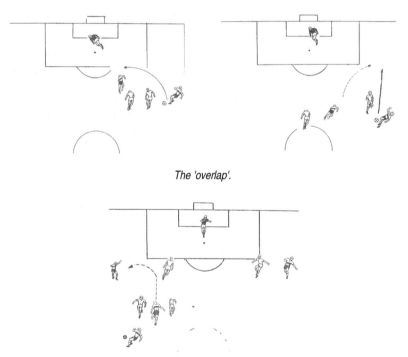

*The 'overlap'.*

*A player runs down the wing to create the 'overlap'. He does not receive the ball but creates space in the middle for the 'inside' pass.*

**2.** *Body position and contact area.*

If the ball arrives from the side or diagonally then the player can play it 'first-time' as long as he takes a few steps backwards beforehand. If the ball arrives vertically then he controls it on the turn and then plays the pass. Sometimes it is also necessary to play the pass with swerve so that at first it gets closer to the opponent only to bend and arrive in the path of a teammate who takes it in his stride.

**3.** *Good awareness.*

It is important that this move is not played automatically just because it is a well-rehearsed and dangerous ploy. If the defender is too close then the player is unable to release the ball as he would like and so should not attempt the move. However, if the player has good awareness and can sense how things are developing all around him then he may decide to try something else instead, such as passing the ball inside to exploit the space left by a teammate who has dragged a defender across to cover the 'overlap' or he may choose to go himself.

These are the main points to follow for the player making the 'overlap':

**1.** *Start the run from behind the ball never in front of it.*

It is very important that the player start his run to make the 'overlap' from behind the ball so that he can take the opposition by surprise and run onto the ball, which travels much faster than he can. The run should also be vertical or slightly diagonal, which means the player usually receives the ball facing the opponent's goal. The run should take the form of a sprint in order to take the opposition by surprise and avoid being marked. Some players make a run from the wing and in front of the ball. These are two serious errors as far as this move is concerned. Why? Because the player gets in position before the ball arrives and he will consequently have his back to goal.

**2.** *Run as fast as possible.*

It is a good idea to run as quickly as possible when trying to create the space for the 'overlap' because it is very difficult for a defender to deal with a player running at pace when he has to turn and begin to accelerate from a standing start. Unfortunately, some players wait for a pass to be made before thinking about making a run and of course this defeats the object of the exercise because the great advantages of speed and surprise are lost.

**3.** *Make runs, check and support.*

Under normal circumstances, a player making a run to play the 'doblada' receives the ball and goes on from there. However, this is not always the case as sometimes (for whatever reason) the player does not make the pass and keeps possession. So now, the player who makes the run is in a 'false' position and may be caught 'offside' and is certainly no longer supporting the player on the ball. Under these circumstances he needs to check and get back into a position to support the player on the ball or stay out wide on the wing to occupy a defender and make space in the middle.

The 'overlap' is a great attacking move because it creates wide-open spaces. The player on the ball analyzes the situation and considers what his next move should be. If there is no clear option then he should retain possession and wait for a teammate to come up from behind him and offer support. Once the player

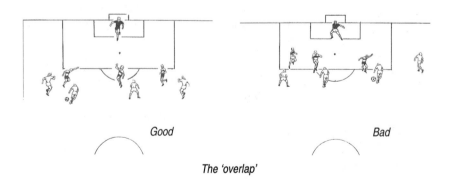

*Good*                    *Bad*

*The 'overlap'*

on the ball senses the run or the proximity of his teammate then various options are available to him:

1. If the player decides that the best thing to do is pass to his teammate then he pretends to head towards the middle of the pitch only to use the outside of the foot at exactly the right time to deliver the ball into the path of his teammate, taking the opposition by complete surprise.

2. If the player on the ball sees that the defenders are aware of his teammate making the 'overlap', he feints to pass to him and cuts inside to have a shot himself or link up with another teammate.

3. It is always a positive move for a player to make a run down the wing. Even if he does not get involved in the build-up directly, at the very least he will unsettle the defense and may even draw a defender out of position to mark him. However, if he is not spotted by the defender but the player on the ball is aware of his run and passes the ball to him then the threat on goal is significant.

4. Truly gifted players are able to totally deceive a defense by spotting the player making the run, feinting to pass to him, cutting inside using the inside of the foot and then immediately playing the ball with the outside of the same foot so that the runner receives the ball in his stride. This is a very difficult move but one that I recommend you practice as it has great merit.

The player making the 'overlap' needs to be aware of the following concepts:

1. The player needs to sprint at full-speed and make sure his teammate on the ball is aware of his run. The player on the ball is unable to see the run as it comes from behind him and is concentrating on the possible options that he can actually see ahead of him. If the player making the run is not seen, make sure he makes a call and is heard.

**2.** The player needs to sprint at full speed and run around the outside of his teammate quite close to the opponent who is doing the marking. Some players either run too slowly or run at a good pace but are too far away from the marker. The result of both these cases is that the marker is not beaten and will continue to 'close down' the player on the ball.

*The best 'goal machine'? Ronaldo!!*

**3.** The player should run at full speed down the wing and at the same time be very aware of what is happening inside him. This observation and analysis of where his teammates and the opposition are will help him decide what to do if or when he gets the ball. If he does receive the ball he should cross the ball immediately or if the circumstances are right, try to get as close to the goal as he can in order to shoot or play a 'goalscoring' pass.

## Perfecting Shooting

Now I want to concentrate on the final objective of the game: shooting. Control and power in the shot are indispensable qualities for any player hoping to take advantage when he is near or in the opposition's goal area. These are the crucial moments in a game that produce goals, decide the outcome and thrill the crowd. The game is all about scoring goals (hopefully at least one more than the opposition) and therefore all the 'serious' action takes place in the final third of the pitch and often involves shooting.

Perhaps you were thinking that I had overlooked this technique and now all of a sudden I am suggesting that shooting is a vital part of the game. But I have seen many technically mediocre players over the years practicing shooting technique incessantly during training.

This makes no sense because the players need the necessary ball skills and technique to get themselves in a shooting position. I am a firm believer that players should learn techniques and skills by following a structured training program that incorporates progression and continuity. For this reason, the players should leave the more complex skills to the end. In other words, once a player has followed my training method from beginning to end and has learned all the necessary techniques then he is ready to start practicing shooting. He is well equipped to be able to create numerous shooting and goal-scoring opportunities.

During this stage of the learning process the player has reached a good technical and creative level and now is the time to concentrate on specific shooting techniques. Starting and finishing-off a move are two totally different things. It is true to say that the player can quickly develop and perfect shooting techniques once he has mastered the creative skills in the game. This makes sense because when he learns to run with the ball, control the ball, dribble and play the 'one-two' a player often practices a bit of shooting at the same time.

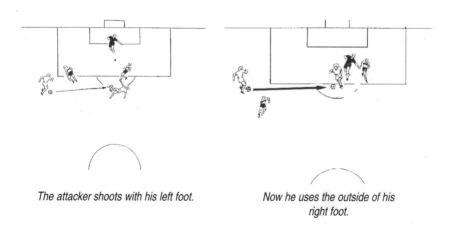

The attacker shoots with his left foot.          Now he uses the outside of his
                                                 right foot.

A player can use either his feet or head when making attempts on goal to display his individual talent. But often a player goes on a tremendous dribble and sets up a teammate to score an easy goal. The goal-scorer forgets about the playing as part of a team when he is in front of goal and only concentrates on his position and trying to have as many chances as possible during the game.

Soccer is all about scoring goals and these are scored with strikes on goal (headers or shots). Without goals the game would not make a lot of sense. Close-range shots with no obstructions need to be accurate and well placed and so it is best to use the biggest contact area possible, the inside of the foot. The idea is to place the ball in the goal beyond the reach of the goalkeeper. From the same distance but in a congested area it is best to use the toe-poke or the outside of the foot as these are quickly executed and largely unpredictable with more chance of taking the opposition by surprise. The full instep should be used to shoot from distance as although placement is important, power in the strike is the overriding factor. The same is true when putting swerve on the ball. It is of no use bending the ball significantly if the shot is so weak that the goalkeeper has plenty of time to get into position and save the ball.

Strikes on goal can also be made on the volley, half volley or as headers. The ball can arrive from any direction, from behind, from in front, from the side or diagonally. There is a tremendous emphasis put on learning to how to volley once the players reach the 14-16 age group. Now they are expected to practice the volley and half volley endlessly. They have already learned the basics of heading technique but at this level the players learn the importance of heading the ball with the forehead or the temple in great detail. The forehead is usually the best area to strike the ball with as the player can keep his eye on the ball until the very last moment. The temples are used when the ball comes from the side and it needs to be directed towards goal. It is less accurate than the header made with the forehead but far more powerful.

The variety and evolution of shots has increased significantly over recent years in order to combat the strong defensive systems being utilized. The traditional shooting technique is to keep the head down, keep the knee of the shooting leg over the ball with the standing leg positioned next to the ball. Contact is made with the boot lace area and the toes point downwards.

Unfortunately it is very difficult to score a beautifully struck shot with power and precision in the modern game.

There are too many people blocking the area in front of goal and so goals are usually scored as a result of the most unlikely and inopportune moments: a toe-poke, a miss-kick, a deflection, a rebound or off the thigh, shoulder or nose. These fortuitous strikes by the attacking team often leave the goalkeeper stranded and unable to react. Players such as Pele, Muller, Quini, Zico, Hugo Sanchez, Papin, Bebeto, and Ronaldo etc... were never worried about the aesthetically pleasing aspects of the game but were more interested in scoring any way they could. Even if they looked off-balance and clumsy on occasion, they were rewarded with countless goals that took the goalkeeper by surprise and left him 'flapping' at thin air. I am not trying to imply that the conventional ways to strike a ball are useless - quite the opposite in fact. If the ball is struck correctly it will travel with precision and power and end up in the back of the net. But this is under 'normal' circumstances and unfortunately players are not always given enough time to produce the perfect 'text book' execution. In other words, an attacking player has to be able to use both techniques, the orthodox and the improvised style.

For example, years ago it was thought that the best way to strike a ball that was crossed into the area was to let it travel to the leg furthest away. In other words a ball crossed from the right should be struck with the left foot and a ball from the left should be struck with the right foot. In this way the player was able to put more body-weight behind the ball with more accuracy as the shooting leg was directly in line with the ball. The other positive benefit is that the angle is that much bigger when shooting in this way. However, the game is played at such a fast pace today that this orthodox execution can be a luxury. If there is a defender near by (and there usually is) a split second could be all the time he needs to make a challenge and intercept the ball. If the player improvises and uses the other foot then he saves that split second and the defender cannot react in time. The time constraints are ever-present in the game and also have an impact on control, passing and dribbling. But more importantly it is a great weapon to neutralize the goalkeeper. If the attacker chooses to shoot using the leg furthest away from the ball then he gives the goalkeeper enough time to get into position and narrow the angle. The goalkeeper does not have enough time to position himself correctly if the attacker shoots quickly using the foot nearest the ball. For the above reasons I recommend that players shoot as quickly as they can by using the foot nearest the ball as it is crossed.

All the above-mentioned players have scored many improvised goals using the foot nearest to the ball to save time and wrong-foot the goalkeeper. They have also on occasion used the foot furthest away from the ball in an unconventional way, using the outside of the foot to speed-up the execution and avoid the challenge from the defender. Of course these types of shots are not powerful and so are usually done very close to goal (in the six-yard box) or perhaps from further out, trying to anticipate the movements of the goalkeeper if he is coming out to challenge for the ball.

Post-war Spanish soccer was famous for its aggressive style and long shots. The introduction of foreign players and coaches changed these characteristics and the style of the game became more technical and skill-based. These days however, long shots are not only a very effective way to score goals but are essential when trying to by-pass the organized defensive formations that prevail. Taking long shots is a good way to 'open-up' a defense because the defenders are conscious of the threat and tend to come up more, thus leaving space for the opposition to exploit. This is very common in basketball and hand ball: when a team does not have a player that can score from distance, the strikers find it very difficult to make space due to the tight marking. However, if a team has the potential to threaten from long range, then the striker has more freedom to move, organize, and generate attacks.

Heading ability is another tremendous advantage when trying to get the better of a well-disciplined defense. Of course any team is capable of playing high balls into the opposition's area all day long and can win games even though they are technically inferior because they have good headers of the ball in attack and in defense. However, very few teams possess real heading specialists that allow them to fully exploit this way of playing the game. Teams are always keen to play with tall players both in attack and especially in the center of the defense. Nevertheless, the crosses into the area are usually poor and predictable and make it easy for the defenders to clear the ball no matter what their height. These days it is common for the ball to be crossed at medium height or hard and low so that the attacker can take the ball on the run and use the power in the cross to direct the ball at pace into the back of the goal. Some players like to anticipate the cross and get to the ball first by producing a 'diving' header.

# Practice Shooting Repeatedly

Despite the great importance of shooting, players spend relatively little time practicing this technique in training. Some weeks shooting practice is not even practiced at all during the training sessions. This seems incredible but it is true. Even when shooting practice is carried out it usually involves all the players lining up, waiting their turn and shooting from the edge of the 18-yard box. On other occasions the coach calls out a name, passes the ball and the player runs forward to shoot. This type of exercise has very little to do with the type of shooting that takes place during a game. Things are made even worse when on occasion the coach privately tells the goalkeepers to make it look as if they are trying their best to save the shots but to let them pass in order to boost the striker's confidence.

Shooting practice should take place on a daily basis and should involve opposition in order to simulate 'real-match' situations. The types of exercises I have just mentioned do not produce this type of situation and so are ineffective and a waste of time.

## Never Criticize a Player for Shooting

Both as a player and later as a coach I was always unhappy with 'greedy' players who shot from impossible angles, especially when a teammate was in space and the pass was the obvious option. However, my opinion changed because of what I am about to tell you.

When I was the coach at Racing Santander (my first spell as coach at the club) there was a young promising winger called Aguilar (who later became an international when playing for Real Madrid). He was a very gifted player but lacked experience and maturity because of his age. One Saturday after training I stayed behind with the player and a goalkeeper to resolve a problem he was having during matches. The player was not clear what to do with the ball once he got to the by-line. I told him that once he got past the goalkeeper he should play the ball back into the box (a goal-scoring pass) and I played the role of a teammate in the area as he practiced the move. Once he had mastered the technique we all left the training pitch happy with what had been achieved.

The next day, approaching the end of the match with the teams drawing, Aguilar got past the goalkeeper and tried to pass the ball as he had practiced but it went straight into the back of the net and decided the match. From this moment on I realized that goals come from the most unlikely positions and when least expected. A player can produce a wonderful shot and not score while another can attempt to make a pass to a teammate and end up scoring himself. Players can miss 'open' goals while at other times goals are scored from impossible angles or under difficult circumstances. You just never know when your shot might produce a goal.

In other words my advice is: **NEVER CRITICIZE A PLAYER FOR SHOOTING.**

*Aguilar was awarded a trophy for his magnificent goal.*

The following is a great exercise for practicing clearances, passing and in particular, shooting: the player receives a high ball, he controls it with one foot, kicks it up and then with a 'scissor-like' movement shoots at goal using the same foot. Once the ball has been struck the player lands correctly in order to avoid injury.

This exercise can be used for various different objectives but by far the most efficient and spectacular is when it is used to shoot at goal. The attacker can be side-ways on to the goal (the half 'bicycle kick') or he can have his back to goal (the 'bicycle' kick). This is very difficult to defend against.

However, these techniques are extremely complex and difficult to learn and for this reason they should be taught as soon as possible. At The School the players start to learn these techniques when they are 10 years old.

These players watch demonstrations by the older players and videos of this technique. At first the players practice on sand or on mats in the gymnasium so that the landing is a lot softer and there is less chance of an injury. Let's not forget that the professionals make this move look simple (sometimes) but in reality it is one of the most com-

*Hugo Sanchez was a real 'goal-scoring machine'.*

plex and difficult techniques to master and there is a serious possibility of sustaining an injury on landing.

Despite what I have just said about shooting being important, I do not think the importance should be over-emphasized too early. The fact is that shooting is only a small part of the game and the players need to practice the other skills that will give them a shooting chance in the first place. Also, the players are very motivated when it comes to shooting and this is one of the techniques they practice in their own time. However, once the player reaches the age of 17 shooting practice should be included in the training sessions. This is especially true when trying to develop the 'bicycle' kick, which should be practiced with a moving ball and with the 'suspended ball'. These skills are also practiced during the 'small-sided' games against 'real' opposition.

This shooting technique has many names around the world: the Brazilians call it 'bicicleta' (the 'bicycle' kick), but it is also known as 'tijera' (the 'scissor' kick) and in Spain it is best known as 'Chilena (the 'Chilean'). The latter seems an unlikely name as Chile is not and has never been an exceptionally strong soccer-playing nation, but nevertheless the technique has its origins in this country. More specifically, the technique was invented by Unzaga playing in Talcahuano. The technique involves the player having his back to goal, leaning backwards as the legs are quickly raised to meet the ball as if cycling upside down.

This acrobatic technique became known some years later as 'La Chilena' in 1927. Colo-Colo went on a European tour and the striker, Arellano, displayed the skill at various Spanish grounds. The public was thrilled by the unfamiliar technique and gave it the aforementioned name. Unfortunately after scoring several spectacular goals using the technique Arellano died in Valladolid after a collision with a defender.

Pele, Van Basten and Hugo Sanchez were some of the all-time greats when it came to executing the 'bicycle' kick. Few people executed the 'half-bicycle' kick better than Pele, the German Seeler and Zico. They all scored memorable goals using this technique and these goals live on as part of the great history of the game.

These five players have separately spoken to me about the technique and coincide on various points:

- They all started to practice the skill at a very young age, perhaps when they were only 10 or 11 years old. Pele and Hugo were able to learn from their fathers who were both professional players themselves.

- They especially enjoyed performing the technique on grass (Pele and Zico often played on the beach) but even practiced it on concrete when playing with friends without worrying about getting hurt. The 'bicycle' kick came to them instinctively and spontaneously, depending on the circumstances of the game and how the ball arrived.

- They all believe that a certain natural ability is required in order to perform this technique but they are all convinced that to perform it well is down to repetition and hard work. All five players have dedicated hour after hour to practice.

*The German, Uwe Seeler, executing*
*'media Chilena' (the 'half bicycle' kick).*

This is how Hugo Sanchez analyzed his technique when talking to the Spanish soccer magazine 'Marca':

**Focus:** "*It is important to focus on the player with the ball who is going to make the pass. Then, keep your eye on the ball as you run into position ready to make the strike*".

**Getting ready to jump:** "*As the ball approaches it is vitally important to judge how and where the ball is going to arrive in order to time the jump perfectly*".

**Once in the air:** "*Contact with the ball is imminent and you need to start the jump trying to put as much impetus in the shooting leg as possible*".

**Parallel to the ground:** "*This is the last stage before striking the ball. Now is the time to concentrate on trying to be as precise as possible in order to get the shot on target*".

**Contact:** "*It is vitally important to have a good contact with the ball or else the previous points will have been in vain. At the end of the day a clean strike is the key to success*".

**The landing:** "*Once the ball has left the boot the outcome cannot be changed. The only thing left to do is to fall safely and land without causing an injury*".

## Advice to Help Score More Goals

Any player with good technical and tactical skill has the ability and the confidence to be able to take players on and create shooting opportunities. On the other hand, many players do not create chances because they need too much time to get the ball on their good foot etc. and so the opportunity is lost. This is why every player should be two-footed and therefore able to shoot with either foot with great effectiveness.

Apart from the constant and systematic training done on the

training ground here is some advice to help players finish off moves with success during matches:

1. A player should always be prepared to shoot without worrying about his position or that of his teammates or whether the shot will be successful or not. Unbelievable goals are always being scored from impossible angles and from incredible distances. Even poorly struck shots can result in a goal thanks to a deflection or a goalkeeping error. Shots are often scored from a long way out because the goalkeeper is unsighted due to a crowded 18-yard box. Poor goalkeeping decisions and poor positioning also facilitate goal scoring.

2. If a player is criticized for shooting by his teammates he should tell them that if he manages to score it is not for himself but for the good of the team. There is no better gift in the game.

## The Attacking Defender

At the start of the 78-79 season, the Gijon coach appeared to be less than happy with Quini. According to the coach the striker stayed up in attack and totally ignored any defensive duties. I listened in amazement and told him that Quini was a real 'goal-scoring machine' and that was how he helped out the rest of the team (what better way to do it?). Gijon won the league that year and of course Quini was top goal scorer.

If I had the same conversation today I would not be at all surprised as these days the coaches expect the strikers to battle, defend and mark the opposing defenders. In October 1992 Esparrago, a coach, was commentating on the Coruña - Madrid match and said: "Madrid played very well during the first half because the two strikers did the invaluable job of putting pressure on the defenders up front".

I respect his opinion but I do not agree with it: despite what Esparrago said about the strikers doing an invaluable job, neither one, Butragueño nor Zamorano managed to score. On the other hand, Bebeto in the other team never chased back once but scored three goals. Which players did the best job do you think?

This way of thinking about the role of the attackers is misguided. A team is made up of ten outfield players and the team does not need all ten defending in order to defend well. At the very most a team needs perhaps seven or eight in order to defend efficiently. This means that once they win possession they have 2-3 players ready to play the counter attack. If all the players play deep in a defensive role then they get in each other's way and invariably leave the ball, thinking a teammate is sure to get it. Once they win the ball there is no one up front to pass to and so to avoid any problems the ball is 'hoofed' up field. The end result is that the opposition get possession easily and mount attack after attack.

My views on this subject are clear: the role of the striker is to score goals and the role of the defender is to prevent goals from being scored. So the attacker does not have to mark the defender. It's the other way round!!

I can imagine lots of you are smiling and thinking: "balance", "spread out and fill the pitch", "the team should work together and for each other". Here is another anecdote to help make my point: some years ago (the obsession about strikers defending had already begun) Carrasco a Barcelona player and now a soccer commentator himself, asked me: "What do think I'm doing wrong? Physically I am in great shape and I can run all day but I still play badly". I told him that he spent too much time chasing back to hassle the opposition and that this was a waste of time and that when he got the ball he lost a yard of pace because of all the irrelevant hard work he was doing. My advice to him was to run less and concentrate on attacking. Knowing he was a great fan of Maradona I asked him to remember when they played together and if he could remember how much time Maradona spent chasing back and marking defenders?

The 'wolf' as Carrasco was known, was a good guy and he asked me: "But doesn't playing that way let the rest of the team down?". On the contrary I said he saved his energy for something even better: scoring goals and making goals. From then on Carrasco's performances went from strength to strength and he became a full international. Spain (down to 10 men) was playing against Austria and the sides were drawing 2-2 half way through the second half. Austria was dominating the game but Carrasco produced some wonderful pieces of attacking play and eventually managed to score the winning goal.

This is what Carrasco told me on his return to Barcelona: "Once one of our players had been sent off I decided to help out more defensively and follow my marker if he went forward. Then I remembered what you told me and stayed up front and on one occasion seeing that the defense were beaten for pace I ran to the center forward's position and this is how I managed to score the winner". And with a sarcastic smile the 'wolf' added: "And now all my teammates are happy with the way I am playing!".

65

*Carrasco in Santander with author.*
*The year was 1989.*

3. A player may simply shoot as a way of stopping a possible counter-attack. If he gets in position he may score, but if he misses then at least the rest of the team has a chance to regroup and organize. I have often witnessed an attacker deliberate too long before shooting only to lose the ball and the other team mount a counter attack and score themselves.

4. I have also witnessed strikers who have not scored in a few matches take it upon themselves to be the creative player in the team or adopt a more defensive role based on hustle and hard work. Unfortunately, this is doing the player and the team a disservice. If a player plays center forward he is in the team to score goals, not to create the build-up. The fact is that every player should be motivated to score goals no matter what his position.

5. If a player is in the clear approaching the goal and the goal-keeper comes out to narrow the angle then take this advice from Puskas and Zico: The Hungarian always shot quickly and low using the inside of the foot as a goalkeeper ran out to con-front him. The ball usually found the back of the net even though he used very little back lift, the shot was not powerful and the ball went near the goalkeeper. Why was this technique

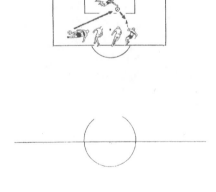

*A shot to the far post and the other striker "Give or don't give, but I'm in support."*

so successful? When goalkeepers are running out to narrow the angle they have great difficulty reacting quickly to a low shot. They are easily wrong-footed and are unable to dive with sufficient speed. So, by the time they dive the ball has usually gone past.

Zico was a master at feinting to shoot and nearly always fooled the goalkeeper and was able to stroke the ball into the open goal. On occasion a goalkeeper would not commit himself and so in this case Zico played another feint only to shoot immediately, leaving the goalkeeper confused and wrong-footed.

6. When referring to crosses earlier in this book I said that if a player gets to the dead ball line he should not cut the ball back and cross with the opposite foot. Nevertheless, moving the ball onto the other foot is a good tactic for making a better angle for a shot on goal. Recently Michel said: "Despite the fact that I am right-footed I scored most of my goals using my left". Although at first glance this statement seems incomprehensible, in fact it makes perfect sense. Imagine him running down the wing, cutting inside and shooting with his other foot to make a better angle. However, his crosses also made lots of goals and these were produced using his right foot and only very occasionally using his left.

7. Years ago a cross was nearly always directed to the far post but today there is far more variety and options available. I always tell players to head for the near post (the post nearest the cross) because this area is less crowded and the attack is finished-off more quickly. Another advantage is that the run to the near post will 'drag' defenders across and leave space behind for a teammate. If a striker wants to meet the center with a header then a good cross always helps. If the ball is struck well then the striker redirects the ball using the power in the cross. The most important thing about making a chance in the area is to anticipate, get into position and get to the ball before the defender.

8. If a player shoots from an angle with the goalkeeper well positioned then I recommend aiming for the far post. One of

*The photo is a clear example of a goal scorer's anticipation and instinct. Netzer takes the free kick and Muller makes his run to be the first player to get to any rebound or parry from the goalkeeper.*

the reasons for this is that the goalkeeper usually covers the near post better than the far post. Another reason is that if the shot is poorly executed it may turn out to be a good cross for a teammate, assuming anyone is supporting on the far post. Also, sometimes the goalkeeper makes a save but only succeeds in pushing the ball towards an opponent who easily places the ball into the open net. Sometimes a shot is deflected by a player in the area and the ball falls nicely for a teammate. It is always a good idea to 'back up' and run into the area when a teammate shoots for the reasons I have just mentioned. Pele, Puskas, Di Stefano, Muller, Zico, Quini and Hugo Sanchez were always in the right place at the right time, ready to take advantage of any rebounds, deflections and saves in the area.

9. It is never easy to score a goal and even more difficult to score an important and decisive one. So any player who tries to score should be applauded even if at times his attempts seem poor. Remember, a player who misses chances is at least getting himself in position to make an attempt and so has a good possibility of scoring sooner or later. I am sure we can all think of players who never venture into the area or have a shot at goal. These players do not have a strike-rate percentage and of course they never miss because they never shoot.

## Puskas and Goals

It is very difficult to practice scoring goals during training as it is it impossible to simulate all the different circumstances and situations that might occur in a game. One day the great Real Madrid team of Di Stefano had finished training and Puskas decided to have a bet with some other players. "Pancho" was a master at scoring goals. He played in the first division for 24 years and scored 512 goals which is a world record.

Puskas took 15 shots from a muddy patch of ground and managed to hit each post five times and the crossbar five times, leaving the goal covered in mud. The players who betted against him were left open-mouthed while those who had confidence in him carried him on their shoulders back to the changing rooms.

Despite his brilliance, during the 1954 World Cup in Switzerland, with Germany winning 3-2, he missed a glaring chance to level the match from inside the six-yard box. Unfortunately, the importance of the occasion and the responsibility weighed heavily on his shoulders and nerves got the better of him.

In other words, even the 'Greats' miss open goals, so we should all be a bit tolerant and understanding when this happens to lesser mortals.

10. Any player who wants to score goals needs to have a good mental attitude. Some players are obsessed with scoring goals and they practice all week to improve their technique. Unfortunately, sometimes a player misses a clear opportunity early on in the game and the crowd starts to whistle. The player is conscious of this, and does not want to make another mistake and so makes no more attempts on goal. Any player who is affected by such things will neither be a good goal scorer nor a good soccer player in general.

**11.** A good goal scorer needs to have a strong character and needs to be single minded. If he scores a goal he is a hero but if he misses he is clumsy and bereft of ideas and talent. A striker always experiences a combination of highs and lows. He should be able to accept success and failure. Any player who lacks a strong mental attitude should look to play in another position as he will not prosper as a striker. All strikers should remember that they can be playing poorly and can be totally marked out of the game for long periods but if they score a goal all this is forgotten.

## Perfecting Speed of Execution

Earlier I mentioned that it is not good idea to practice specific shooting exercises until the player has good ball skills, is able to play as part of a team and is able to play well against an opposition. When a player starts this training he should also start to concentrate on another special skill: speed of execution.

The player is not expected to concentrate on speed of execution before he reaches this level because it is tremendously difficult to achieve. The player needs to combine physical, mental and technical speed (this is not always the case if the player 'really' knows how to play the game).

The player first needs to execute the technical skills properly without worrying and performing them at speed. Once the player has mastered the technique, he can start to concentrate on progressively trying to improve how fast he produces the skill.

Some coaches confuse the speed of execution with the skill itself but these are totally different considerations. The skill involves the ability to assimilate new movements quickly. By this I mean learning the skill properly, which involves performing the technique with precision. These are the considerations involved in learning a technique:

**1.** The precision required to perform the movements.

2. The complex coordination required to perform the movements.

3. The time taken to be able to achieve the necessary movements. This refers to the time taken to learn the movements the skill requires.

On the other hand, speed of execution has the following considerations:

1. The cognitive capacity of the speed (Perception, decision making, reaction speed and anticipation).

2. The speed of the technical coordination (technical skills and a 'feel' for the ball).

3. The speed of movement without the ball.

What I mean by speed of execution and quick thinking during a game is the ability to analyze situations quickly, to react quickly and how quickly the player controls or plays the ball, how quickly he dribbles, passes or shoots when in a limited space or when being put under pressure by the opposition.

The performance level of any player depends on this type of speed and quick thinking. Some players are very skillful, extremely quick, with breath-taking speed off the mark and with an excellent jump, but they do not produce good performances because they are unable to apply these qualities correctly in the context of the game. They do not fully understand the tactical aspects of positioning and constructing a move or they are just simply persistent daydreamers who lack concentration.

It is very difficult to achieve speed and precision at the same time because these are antagonistic forces. A perfect technique can be achieved slowly whereas if the skill is performed more quickly the technique is not as precise. However, all the great teams over the years have had players in the team with the ability to perform fantastic skills at speed. Soccer teams are always made up of players with different strengths and weaknesses. The secret is to get the balance right. For example, a slow but technically gifted player able to 'read' the game and distribute the ball well is complimented by other less skilful players who are able to run at pace in order to take advantage of the 'defense-splitting' passes.

Coaches involved with players (of a high standard) should get them to concentrate on producing the technical skills as fast as they possibly can. They should insist that the 'rounds', small-sided games and games are play work on producing his skills as quickly and efficiently as he can.

Once the player reaches this stage he will normally be comfortable on the ball with a full repertoire of ball skills. Although his technical and tactical knowledge is fairly advanced he plays the game relatively slowly. However, this is not always the case as some players have a problem because they try to play too quickly. They are unable to 'read' the game or choose the right option at the right time because their undoubted speed is not matched by their technique and knowledge of the game. The only way to sort this problem out is by getting the players to do very complex technical and tactical exercises on a regular basis.

Speed of execution is often affected by motivational and/or emotional considerations. The need to succeed and the fear of failure mean that the player takes a split second longer to execute the action.

In summary, it is important for coaches to help their players to develop cognitive processes, concentration skills, anticipation, 'fighting' spirit, positive thinking and will power. Any player needs these qualities and the ability to 'read' the game and play with intelligence.

Technical and tactical considerations at pace should be omnipresent during training sessions. The theoretical side of training such as analyzing videos and studying tactical exercises for homework compliments the practical side of the game and together they help the player develop a good knowledge and understanding of the game and faster speed of execution. This type of constant and progressive training helps the player to produce less errors during a match. These mistakes usually occur because of an inability to 'read' the game, poor anticipation and human error.

During training the players should be expected to increase their perception and anticipation skills by practicing playing the game under pressure due to limited space and time. This is particularly true when playing in the final third of the pitch as players need to get used to creating goal-scoring opportunities by playing the 'one-two' or dribbling under difficult circumstances where time and space are at a premium.

The following will give you some indication about the sort of split-second timing that takes place during a game. The player should know what he is going to do with the ball even before he gets it in the opponent's area. If this is not the case then he loses valuable time. This is how quickly a player needs to think: two

## Hugo Sanchez

Defenders are less than happy when the opposition plays 'one-touch', as this doesn't give them a chance to react and leaves them stranded.

Of course, shooting first time is even more difficult to defend against and leaves the opposition totally powerless to respond. There has never been a better example of striking the ball first-time than Hugo Sanchez. During the 1989-90 season he was the league's top goal scorer with 38 goals. His goals came in a wide variety of circumstances: free kicks, penalties, using his left, using his right, headers, diving headers and 'bicycle' kicks etc. But the most extraordinary statistic (and it seems almost unbelievable) of all is that all his goals were scored 'first-time'. He only needed 'one-touch'.

tenths of a second to see where the defenders are, one tenth of a second to spot a teammate and another tenth of a second to pass the ball. If the player is not able to perform at this speed (even though the move may be successful due to poor opposition) he will never become a top player.

The only way to be able to play a fast game is by training at a good pace and intensity over a long period of time doing exercises that are as similar as possible to playing the game itself. If this is not the case then the player will notice a tremendous difference between what he does during training and what is possible during a proper match.

The type of training I recommend conditions the body and the nervous system to actions and the speed of movement. The mind also becomes accustomed to making quick decisions depending on the circumstances in the game. This does not come naturally to most players. A player must work hard over several years to condition his mind and body to function in a certain way and at a certain speed.

Specific emphasis should be given to twists and turns, speed off the mark, subtle changes in direction, playing in a confined space and particularly running with the ball at speed. As I have already mentioned (but it is worth mentioning again) a fast player is of no use whatsoever if he cannot control the ball and does not know what to do with it.

It is also significant to point out that a player can only gain the maximum from training at a good pace if he is not tired. For this reason, the breaks should be frequent and lengthy when doing this type of training exercise. It is also advisable to incorporate frequent stretching, jogging and walking activity in order to keep the neuromuscular system working at its best. All players are different and some recover from physical activity more quickly than others so it makes no sense to make them rest for the same period of time. The rest periods should suit the individual needs of the players. Some have trained more than others and some are fitter than others and some have less stamina than others.

I should make it clear that during this type of training to

Caminero, Aguado, Ivan Helguera and Seedorf all know how to 'play'
using their arms. (All players do it)

*Raul soon understood and learned the importance of using his arms. Perhaps this is the very thing that helped him to demonstrate his true talent. Here he is seen competing with the Basque player Urrutia, a great player, who seems to know a thing or two about using his arms himself.*

improve the speed of execution (just as in any other) the players should be divided into groups according to their ability as this helps with continuity and progression

## Use Your Arms

At this stage the gifted player learns how to make full advantage of his arms during a match. Spectators can usually perceive good play when watching professionals and they enjoy the headers, passes, shots and if they are knowledgeable, the tactics as well. However, they fail to spot the subtle use of shoulders, arms and hands which takes place throughout the whole game.

Professional players use a range of tactics, some legal and some totally illegal that the referee is unaware of or fails to spot because he was never a player himself or if he was he never made it as a top professional. The top players are well aware of this and use less than official tactics to exploit the situation in the following ways:

1. Soccer players, unlike sprinters, do not help generate speed by using their arms when running. Instead, they run with their arms slightly bent to achieve better balance. However, when they are competing with an opponent the players will extend their arms firmly to the side in order to obstruct the defender, impede his progress or keep him from getting to the ball. This is legal.

2. This arm position is also used when jumping for the ball against an opponent. This is because it is important to make space, get into position and hold an opponent off. If the arms are not held in this position then the jump will not be as high and it is difficult to compete for the ball against an adversary. This is legal.

3. Some players, when running alongside an opponent, try to put him off or break his rhythm by hitting, pushing on the side, back or bottom with the palm of his hand. This same tactic is used if the opponent has the ball and is about to pass or more importantly shoot as it has an adverse affect on accuracy and power. These are all illegal.

4. On other occasions players surreptitiously 'grab' or hold their opponent using one of the following methods:

   a) The opponent is held slightly and then released and then held again and released and so on until finally he loses the ball or the chance is lost.
   b) The player holds his opponent back and is not released until or unless there is no possibility of getting to the ball. (Both these tactics are illegal).

5. Some attackers when they receive the ball with a defender in close attendance 'sneakily' 'pinch' him in the chest as they quickly turn to make a run or if close to goal to shoot. (This is illegal).

## Migueli and Toshack

When I think about the different strategies players use to resolve given situations in a game (not always legally) a certain memory always springs to mind which involves an experience I had coaching Barcelona.

We were playing Liverpool in the semi-final of The European Cup. We knew all about the English team and prepared for the match by studying the players on a collective and individual basis. I spoke to Rife about the aerial threat posed by Heighway who had a knack of arriving at the far post. Rife seemed very relaxed and said: "Don't worry I know what to do to keep him from getting a clean header on goal. When I jump with him for the ball I'll bang my hip against his and we'll both fall to the ground. I won't get to the ball but neither will he".

Later I spoke to Migueli and discussed the problems caused by Toshack (now a coach at Real Sociedad). Migueli was good in the air but so was Toshack and he was a lot taller. Migueli seemed unconcerned and replied: "Relax boss, I know he's got a height advantage but as we jump I'll place my head against his Adam's apple. The harder he tries to head the ball the more pain he'll be in".

As I have said repeatedly, in reality there are always two sets of diametrically opposed tactics going on in a game: the ones we can see and the ones we can't see. Never forget it.

*Migueli is probably the best defender I have ever coached.*

**6.** When about to jump and compete for a ball with a defender, some players grab their shorts just as they jump. Obviously the opponent is unbalanced and is unable to jump effectively. (This is illegal).

The masters of these 'professional' tactics are the Italians. In the European Cup final between Juventus and Ajax, Finidi got to the dead ball line and crossed. Kluivert beat his marker to the near post and got ready to shoot. The defender, seeing that a goal was imminent, nudged him in the back as he was about to shoot. The striker lost his balance and hit the ball with his knee and it went wide of the goal. According to the match commentator "the defender was unable to make a challenge but did enough to put the striker off".

I have known lots of very talented players who once they made it to the professional game were unable to show their true talent because their opponents used arms, obstructions and shirt-pulling to stop them. These players were not 'clever' enough to make it at the top level.

Once the players have reached this level they should understand that being a soccer player is not just about talent, quality and skill but there is also another very important factor: the shoulder to shoulder challenge (sometimes body to body). They need to understand this and adapt their game accordingly.

During the recent World Cups in Mexico, Italy and USA 90% of the goals were scored from inside the 18-yard box. This means that goals are scored or prevented in a very populated area where space is tight and the use of the body and arms is imperative. Goals can only be scored if the player anticipates and moves rapidly. He must analyze the situation intuitively and instinctively, deciding quickly what offensive movement to make. But on occasion the player needs to shield the ball or the space from his opponent and this is where he uses his body and arms to great effect.

The attacker has to overcome the obstructive tactics employed by the defenders by undertaking special training where he practices stopping suddenly, changing direction, making dummy movements and runs and by improving his explosive speed over a short distance by practicing sprints from a standing start. The player needs to move in any direction off either foot and should keep the defender guessing by being unpredictable and constantly moving.

Nevertheless, it is not always possible to avoid the physical contact and confrontations so the player needs to practice these as well and learn how to deal with them and overcome them.

The idea during these exercises is to pass, dribble and shoot as quickly as possible, while your opponent holds you, pushes you and generally obstructs you. The player should shield the ball as best he can and this includes using arms. He should also do his best to overcome the problems being posed by the opposition in order to keep possession and finish off the move.

These exercises should be played with the right attitude and involve constant repetition. It is a good idea to play with the professionals to learn how they use the body and arms to their advantage. This is a privilege and should be taken seriously as there is a danger that the players (seeing it as a dream come true) will be in awe of their local heroes and will not learn as much as they should from playing with them. The only difficulty is that the professionals are so much better than the players that they do not need to use their arms etc. to keep them at bay. For this reason, these sessions should be performed on a daily basis if possible so that the better players will sooner or later force the professionals to use these tactics to keep possession of the ball. When this happens, the players learn the 'tricks of the trade' and how to combat them.

Once a player has developed good technique and tactical awareness on an individual basis he needs to concentrate on using this ability to play as part of the team. The team is made up of exceptional players with wonderful individual talent but will only perform well if all the separate entities gel and play as one. Good soccer is made up of the inspiration, intelligence and individual magic of the players and their ability to work together as a unit in an atmosphere of well-ordered discipline and cooperation. Either way, a well-balanced team always needs individual 'flair' players and grafters. If all the players are 'flair' players, who is going to make the runs into space? Who is going stay back and play a more defensive role? On the other hand, if all the players are workers it would be better to start them working in a factory somewhere…

Naturally enough, all the work the players do in training is to get them to perform to a high standard on the pitch during a match and so any strengths and weaknesses are easily spotted on the field of play. It is important for the players to understand the system and work together as much as possible. Even though normally there are three or four players who lose concentration on an individual basis during a match, the team still plays as a unit and works hard for one another.

On the other hand, a player can have an inspired game on an individual basis but he does not follow the plan and work with his teammates, leading to a lack of discipline that totally undermines the efforts of the rest of the team. Anyone who has ever seen the Milan team under Capello, or Laudrup, Stoichkov and Bakero at Barcelona will know that teams with talented individuals can still play as a unit.

But there are also many teams whose talented players have the wrong mental attitude. They do not work well as part of the team and are frequently jealous and egotistical. The team therefore fails miserably to reach its potential.

## Do the Players Adapt to the System?

One of the great problems with playing a system is that many coaches believe the system should be adapted to suit the players. In other words, the coach adopts the system to play to the strengths of his players and tries to cover up their weaknesses.

Knowing that soccer is full of discrepancies and is certainly unpredictable, it seems almost unbelievable that the majority of people (critics, commentators, players and fans) agree that the system should be arrived at in this way even though there is no basis in fact to support this view as the following demonstrates:

1. Anyone who believes in this way of choosing the system is also in favor of 'multi-purpose' players who can play anywhere on the pitch as attackers or defenders. This in itself is hard to understand because if the players are so flexible and talented then surely they should be able to adapt to any system.
2. I started playing soccer just as the W-M system was being introduced to Spain. If any of the teams using this system lost a match then the usual arguments and criticism were heard: "This system might be all right for the English but it is not good for us". Soon all the teams adopted this system.

3. Then the 4-2-4 line-up arrived. The same thing happened and the cynics voiced their opinion after every defeat: "Our game is based on tenacity and hard work. We should leave the 'fancy' technical play to the Brazilians". Of course, slowly but surely this way of playing was adopted by all the teams.

**4.** Next the 'Sweeper' was introduced along with tight man-to-man marking. This system was branded ultra-defensive when in reality it was a very intelligent tactic to help launch the counter-attack. This system also became widespread throughout the game.

**5.** Today, nearly all teams play a multiple zonal defensive system as far up the pitch as possible, putting pressure on the opposition. The goalkeeper is often used to support and run off his line and the team plays without 'real' forwards.

How many players can realistically play in any position? How many coaches adapt the system to suit the players? I think the answer to both these questions is in reality very few.

These are my ideas on the subject:

The coach arrives at what he thinks is a good system thanks to his experience and knowledge of the game. He positions his players where he thinks they will perform best for the team.

The coach has to weigh the player's strengths and weaknesses before deciding where he should play. Apart from a few exceptions, the player is normally selected in a position where he can perform at his best, whereas if he is played elsewhere his value to the team and his own personal performance is much less. Sometimes there is no comparison. Have you ever thought how Ronaldo would fair as an out-and-out winger? How about Bebeto as a midfield general? Why not use Ferrer as the 'brains' of the team?

I am sure that some of the people who advocate picking

*The author with the Barcelona youth team after becoming Spanish Champions.*

the system according to the players think that what I have just said is exactly what they believe in. Nothing could be further from the truth. No matter what the system, players always have to mark, make space, defend, attack, intercept, pass and shoot etc. And all teams are made of fast, slow, technical, brave and not so brave players. The great skill of the coach is to know which players should play in which positions in order to compliment teammates and thus get the best out of individuals for the benefit of the team. This is a tremendously difficult job that requires total dedication, knowledge and a real understanding of the game. If one day you become a coach and you are fortunate enough to have Ronaldo in your squad but you do not pick him or you play Laudrup as 'sweeper' you should face the fact that you are not cut out for this profession.

On the other hand, 'Great' coaches have left their 'mark' on every club they have ever been in charge of by making them play in a certain way. The new team soon plays using the same system and with the same style as the previous team. Coaches like Benito Diaz, Helenio Herrera and Scopelli; later Menotti, Venables and Tele Santana; these days Capello and Cruyff (who brought the Ajax system with him) have all put their 'stamp' on every club they have coached and offer clear proof that I am not mistaken in what I say. When I was at Barcelona, the Youth team were Spanish Champions fives years in a row. Of course, the players were different each year but the system remained the same.

After clearing up that point I would like to move on and talk about how to develop and how the players learn to play as a team.

The method was learned in the previous level and now it is time to develop these ideas still further and head towards perfection.

The method is used along with the 4-3-3 system explained in the previous level to get the players to play as a unit. The idea is to work together as a team to support one another and cover all the space on the pitch, not allowing the opposition time or room to maneuver. The whole team has to cooperate and play as a unit or else the system is undermined.

These are some of the most common movements involved:

If the team is dominating the game and the right-sided midfield player has the ball then the defenders come up and fill all the space behind him. There is no need to worry about the opponent's attackers as they will be 'offside'.

As the player on the ball advances, obviously his teammates look to make space and make themselves available. The right-winger stays out wide, the center forward looks to play the 'doblada' down the middle, the left-sided midfield player stays in his zone, conscious that there may be a sudden change of direction and he will quickly run out wide of the winger who moves inside. The center-midfield player stays back in a defensive role in case there is a sudden counter-attack.

If possession is lost then in theory nobody runs back chasing after the ball to win it back. Obviously the strikers are the first line of defense and they try to impede, stop or at least make a challenge for the ball in the opponent's area. Once the ball is lost, the players at the back (with a good view of the game) will call for the team to drop back in order to do what Tassara says: limit space to create space.

The great advantage of playing as a unit (despite what the critics say) is that it is a good energy-saving tactic. Any team playing the counter-attack has to run 70-80 yards to get to the opponent's danger area and then run back. Using this system, if there is a counterattack and attackers are all up in support, when the ball is lost they do not run back but they defend from where they are. The attackers become the first line of defense. Over a match this saves the players a tremendous amount of energy.

Apart from saving energy, playing as a unit offers other advantages:

- The idea that a team defends even in the opponent's half is very off-putting for defenders as they are used to be hassled into playing quickly when they have the ball in their own area.

- If the attackers actually manage to win the ball, there is a good chance they will score because they are close to goal and the defender has little time to react and make amends.

## Playing the 'Cerrojo' Defensive System?

At this level, the players in defense still concentrate on covering, supporting one another and dropping back, always trying to mature and develop tactically. By the end of this level the players play the 'Cerrojo' defensive system, which if mastered allows the defenders to play 'flat' in a line, but this is usually introduced in the next level.

The 'Cerrojo' defensive system.

1. The 'sweeper' runs to challenge the player on the ball.

2. Now he moves forward to challenge. He is no longer the last defender and an opponent is now 'offside'.

The attack is not going to be easy. The defense is playing well as a unit.

It only takes one player to forget his role and position. The defense is no longer playing as a unit and there is a potential threat on goal.

This system allows a team to play with a split defense. One of the defenders moves up to midfield (unless the opposition plays with three forwards) two others man-mark the opposition's central attackers, while the fourth plays as a 'sweeper'. It is his job to intercept passes and cut out any ball that gets past his team-mates.

He needs to be able to 'read' the game well because he has to anticipate and imagine what might happen before it actually takes place. He should also be strong and have good timing when challenging for the ball.

Apart from the above the 'sweeper' has other equally important responsibilities. He always plays behind the other defenders except when the opposition attack and get close to the 18-yard box. When this happens he plays in line with the other defenders, does not stand in the 18-yard box and gets ready to challenge the opponent with the ball. Under these circumstances, the goalkeeper acts as the 'sweeper' as there is not a great distance between him and his defenders.

The 'sweeper' moves from one side of the pitch to the other (depending on where the attack is coming from) covering his teammates. If the ball is played deep he only runs across to deal with it if he thinks he has a good chance of getting to it first. If he cannot get to the ball before the opposition then he drops back to the 18-yard box. He also drops back to this position when an opponent is running with the ball towards the area. The idea of dropping back is to limit the space for the opposition to play in and to give the defense time to regroup and take up their positions.

Let's look at the examples above: In picture 1 the 'sweeper' runs out to challenge for the ball. This decision produces one of the following outcomes:

**a)** The 'sweeper' is beaten and the opponent has a clear run on goal.

**b)** The player on the ball passes it to his teammate who makes a run to get beyond his defender.

**c)** The 'sweeper' commits a foul and because he is the last defender he is 'sent off'.

The situation is very different in picture 2 as the 'sweeper' has decided to drop back:

**a)** In this case the other attacker who tries to make space for himself is now perfectly marked. In fact, if he does not check his run he will be caught 'offside'. Either way his marker is in the correct position to deal with any possible threat.

**b)** The 'sweeper' will not be 'sent off' if he commits a foul as he is not the last defender and if he is beaten his teammate can intervene.

The method is taught to the players at length on a progressive basis throughout the different levels and gradually they understand the concepts and master them. However, if the players manage to master the following defensive and offensive ideas

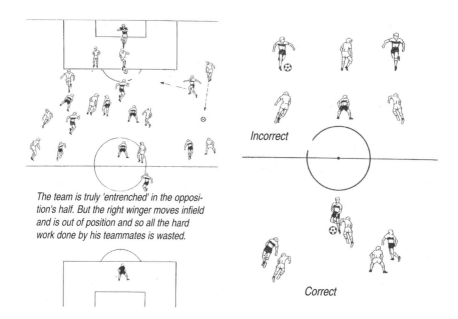

The team is truly 'entrenched' in the opposition's half. But the right winger moves infield and is out of position and so all the hard work done by his teammates is wasted.

*Incorrect*

*Correct*

as well then they play even better both individually and as part of the team. They will become 'multi-talented' players as these concepts ('dropping' back, covering, the 'one-two' and the 'doblada' etc.) can be applied to any system that has a good balance between defense and attack. Here are the concepts:

**1.** Any team playing deep in the opposition's half should make sure they play as a unit, occupying the space effectively to make it as difficult as possible for their opponents to leave their own half. This is seen is picture 1 on the following page. However, all the good work is spoiled as the right winger leaves his position and goes 'chasing' the ball, giving the opposition the space to move forward more easily.

**2.** For this reason the central midfield players need to make sure that their opposite numbers are 'closed down' and given little time or space to play or else the tactic of playing as a well-disciplined unit breaks down. If the opposition has a midfield player deep supporting the defense and the other two playing further forward then the midfield players have to position themselves and mark accordingly.

The opposition may play two midfield players deep and another further forward supporting the strikers. In this case we mark the midfield player supporting the attackers and play two midfield players further forward marking their opposite numbers. In other words, whatever the opposition's midfield does, we do.

If this is the case then there will be midfield players without a marker (this is an advantage or a disadvantage depending how you look at it) which undermines the system of playing as a unit. If the opposition plays with four midfield players then one of our defenders moves forward and plays in midfield to mark the extra midfielder.

3. Interchanging positions is a way of keeping a reasonable control and cover over the whole pitch in order to carry out attacks or counter-attacks. So, when a defender is involved in an attack and runs forward and is obviously out of position as he cannot be in two places at once, then another player has to drop back and cover and play a defensive role until the defender returns to his position.

This is a good way to prevent dangerous counter-attacks because once the opposition gets the ball (and they will sooner or later) they do not have any free space to exploit. The defender playing as a temporary attacker will generally run back to take up his defensive position once the attack he was involved in ends. He should be taught during training that he does not have to frantically run back as his position has been filled by a teammate but instead he should start defending from his advanced position by either challenging for the ball or marking someone, thus making it difficult for the opposition to break out of their own half.

Any player hoping to play this type of system needs to be both intelligent and interested in working hard for the team. Some players find it difficult to sacrifice their individual 'urges' and concentrate totally on playing a disciplined role for the benefit of the whole team.

4. However, the system is not just about correct positioning. There needs to be a clear distinction between good but static

positioning and good, dynamic positioning that involves constant movement and anticipation. Modern soccer is based on movement, anticipation, vision, speed and teamwork. Players need to be able to 'read' the game and they need the necessary knowledge and understanding of the 'logic' of the game to be able to anticipate the likely outcomes of any particular move. It is just as important to know what to do when a teammate has the ball or when the opposition has it.

These qualities are important both in defense and in attack but they have a particular emphasis when referring to anticipation when marking. The most important thing about marking is good positioning. We often see professional players stand behind their opponent, but this is not the best position to mark a player. Instead, the player should stand to the side of his opponent as explained in the previous level. This marking technique is perfected during this stage of learning.

**5.** A team can organize its defense in various ways when playing with a 'sweeper'. The defense can be mixed, zonal or man-to-man marking. The latter gives a team far more freedom and space in which to express itself. The Ajax teams in recent years and Cruyff's Barça team played with this system and proved that marking on an individual basis is not an outdated concept.

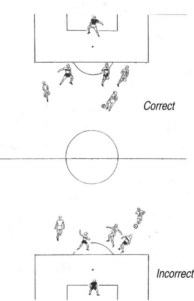

*Correct*

*Incorrect*

**6.** The players should be very sure of what their attacking role involves. They have to know how and when to rotate positions, to cover defensively and when to move forward and help 'unlock' even the most well-organized and disciplined defense.

The French refer to these movements as 'Tourbillon' and the players are very familiar with this tactic: if you are in my position covering for me, I will take up another teammate's position as he is in yours covering for you.

## **M**ove Away to Create Space

**7.** All the great teams over the years worked tirelessly for each other and always supported the player on the ball. At the same time other players would make runs or dummy runs in order to unsettle and surprise the opposition. If the markers follow the player making the run then this creates space for other players to exploit. If these runs are not made, the defense keeps its shape and discipline, thus reducing the space and the possibility of a successful attack. This is why the method encourages the players (all players) to 'open up' the opposition's defense by playing the 'doblada': this move means that the ball is received deep in the opposition's half in front of goal or produces space in front of goal for teammates to exploit. Remember, always move away to create space.

**8.** Of course these runs need to be perfectly timed and do not involve all the players. How many times have we seen a midfield player win the ball in the middle of the pitch and look to play a quick pass to release the forwards but he cannot because they have mistimed the run and have already set off towards the opponent's goal? On other occasions the attackers wait and wait for the perfect time to make their run but the midfield player does not release the ball. Both cases mean that the defenders drop back and restrict the available space with the likely outcome that they will win the ball and perhaps start a dangerous counter-attack. In other words, 'forcing' the defenders to drop back and play deep has the

*Alejandro Scopelli was one of the best coaches of all time.*

same effect as when we set the 'trap' of playing deep to restrict time and space looking for the counter-attack. We try to hassle them and restrict their time and space in order to create some for us. Put simply: closing down the space to create space.

9. Years ago, the sadly departed, extraordinary coach, Scopelli, discovered that the runs made by forwards were often detrimental to the attack because they were too close to their teammate on the ball, which caused problems. I always tell the players to make their run to create space and alternatives and not to run towards an area that is already being covered by a defender. For example in a) (on page 93) the number 8 runs with the ball towards the number 9, who runs to the right. His marker now faces a dilemma: should he run with him or stay to challenge the player on the ball. Whichever decision he makes he is in a lose-lose situation. If he follows the number 9 then the number 8 is free to run at goal, whereas if he stays to

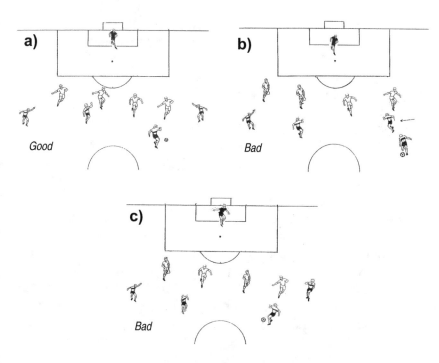

a) Good

b) Bad

c) Bad

challenge for the ball then the number 8 passes it to the number 9 who is in space. However, in b) the number 9 is running in the wrong direction towards another defender (this is very common) and so he is making the attack more difficult. The left back challenges for the ball and the number 9 is not in space to receive a pass as he has run towards the space covered by the central defender.

10. Poor tactical awareness also causes attackers to lose possession, to waste good goal-scoring opportunities or finish a promising attack. Here are some examples:

a) This is a '4 v 4' counter-attack. The most logical thing to do in this situation is for the player on the ball to run at the defenders to create a '2 v 1' with a pass to the winger.

b) However, the winger does not have a good tactical sense and runs towards the zone which is being covered by the central defenders. In this case the defender's job has been made easy: the central defender marks the winger and his marker challenges the player on the ball.

c) On other occasions the winger makes a good run but the player on the ball runs towards the central defenders and so loses the opportunity of exploiting the '2 v 1' situation.

11. Perhaps the secret of my method is the positioning of the wingers. If they position themselves correctly they help the team tremendously: challenging for and winning the ball when the opposition attack and they act as the 'beacons' out wide so that their teammates know they can always pass the ball to them. They are capable of producing wonderful moves and they always produce and score goals. Having said this, this is more difficult than it sounds as positional sense requires a lot of hard work. Sometimes they are too keen to get possession and they ball-chase (nearly always a waste of time and effort) leaving the wing and only returning to their position when a teammate gets the ball. When they are not in position it is impossible to use them as 'beacons' to start a quick counter

attack. And finally, when the player starts to keep his position there is another problem: his teammates never pass the ball to him, which means that the defense always has a numerical advantage.

I should like remind you that throughout the whole process of learning my method the players follow the ideas on the blackboard (and by watching videos) and they practice what they have learned on the pitch. They practice defensive and offensive play and perfection is reached via the competitions and small-sided games.

## Tactical Tests

The players continue to be tested on their knowledge and understanding of the 'logic' of the game (on a practical level this is done during every training session) through a series of diverse questions.

Here are some examples of questions and answers:

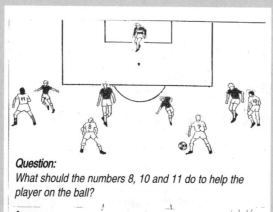

*Question:*
*What should the numbers 8, 10 and 11 do to help the player on the ball?*

*Answer:*
*The number 8 should quickly run towards the player on the ball so that he can play the 'one-two'. The number 10 and number 11 should help their teammates by staying out wide and keeping their markers with them.*

**Question:**
1. From this position the number 10 should cross the ball instead of cutting it back. Why?

**Question:**
2. If the number 10 gets past his marker and runs to the dead ball line how does this affect the movements made by the number 11 and the number 9?

---

**Answer:**
1. Because either the number 11 or the number 9 can move into the box and meet the cross on the run in front of goal.

**Answer:**
2. They will run towards the penalty spot anticipating that the ball will be 'cut back' towards this area.

*The number 10 is poorly positioned because if the number 6 passes the ball to him the opposition's midfield are not beaten. The number 8 should not be running in this direction because it stops any possibility of the number 6 and the number 10 playing the 'one-two'.*

*The number 2 should come out to challenge for the ball. If he is beaten then the number 3 comes across to try to stop the advance while the number 4 marks the player previously marked by the number 3 and the number 6 marks the player previously marked by the number 4.*

As you can see, I do not agree with the majority of people who believe that tactical knowledge should only be gained in theory while the technique is achieved with practice. I strongly believe that both theory and practice should be learned hand-in-hand with constant repetition of the moves and executions.

## Improve Your Stamina

Unfortunately, during the early stages of learning the majority of coaches ignore the technical/tactical side of the game and only concentrate on physical fitness. This is a terrible mistake and it means that the players do not train specifically for soccer at all. They do not get to understand the game and how it works or practice the necessary techniques and skills the game requires.

Furthermore, this physical fitness training creates a disparity between the physical capacity and the more technical motor and coordination skills. For example, if a player works hard in training on improving his jumping ability he also needs a way of sending the instructions to his brain to head the ball at the highest point of the jump. This can only be achieved by repeated heading practice and becoming familiar with the coordination of the movements. It is no good being able to jump high without knowing when or how to head the ball.

Coaches with a good knowledge of the game concentrate on teaching the players how to play soccer and do not have any specific training sessions with the emphasis on physical fitness. This does not mean that the physical fitness side of the game should be ignored, but it is definitely a secondary consideration. During the early years of development the player gets in shape and keeps fit by actually playing the game. No special physical fitness training is needed.

However, once the initial learning stage is over and the player is in his 'prime' for acquiring new skills and techniques he may find that he is held back by a lack of strength, speed and flexibility. This keeps him from taking the huge step necessary to develop from a competent beginner to an accomplished player. This is when the physical conditioning work becomes more intensive and it is based on physical exercises that are very similar to those used to practice technique.

Fatigue also affects the ability to think clearly and to execute difficult techniques. A tired player makes poor decisions and has more misunderstandings with his teammates. Techniques and skills that are normally easy to perform become impossible if the player is suffering from fatigue. In other words, the coach and the player need to be aware that performance levels and the ability to execute techniques properly throughout a season are seriously influenced by the player's stamina and fitness.

For this reason, at this level the players practice the technique and stamina work in the same activity so that the skill is not adversely affected by fatigue. This work is performed on a regular and progressive basis and if the problem is particularly acute then the technical and stamina activities are done separately.

Nevertheless, do not forget that if speed stamina work is carried out more than once a week, it will have a negative impact on the player's basic stamina and speed. This is particularly dangerous for players who have reached this level and hope to become professionals. The more mature players and professionals are used to this heavy workload and have learned to cope with it, but any player who is pushed to the limit will sooner or later pay the consequences. At best his performance levels will suffer and at worst he will suffer from 'burn out' and over exhaustion and leave the game.

It is interesting to point out that many people think that sometimes there is a pause in the learning process because the player has a lack of stamina, but it is usually that he has not yet developed the necessary coordination skills and speed required. When this happens it is a good idea to help improve and develop coordination by having the player practice the basic skills involved in soccer itself by way of obstacle races. This is a great way to instill confidence and greatly improve coordination.

There are also some specific exercises to help increase and develop stamina. I would like to recommend the great technique created by the Italian Bosco. This is ideal for players at this age and I have made a few slight alterations so that the technique can be carried out with a ball. This method has been developed to increase stamina in the soccer player and involves: sprinting for 10-20 yards for a certain period and then relative rest by jogging for 30, 70 or 110 seconds. This slow run allows the Karvonen formula to be used to monitor the players' optimum pulse rate during the sprints. This is how it works:

1. The player's resting pulse rate is taken.

2. The maximum pulse rate is established after the energetic sprint.

3. Finally the difference is calculated between each and then 6 is added to this number.

Here is an example. A soccer player's resting pulse rate is 56 beats per minute and his maximum pulse rate is 190 beats per minute. So, 190-56 equals 134 + 6 equals 140. Therefore this player's optimum pulse rate is 140 beats per minute. This means that the player needs to run at the speed that will make his pulse rate rise to 140 beats per minute. When this happens he is able to successfully eliminate the lactic acid from his body. In other words, at this level his body produces lactic acid but he is able to deal successfully with the build-up and there are no negative effects. Bosco claims to have monitored this phenomenon during soccer matches. The physical effort lasts from 12 to 24 minutes (1 x12 or 2 x 12) with an 8-minute break between the sets. This is how I have adapted the technique in my method using a ball:

- When doing the sprints, the player can shoot, kick a moving ball on the run without breaking his stride; or try a control and shot or perhaps a volley. All three of these elements (or two or just one) can be incorporated into the activity, depending on the length of the sprint.

- During the exercises where the pulse rates are taken it is appropriate from time to time to introduce a ball, kick it 10-20 yards, chase after it and keep on running with it.

Players at this age should not do as much resistance and stamina training as adults. There should always be a 72 hour resting period after a demanding workload (this includes matches) and this is by no means an excessively long break. A relatively low-intensity daily training session also helps with the recovery process. Training is a bit like eating. We do not eat one heavy meal after another but need to take a break and follow a heavy meal with a light one. This is the same as far as training sessions are concerned. Nobody can do one intensive session after another.

I am not a great fan of all the physical fitness tests that are carried out on soccer players as they are too general:

1. The evaluation has little relevance as far as soccer is concerned. Just because someone gets a good score this does not mean he can use this to an advantage in a game.

2. The players approach these tests in different ways. Some are very motivated and try their best and others have little interest

and go through the motions. The reserves and substitutes are usually more motivated than the established players as they feel it is an 'objective' test that proves their qualities.

3. Finally, let me just say that none of these fitness tests prove anything in a soccer context and do not give even a hint as to how well a player will perform during a match.

I gave a first division team and a third division team the Cooper test and after the 12-minute run I found no significant differences - quite the contrary, the results were virtually identical. On average the professionals ran 3,016 meters and the semi-professionals (far more motivated) achieved an average distance of 3,009 meters. More evidence (if it was needed) that there is no correlation between these results and soccer ability.

Having said this, I am not suggesting that these tests are a waste of time. A player does the Cooper test and after he finishes he has a pulse rate of 166 and 142 after a minute's rest. If after two months he repeats the test and his pulse rate is 149 and 125 respectively then this is a clear indication that his aerobic fitness has improved. If there is no improvement then this indicates that the player's aerobic fitness levels are insufficient. The necessary steps need to be taken in order to remedy the situation. But it goes without saying, that when this fitness level improves he will not suddenly become a better soccer player. All it does is give him the necessary energy to allow him to produce his existing soccer skills as efficiently as possible for longer periods throughout the match.

# Improving Speed

Sometimes a game lacks vitality and spectacle because it is played at a slow pace. There is usually a good reason why players find it impossible to perform any quicker. The first reason concerns how quickly the muscles respond to the electrical impulses asking them to flex and contract (reflexes). A player can think quickly and move slowly and vice versa. Unfortunately, the two processes (reaction and thinking) do reach their peak at the same time: motor reaction speed peaks between the ages of 18-25 whereas the speed of movement increases notably between the ages of 8-12 and reaches its peak around the age of 16.

It is very important for players and especially coaches to understand that the speed with which a muscle contracts depends to a large extent on the amount of fast-contracting muscle fibers ('sprinters'). Players are born naturally quick and with good acceleration if they have an abundance of this type of muscle fiber. Children have a lot more so-called 'intermediate' fibers than adults. Children have 13% and adults 2-3% to be more exact. My method tries to train these players from a young age so that the intermediate fibers can develop into 'sprinters', changing the muscular structure and making the players quicker. So when the players reach the age of 17 they will have developed an improved natural pace that will help them perform well when the specific emphasis on the training session is speed. However, if the players put too much emphasis on resistance training during the formative years then the aforementioned fibers will develop into 'slow' ones at the expense of speed.

The length of the rest periods in between the speed training sets depends on the individual player. For well-trained players and professionals this period usually lasts between 2-4 minutes. However, at this age the players need even more rest to recover totally. For this reason I recommend that the rest periods in between sets are as follows: the first and second, two minutes, and the third and fourth, two and a half minutes. The fifth and sixth three minutes and so on. The players should stay active during the breaks and do some stretching exercises.

The amount of repetitions done depends on the fitness of the players. Nevertheless, if the coach detects that the players are slowing down then he should end the particular exercise and call for a break.

# Improving Strength

Strength is a fundamental necessity for every athlete and this is also true in soccer. Although 'pure' strength, what you might call 'brute force' is not a pre-requisite in the game, many of the movements carried out require this characteristic.

Soccer players need to have what we might call 'explosive power'. They have to be able to produce short but intensive bursts of strength. The legs need to be especially strong in order to run, twist and turn and change pace rapidly. The legs produce the strong challenges and powerful shots that some people refer to as 'rapid power'.

Soccer strength is defined as how well and how quickly a player can move his body weight. The ability to achieve momentum by controlling the body weight allows the player to produce a powerful shot, a long throw-in and high jump etc.

There has to be a distinction made between the two different types of strength: the absolute and the relative. Soccer players want to develop their ability to achieve good relative strength such as stamina as well as absolute strength which manifests in the 'rapid power' mentioned above. This type of strength is needed to produce movements at an explosive speed and the stamina helps the player to produce these movements over and over throughout the match.

The most common way to develop the explosive power is to use exercises from other sports, even though soccer-specific exercises are more than adequate. The soccer player's speed and strength develops over time by simply shifting all of his weight off the ground. So this type of exercise is not dependent on any special apparatus or high-tech gymnasium.

The desired progress and development is best achieved by utilizing the specific motor skills used in the game (technical movements done as quickly as possible) together with the games and competitions that are done at full speed but with no additional resistance built-in.

At this stage the players start to practice special acrobatic techniques in front of goal (until now only the goalkeeper has done this type of work): the attackers take up all sorts of positions in order to make a good strike at goal, the defenders learn to move with more agility and flexibility in order to clear the danger and the midfield players practice both these disciplines.

These are the objectives for explosive power training:

- To prevent injuries as the technique involves explosive and sudden movements.

- To achieve better flexibility, agility and coordination to allow the player to cope with difficult balls, primarily in the final third of the pitch near the goal areas.

- To achieve a greater control and efficiency when producing techniques involving both speed and power at the same time. Techniques with the ball: powerful strikes with the head or feet, clearances and long passes, throw-ins and when challenging for the ball. Techniques without the ball: jumps, runs, acceleration, twists and turns and changing pace as quickly as possible.

The player needs good upper body strength in order to help with heading, dribbling, feints and dummies, challenging for the ball and changing direction. He also requires good mobility, a flexible vertebrae and pelvis musculature.

In particular, flexible hips are extremely important for the soccer player. Training needs to focus on developing the required flexibility in these areas. The player's center of gravity and balance is located in the hips. The back and stomach muscles need to be developed and strengthened as back pain and pelvic injuries are almost always due to poor musculature in these areas.

'Explosive power' should not become part of a special training routine until the players have reached the age of sixteen. Practicing soccer-specific exercises such as sprinting after the ball and jumping for headers is enough to develop this strength. Once the player reaches the age of seventeen or eighteen he starts to concentrate on progressive training sessions designed to improve his explosive power and physical fitness.

It is not important for the player to undergo any specific mobility training when he is a youngster. Thanks to his elasticity and suppleness he is able to run and jump without any specific preparation beforehand and without any risk of injury. However, once the player reaches this stage he has to train the soccer-specific muscles so that he does not suffer stiffness and incur injury. So it is important for the player to stretch and relax often. During a training session these activities are best done during the warm up and during the breaks between sets when undertaking strength, speed and stamina work.

In this way the tired muscle groups are rested and revitalized in preparation for the next training exercise. The player should pay special attention to the quadriceps ( the main muscle used for shooting) as this muscle has a tendency to stiffen up and contract and therefore needs to be relaxed and stretched regularly, particularly after a strength-related activity.

Let me remind you again, now that we are talking about physical fitness, that having tremendous physical fitness does not make you a good soccer player. Also, some players' performance levels drop near the end of a game and the spectators attribute this to poor physical fitness. However, the reason for this could be a personal error made by the player or a tactical change in the team or opposition. This could even be a poor refereeing decision that the player is not happy with and so he is distracted, loses concentration and his performance suffers as a result.

# Psychology in Soccer

In the previous level the player started to learn how to relax and use his imagination. By this level he should have mastered all the necessary technical and tactical aspects and start to dedicate more time thinking about the psychological aspects of the game, mainly concentration and motivation.

This type of training depends to a large extent on the knowledge, attitude and dedication of the coach. He should be aware from the outset that no two players are alike and that he needs to treat each player with sensitivity, tact and understanding as this is a very difficult age.

The coach needs to know each player on an individual basis, how he thinks, how he is motivated or disheartened in order to have any realistic chance of using psychology with any effectiveness. These are the points the coach needs to bear in mind:

1. An overall knowledge of the player (physical characteristics, temperament, social behavior and his normal confidence level).

2. Psycho-motor behavior. (understanding and assimilation of the specific movements in the game, perception and consistency).

3. Reactions when practicing the sport (both when training and playing in a match).

The coach should also be aware of what is known as 'invisible training'. What does the player do in his spare time? How many hours does he dedicate to training and to studying? What is his diet like? How many hours does he sleep? What is his relation with his parents and brothers and sisters? Has he got any friends? Are his friends in the team? How does he get on with them? All these factors are important and if the answer to the majority of these questions is positive then this gives the player the necessary stability to help overcome difficult aspects of the game and make good progress. If the answers to these questions are negative then the player has less chance of doing well in the game.

Motivation is a key factor at any stage of learning. Each player is nervous and anxious to perform well during training and it is up to the coach to dispel these self-doubts. He needs the ability to relax the player and develop his learning and understanding on a gradual and progressive basis.

Nevertheless, no matter how good the coach is, at the end of the day it is largely down the player himself to be self-motivated. The player needs to be his own biggest fan, 'psyching' himself up before each encounter. This inner 'strength' has a far greater influence on the player than any external influences. This positive thinking (motivation, attitude and determination) helps the player set and achieve his targets. These targets should be clearly defined and should be realistic and achievable. The player needs to be aware of how he performs during training and matches so that he can exploit his strengths to the full and eliminate his weaknesses.

It is worth pointing out that the player's motivation is not an 'overnight' phenomenon but is a result of his experiences over many years. These motivations (the need for power, praise or sacrifice to achieve a greater performance) mean that unless the coach is careful the team's performance may be sterile and ineffective because all the players are pulling in different directions.

This is an important consideration at any level but even more so when the play reaches this stage of development. At a young age, a child is motivated to learn because it comes easily. Once a player reaches 17-18 he is beyond the ideal age for learning and his neurons and motor responses are largely fixed (he is no longer a 'sponge' learning easily and naturally) which means that he only make real progress thanks to his own determination, will-power and his interest in becoming a better soccer player.

Remember that motivation is seriously affected if the player is expected to complete repetitive, simple and monotonous exercises over and over. Motivation is also affected in a negative way if the player plays against a weak opposition or a rival that is far too strong for him on a regular basis. However, playing against a better team occasionally acts as a positive influence on the player and invites him to strive to improve his game and compete at a higher standard.

We also need to take pressure into account. Any player who has excellent technical and tactical qualities but is unable to take the pressure during a match will find it very difficult to make any progress in the game. The player should be brave and take risks during a game. I am referring both to physical bravery and mental strength to be able to try a risky move that may go wrong and make him stupid. This all depends on the personality of the player. The player can easily be influenced by the score (if his team is winning then he tries things and plays with confidence), the opposition or the attitude of the crowd. A good player needs to make difficult decisions during a game and deal with the consequences, good or bad. He needs to do his best to ignore and 'block-out' the often intense pressure put on him during a match.

Motivation is linked closely to concentration. If the player is motivated and enthusiastic then his concentration levels increase as a result. However, if his spirits are low and things are not going well then there is every possibility that he will lose concentration and become distracted.

It is very common for coaches to ask their players for greater concentration. These coaches are usually the ones that are only interested in winning at all costs. However, this is where their involvement ends as they offer their players no guidance or constructive training on how to improve and maintain concentration levels. Just as there are games and exercises to improve passing and shooting, there are also ways of improving concentration. The player is helped tremendously by doing a series of mental exercises and learning not to be distracted by external influences. (you will find some of these techniques in the games and exercises that follow this section).

## Psychology and Soccer

As far as psychological strength is concerned there has never been a better example in the game than Franco Baresi. He finally retired in 1997 (at the same time as another 'great' player: Koeman).

He started his career at the age of 17 with Milan and stayed at the club until he retired from the game at the age of 37. He won many caps for his country, he also won 6 League titles, 3 European Cups, 2 Intercontinental Cups, and 7 SuperCups.

Baresi was not very fast and only 1'76" (seems hard to believe but it is true) but was considered to be the best player in the world without the ball. His tremendous concentration and intuition allowed him to remember every moment in the match, thus allowing him to get to the ball before his opponent. This was his great secret!

When I asked him in Madrid about this gift he said: "I am so focused during a game that I only see the ball, the movement of my teammates and the opposition. A stand could collapse and I wouldn't notice because I am anticipating my next move. So when the opposition kicks the ball long it is easy for me to intercept it and pass it to any of my teammates".

*Franco Baresi. A great athlete? No. Still a great player.*

Nevertheless, these exercises will only be of use if the player has learned to use his imagination. This is why the player was introduced to exercises involving the imagination in the previous level and continues to practice them during this one.

It is useful to know that any intensive training of this type will produce a drop in performance in the short term. This is due to the mental effort and concentration involved during these exercises. However, over the long term, these exercise will facilitate improved reaction time and concentration levels.

Usually, the player with the quickest reaction time is the one that has consistently high concentration levels during the game. On the other hand, inconsistency and a lack of concentration make the player's reaction times slower.

In summary, in order to play well the player needs good concentration, motivation, understanding and the ability to think quickly. The player also needs to move intelligently (sometimes a player has a great game just by 'patrolling' a certain zone).

The ability to concentrate is a pre-requisite to playing well and this ability can be enhanced and developed during a structured and progressive training program. From this stage on the player needs to work on all of the following: the psychological aspect of the game (concentration and motivation), physical fitness, technique and tactical knowledge.

**A note on the 'age' recommended for the exercises:**

It has always been clear to me that players and professionals should not follow the same training programs. The professionals have obviously reached a very high standard and are able to 'play' and 'read' the game, but the youngsters (because of their youth and inexperience) lack the necessary skills and craft that the game requires. The latter need time to really appreciate and understand the 'secrets' of the game.

As I developed my ideas further as a coach I realized that there should also be some sort of 'guideline' to indicate when players should carry out certain exercises. I have therefore recommended an appropriate age for the exercises that follow although this only serves as a 'guideline' as more important than age is ability. If the child has the ability to do the exercise then he is ready, but if this is not the case then the training will at best have no benefit and at worst be counter productive.

This point was made clear to me when in 1976 I visited Manchester, England, to watch the legendary George Best give a training session to a group of 8-year olds. The ex-soccer player (and a beginner as far as coaching was concerned) went through a series of exercises that only served to show off his talents. Unfortunately the youngsters themselves learned very little.

To give you an idea of what I mean let's have a look at the first and last exercises during the session. The first involved Best flicking the ball up high and amazing the youngsters with his ball-juggling skills. Then, standing on the penalty spot he kicked the ball up 3-4 yards, let it bounce and scored a fantastic goal on the half-volley. Afterwards he threw the ball up so that all the players could have a go (one by one) but the vast majority found it too difficult to even make contact with the ball and those that did only managed to hit the ball with the shin or the toe. The last exercise was more like an exhibition of how well Best could score from free-kicks. He scored several goals by kicking a ball with power and swerve around and over a 'dummy' wall. Then the players were asked to do the same and produced a parody of what they had just seen. As with the first exercise, this one was also beyond their current capabilities.

This experience was one of many that helped me to clarify my ideas about training and this is why my training method has a series of well-balanced and progressive exercises aimed at players of a certain age or of a certain ability.

However, none of my recommendations are set in stone as I feel it is up to the coaches to decide what training routine is best for their players and when best to do certain exercises. Compare any two players of the same age and you will find that they are totally different. Each player in the team will have his own individual characteristics that make him different from all of his teammates.

Nevertheless, the majority of coaches still persist with traditional training routines that have been around for many years. These programs are largely outdated and leave a lot to be desired. Some coaches just copy what they have seen others do on the training ground. Others buy a book and follow any 'example' to the letter without tailoring it to the needs of their players. Basically, copying somebody else's ideas in this way is like expecting one sick patient to take the same medicine as somebody else no matter what his illness.

This is why I always explain each game or exercise, outlining the objectives and an appropriate age for them to be played or carried out. I am always conscious of age, ability, intensity and pace but the most important thing is to be flexible and have complete freedom to change any exercise to suit the needs of the individual players involved.

# Games for
## 17-18 Year Olds

| No. | Objectives | Age | Developing the Games | Common Problems |
|-----|-----------|-----|---------------------|-----------------|
| 1 | Positioning. Speed of execution. Speed and stamina. Control without touching the ball. | 17-18 | '7 v7' played along the width of half the pitch. The game involves a maximum of two touches, positioning, fitness and especially what we call 'invisible' control (letting the ball do the work). The player has to think what he is going to do with the ball even before it reaches him. This can be performed anywhere on the pitch - at the back receiving a pass from the goalkeeper, in midfield or in attack when shooting or playing a 'defense splitting' pass. A point is earned each time this control is performed correctly. Each goal is worth 2 points. The team with the most points at the end wins. | What usually happens is that players with good ability run with the ball without touching it while they look around to see what to do next. The ideal is for the players to control, touch and pass almost in one movement. The players find it difficult to do the 'invisible' control. |

| No. | Objectives | Age | Developing the Games | Common Problems |
|---|---|---|---|---|
| 2 | Ball control. Concentration. Fast reflexes. Positioning. Anticipation. Ball skills. 'One touch'. | 17-18 | A 'round' '4 players on the outside v 2 in the middle'. When a player makes a mistake he changes places with one of the players in the middle. Pitch size 18 x 18yds but flexible. In other words, if a player has to go beyond the confines of the pitch temporarily, the rest of the players should go with him and the round is the same size but in a slightly different place. The game involves keeping the ball in the air. The players in the middle can move about. If the player receiving the ball decides he can pass the ball 'one touch' to another player or control and pass without using his hands then he is free to do so, (usually the players receive the ball and control it with head, chest or thigh and then gather it in their hands and then pass it). Any player can control the ball on the run and pass in order to avoid the players in the middle. The 'round' has a tactical emphasis, as each player on the ball must be supported to his left, right and in the middle. The latter is further away in order to have space to maneuver. Remember, possession is not lost when the players in the middle touch the ball but when the ball bounces. | The players do not make space effectively. The ball is received and almost in one movement taken in the hand. The ball should be fully under control first. The players stop when those in the middle get near them or when the latter touch the ball. The players in the middle make little effort and so the game loses its appeal. |

| No. | Objectives | Age | Developing the Games | Common Problems |
|---|---|---|---|---|
| 3 | Ball control and passing. Positioning. Anticipation. | 17-18 | Pitch size 9 x 6yds. The ball has to strike the wall above the line 4yds from the ground (so that the players get used to controlling the high ball). The game is played '2 v 2'. The game is started from beyond the baseline with a volley. Once the ball rebounds off the wall it has to be controlled and passed without letting it bounce. The players can only pass the ball to each other once (playing 'two-touch') before kicking it against the wall. | Letting the ball bounce. Taking more than two touches on the ball. Passing too often to the teammate or not at all. |

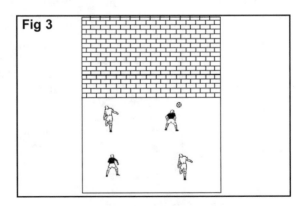

| No. | Objectives | Age | Developing the Games | Common Problems |
|---|---|---|---|---|
| 4 | Getting a 'feel' for the game. Speed of execution. Ball control. 'Killing' the ball. Anticipation. Intercepting. | 17-18 | Pitch size 25 x 25yds. A 'round' with 7 players in total. 4 attackers on the edge of the pitch (one near each corner) with 2 defenders and 1 attacker in the middle. This is a normal 'round' with the following exceptions: the game is obligatory 'two-touch'. The idea is to 'kill' the ball on the turn with the first touch and then pass it (in another direction) in the air with the second. If a player makes a low pass he swaps with one of the defenders in the middle. He also swaps if he controls the ball but fails to pass in the required direction. The attacker in the middle should be alert and very mobile in order to make space for the passes. | Neither control nor passes done as stipulated. The players do not play the obligatory two touches. The attacker in the middle is either static or he stands beyond the playing area. The pace of the game depends on the effort made by the defenders. If they are lazy then this game is easy for the attackers. The coach makes the players swap roles regularly as playing in the middle is tiring. |
| 5 | Coordination. Balance. Ball skills. Ball juggling. Speed. | 17-18 | Any number of players each with a ball. The idea is to kick the ball over the head, turn quickly and run with the ball, always keeping it under control and never letting it bounce. The same sequence is performed again using the other foot and so on. A point is awarded each time the ball goes over the head and is controlled successfully. The winner is the player who achieves the most points in the allotted time. | The ball does not go over the head but goes to one side instead. After kicking the ball over the head some players try to control it on their foot when it is far easier to use the thigh. |

| No. | Objectives | Age | Developing the Games | Common Problems |
|---|---|---|---|---|
| 6 | Coordination. Balance. Ball skills. Ball juggling. Speed. | 17-18 | Similar to the previous game. The players juggle the ball and keep it up next to a neutral zone 5yds wide. When they are ready they can kick the ball high across the 5yd-zone and sprint across to control the ball before it bounces. The player then has to get back across in the same way. 1 point is awarded each time this is achieved. | The players do not run as fast as they can and so do not get to the ball before it bounces. The same is true if the ball is not kicked high enough. The ball does not go across the 5yd-line and is controlled in the neutral area. This is incorrect. Controlling the ball on the foot and not the thigh. |
| 7 | Coordination. Balance. Ball skills. Ball juggling. Speed. | 17-18 | Any number of players each juggling a ball, not letting it bounce. The idea is for the players to juggle the ball between the instep and below the knee for 5 minutes, first with one foot and then the other. When this has been achieved successfully with both feet the player earns 1 point. | Some players keep their arms very close to their bodies. They should be slightly raised to help balance. Lack of balance when standing on the stronger foot. |

Fig 4

Fig 6

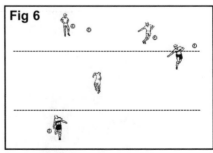

| No. | Objectives | Age | Developing the Games | Common Problems |
|-----|-----------|-----|---------------------|-----------------|
| 8 | Coordination. Balance. Ball skills. Ball juggling. Speed. | 17-18 | The same as the previous game but the players now have to juggle the ball for 5 minutes only using the instep. | The same as in the previous game. |
| 9 | Ball skills. Vision. Control. Cooperation. Balance. Coordination. | 17 | Groups of 3 players keeping the ball up. Each player keeps the ball up 4-8 times. Then the player kicks the ball up higher and calls out the name of one of the other two players. These have their back to the ball. When the player hears his name he turns quickly to control the ball before it bounces. The game continues in this way and once all 3 players have had a turn without the ball bouncing, the team earns a point. The team with the most points wins. | Not taking the required number of touches. The ball is not kicked up high enough to give the next player time to get to it before it bounces. Forgetting to name the next player and so the ball drops to the ground. |

**Fig 9**

| No. | Objectives | Age | Developing the Games | Common Problems |
|---|---|---|---|---|
| 10 | Ball skills. Balance. Trying to become two-footed. | 17 | 4 groups of 4 players compete on an individual basis in a ball-juggling competition. Each player uses one foot and keeps the ball low, balancing on the other leg. After a while they use both feet. The winner is the player who makes the most touches in the allotted time (the exercise usually finishes when the players stop, this is unlikely to be longer then a minute). Groups are then formed according to how players have performed in each round. | Poor balance. Arms should be raised slightly to help balance. |
| 11 | Ball skills. Balance. Trying to become a complete player technically. | 17 | 4 groups of 4 players compete on an individual basis in a ball-juggling competition. In this game however, the players must juggle the ball in the following way: on the right thigh, then left thigh, left foot, right foot, head and then start on the right thigh again and so on. | The players do not use the right parts of the body in the correct order. Usually they forget to use the weaker foot. |

Fig 10

| No. | Objectives | Age | Developing the Games | Common Problems |
|---|---|---|---|---|
| 12 | Coordination. Balance. Ball skills. Ball juggling. Agility. (Some players can start this exercise in the previous level). | 17-18 | A random number of players are keeping the ball up. They try to keep the ball under control as they sit down and stand up again. The player should keep the ball close to the foot as he bends his knees, lowers his center of gravity and sits down. The ball is kept low until suddenly it is kicked up high so that he can quickly stand up, prevent the ball from bouncing and get it back under control. Each time a player does this successfully he earns a point. The winner is the player who earns the most points in the allotted time. | The players try to sit down from a standing position when really they should lower their center of gravity and sit down slowly. The ball is not kicked high enough, which does not give them enough time to stand up and control it before it bounces |
| 13 | Coordination. Balance. Ball skills. Ball juggling. Agility. | 17-18 | The players have to make one touch with the right foot and one touch with the left. Then two touches with the right and two with the left. This increases up to ten touches with each foot. Once this has been successfully achieved the players have to sit down and stand back up, keeping the ball under control at all times. Two points are awarded if both parts are performed correctly. One point if the sitting down and standing up part fails but the touches are ok. The winner is the player who earns the most points in the allotted time. | Not playing the required number of touches. Some do more and some do less. Trying to sit down without lowering the center of gravity. Not kicking the ball up high enough to allow enough time to stand before it bounces. |

| No. | Objectives | Age | Developing the Games | Common Problems |
|---|---|---|---|---|
| 14 | Technique. Speed. Changing pace and direction. Controlling the space around you. Concentration. | 17-18 | 4 cones positioned to form a square 10yds apart. There are 3 players and a ball on two cones (never the nearest to each other). On the signal a player from each group sets off with the ball. The players run to the cone to their right, go round it and then head diagonally to the cone furthest away. The players should not interfere with each other as they cross. They go round this cone and then the final cone before heading straight back to the group to hand over the ball to the next player and so on. The first team to finish wins a point. These cones can be organized all over the pitch so that the whole team is doing the exercise. | Some players have poor orientation skills. The changes in pace are not applied correctly. (The players should slow down around the cones and speed up when running between them). |

Fig 13

Fig 14

| No. | Objectives | Age | Developing the Games | Common Problems |
|---|---|---|---|---|
| 15 | Technique. Speed off the mark. Speed. | 17-18 | 4 cones are positioned in a line 4yds apart with 2 players with a ball at each one. Another line of cones is parallel 5yds away and the players are facing these cones. On the signal a player from each cone runs with the ball to the cone 5yds opposite, goes round it and returns then hands over to the next player who sets off quickly. Then the next players have a go etc. This game is very intensive and therefore there should be regular breaks. | The ball is kicked too far from the foot. It should be 'stuck' to the boot. This game is all about speed but if there are no breaks it turns into a test of stamina. |
| 16 | Ball skills. Ball juggling. Coordination. Agility. Speed of execution. Dribbling. Shooting. Speed. Stamina. Playing in goal. | 17-18 | 15 players near the middle of the pitch split into groups of 3; 1 in the middle and 1 on each wing. 2 goalkeepers alternate in goal and compete with the other to see who concedes the least number of goals. The players in the middle are carrying a ball and on the signal they throw the ball up and control it moving towards the edge of the 18-yard box. If the ball bounces the player needs to pick it up, do a forward roll and then continue. At the same time the other 2 players in the group run with the ball as fast as they can down the wings. They zigzag in and out of 3 cones 5yds apart. Once they reach the cone at the 15yd mark they leave the ball and sprint around the 3 remaining cones (to the 30yd mark). If by the time they have finished the | The players find it hard to follow the sequence. They forget to do a forward roll when the ball bounces. They do not get the knee over the ball to keep it down. Once they have finished the course if the player in the middle has not shot they forget to try and get the ball off him. |

| No. | Objectives | Age | Developing the Games | Common Problems |
|---|---|---|---|---|
| 16 (cont.) | Ball skills. Ball juggling. Coordination. Agility. Speed of execution. Dribbling. Shooting. Speed. Stamina. Playing in goal. | 17-18 | player in the middle has not shot, then they compete for the ball and try and shoot themselves. If this confrontation takes place then obviously the player in the middle can drop the ball to the ground and try to dribble and get his shot in. Each player has a turn in each position. The player with the most points after the allotted number of repetitions is the winner. This is how the points are awarded: if the player in the middle shoots before being challenged he earns 1 point; another point is awarded if the ball is on target or hits the post or crossbar and another if he scores making a possible total of 3 points. The first of the two wingers to get to the 'shooting' area earns a point. If one of them manages to win the ball they can earn another 1 or 2 points and in this case the player in the middle gets nothing. | |

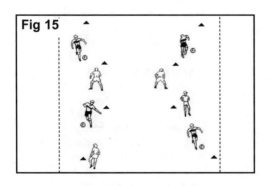

Fig 15

| No. | Objectives | Age | Developing the Games | Common Problems |
|-----|-----------|-----|---------------------|-----------------|
| 17 | Ball skills. Ball juggling. Coordination. Shooting. Agility. Playing in goal. Particularly speed and Speed of execution. | 17-18 | This is very similar to the previous game with the following differences: The distance traveled is only 10yds, the players on the wing only run around 2 cones always with the ball. The point system is the same. | The players find it hard to follow the sequence. They forget to do a forward roll when the ball bounces. They do not get the knee over the ball to keep it down. Once they have finished the course, if the player in the middle has not shot, they forget to try to get the ball off him. |
| 18 | Speed. Changing direction. Coordination. Shooting. Playing in goal. Concentration | 17-18 | 5 players are all playing at the same time: 1 is in goal, 4 players start from near the halfway line. There are two parallel lines of 6 cones, the first cone in each is 5yds away from the 18-yard box and the rest are evenly spaced in a line (slightly zigzagged) back to the halfway line. 2 players and a ball are positioned on each line at the penultimate cone to the halfway line. The exercise is as follows: on the signal one of the players in one group sets off with the ball and zigzags around the cones. Once he is round the last cone (but not entering the 18-yard box) he shoots. On the same signal the other player in each group runs towards and goes round the cone on the half-way line and then sets off after his teammate running around all the cones. If he catches him he tries to win the ball so that he is the one who gets to shoot at goal. As this group is finishing | The play should be 'explosive'. Some players do not fully understand the game. Some do not start to run round the cones on their 'good' side and this causes problems when they have to shoot. If the player on the ball is caught by his teammate he lets him have possession when he should try and keep it. Sometimes the chasers are so keen to catch the player on the ball that they forget about the cones. |

| No. | Objectives | Age | Developing the Games | Common Problems |
|---|---|---|---|---|
| 18 (cont) | Speed. Changing direction. Coordination. Shooting. Playing in goal. Concentration | 17-18 | the other group sets off and does the same. When running down the right the shot must be taken with the left foot and vice versa. Various groups take turns playing this game as a lot of time is needed for recovery. The players also alternate with and without the ball and on the right and left. 2 or 3 goalkeepers also take turns in goal. | |

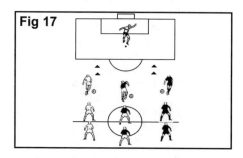

Fig 17

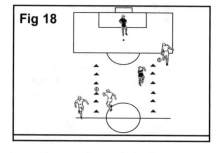

Fig 18

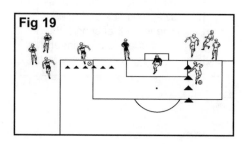

Fig 19

| No. | Objectives | Age | Developing the Games | Common Problems |
|---|---|---|---|---|
| 19 | Running with the ball. Dribbling. Shooting. Speed of execution. 'Explosive' strength. Winning the ball. Teamwork. Playing in goal. | 17-18 | 2 goalkeepers alternate in goal and 2 groups of 8 players. Pitch size 30 x 30yds. There is a line of 4 cones 5yds to the right of the goal post stretching up from the touch line towards the edge of the 18-yard box. There is a line of 6 cones 5yds to the left of the goal and parallel to the touch line (each cone 1yd apart). 4 players at each set of cones, team 'A' ( next to the line of 4 cones) and team 'B' (next to the line of 6 cones). The latter stand at the first cone of 6 each 1yd apart. These cones run parallel to the 'dead ball' line and about a yard from it. On the signal the first player in each team sets off and zigzags around the cones. Once the player in team 'A' goes round the last cone he turns and shoots. Once the player on team 'B' goes round the last cone he passes the ball back to a teammate and sprints after it to challenge for the ball. Whoever wins the challenge gets the chance to shoot. Once this is finished the second player in each team sets off and so on. The teams swap courses and roles. The team that scores the most goals is the winner. | Not dribbling around all the cones. Not playing a good pass to the teammate who will compete in the '1 v 1'. Poor choices are made when trying to score: not confident enough to play a feint or dribble or they do the above and forget that the end result should be a shot on goal. |

| No. | Objectives | Age | Developing the Games | Common Problems |
|-----|-----------|-----|---------------------|-----------------|
| 20 | Strength. Speed. Coordination. Changing direction. Shooting. Playing in goal. Concentration. | 17-18 | 2 goalkeepers in goal and 2 teams of 6-8 players each in line with one of the goal posts on the edge of the 18-yard box. On the signal 1 player from each team sets off with the ball running towards the midfield to attempt the following circuit: go round a cone 5yds away and another 3yds away in a diagonal direction and a third also 3yds away diagonal to the second. Then the player heads back to the first cone and once he gets there he steps on the ball, leaves it and sprints around the second cone. He runs back to collect the ball, goes around the first cone and shoots. The first player to shoot earns 2 points. An extra point is awarded if the shot is good and an extra 3 if a goal is scored. This is a very tiring activity so long breaks are needed and the players swap teams and roles regularly. The goalkeepers alternate and need to keep on their toes as the shots come hard and fast. The team with the most points is the winner. | The pace of the game is not 'explosive'. Sometimes shots are made before the last cone has been passed. Some also forget to step on the ball and go back. Some goalkeepers only try to save the first shot on goal and ignore the ones that soon follow. |

| No. | Objectives | Age | Developing the Games | Common Problems |
|---|---|---|---|---|
| 21 | Running with the ball. Dribbling. Feints and dummies. Peripheral vision. Changing pace. Craft. Astuteness. | 17 | Pitch size 18 x 18yds. 3 'rounds' of 6 players each with a ball. 2 players are carrying a bib. These try to touch the other players or the balls. The players should all dribble and use feints and dummies (the latter also applies to the chasers). If a player is touched he is given the bib and now he has to 'tag' other players. If a chaser is fooled then he has to stop and pursue somebody else (no personal duels allowed). After the first game the players are put in different groups depending on how long they had a bib or how many times they were 'tagged'. | Not changing pace. Not playing feints and dummies. Going beyond the specified playing area. The players with the bib go after the same player at the same time. Players often leave the ball behind. |

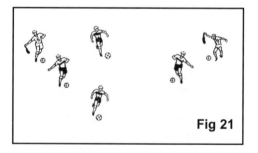

**Fig 21**

| No. | Objectives | Age | Developing the Games | Common Problems |
|---|---|---|---|---|
| 22 | Running with the ball. Peripheral vision. Feints and dummies. Winning the ball. Shooting. Goalkeepers work on paying attention and concentration. | 17 | Half the pitch. 3 goals, 1 being the goalmouth and another on each wing. A goalkeeper in each goal and 18 players and 9 balls on the pitch. On the signal all the players rush to claim a ball. If successful the player has to try to 'beat' another player by dribbling and using feints and dummies. If successful he can shoot. The player without a ball tries feints and dummies to try to win one. If successful he tries to 'beat' another player before shooting. All players must play a feint before shooting to try to fool the goalkeeper. If the goalkeeper is busy trying to save another shot the player has to go to another goal. If a goalkeeper saves a shot he immediately puts it back in play. If the shot goes 'high and wide' the player who shot has to collect the ball, give it to another player and try to win it back. | Not playing feints in defense or when attacking the goal. Various players go after the same player. The players without a ball often lose interest and ball watch. Balls that miss the target and travel a long way are not collected, which means sometimes there are very few balls in play. When this happens, the game loses pace and intensity. |

131

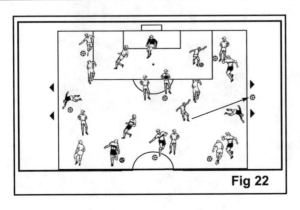

**Fig 22**

| No. | Objectives | Age | Developing the Games | Common Problems |
|-----|-----------|-----|---------------------|-----------------|
| 23 | Running with the ball. Dribbling. Speed off the mark. Changing direction. Strength. Coordination. Peripheral vision. Controlling the space around you. | 17-18 | This game looks simple but if played properly it is very complicated and beneficial. Pitch size 20 x 20yds. 6 players run slowly, each with a ball. On the signal each of the players try to touch all the other players. Of course they have to run with the ball and keep it under control at all times. The coach sets an appropriate time limit for this game (usually a minute is more than enough). The first player to touch everybody earns 3 points, the second 2 and the third 1. This game is played several times and at the end all the points from each game are added together. A competition can be organized for the whole team. | At first the play is chaotic. The more intelligent players soon pick it up. Some players cheat. Some are convinced they have touched all the players but they soon realize their mistake when they count up all their teammates. |

Fig 23

| No. | Objectives | Age | Developing the Games | Common Problems |
|---|---|---|---|---|
| 24 | Running with the ball. Dribbling. Speed. Speed off the mark. Changing direction. Shooting. Coordination. Concentration. Playing in goal. | 18 | Two goalkeepers take turns playing in goal. An imaginary line runs all the way from the edge of the 6-yard box up to the half way line. There are 2 lines of 7 cones 2yds apart in a zigzag formation, one set on each side of the imaginary line 4yds beyond the edge of the 18-yard box. There is a player with a ball at the first cone and a player with a ball at the last cone in each row. The 4 players set off on the signal and go in and out of the cones. Once they have gone past the last one they shoot before entering the 18-yard box. Then 4 other players go and so on. The players then go again and they do the same with the other set of cones. If they start from the last cone during the first run they start on the first cone this time. The goalkeepers have a difficult job because the shots are almost simultaneous and so they save what they can. The points system is as follows: 1 point for getting the shot on target or hitting the woodwork and 2 points for scoring. The team with the most points at the end wins. | If a player catches up to another, he stops when he should pass him. Some go too quickly and lose the ball. Others forget a cone or two. Some players complete the course quickly and then take a long time to shoot. This game can also be played with cones nearer the wings to give more of an angle for the shot. |

| No. | Objectives | Age | Developing the Games | Common Problems |
|-----|-----------|-----|---------------------|-----------------|
| 25 | Running with the ball. Dribbling. Changing pace. Twisting and turning. Coordination. | 17 | Pitch size 18 x 18yds. 8-10 players running with a ball each around 18-20 randomly positioned cones. On the signal each player has to change pace and dribble around a cone as fast as he can and then revert back to the relaxed trot. The coach varies the time randomly between signals. | Two players head for the same cone. One of them should turn and look for one that is free. Lack of pace. Slow to react to the signal. |
| 26 | Passing. Control. Running with the ball. Dribbling. Winning the ball. Physical work. | 17 | 6 players (3 pairs, with only 2 pairs playing at any one time). The two pairs face each other (only one pair have a ball each)and are 20yds apart. The game starts with the 2 players with a ball each playing a long pass to the 2 players opposite. These players control the ball and run with it towards the players who just passed to them. When the players meet a '1 v 1' confrontation ensues. No matter what the outcome the players swap roles so that the 2 players who received the pass now play a pass to the third pair and the players who made the pass wait to receive a pass from the third pair once they have had their turn. | Poor passing. The players should make sure the passes are accurate. The '1 v 1' confrontations are too low key. They should be played as if in a real match. |

**134**

Fig 25

| No. | Objectives | Age | Developing the Games | Common Problems |
|---|---|---|---|---|
| 27 | Ball skills. Technique. Agility. Controlling the body. Coordination. | 17 | 3 cones form a triangle with each side measuring 5yds. There are 3 players and 1 ball at 1 cone and 3 players and 1 ball at one of the other cones. The game starts when a player from each group sets off around the course keeping the ball in the air. If the ball bounces, the player has to pick it up, do a forward roll and continue around the course keeping the ball up. When the player gets back to his cone, the second player takes over and when he has finished the third player sets off. The ball should not bounce during the 'hand over'. Play is stopped when the player in the chasing team catches the player ahead of him. Play resumes in the other direction and the player that was caught now acts as the chaser. The team that catches the opposition the most wins. | Some players do not do the forward roll. If the 'hand over' is not performed correctly and the ball bounces, the player at fault should do a forward roll. |

**Fig 26**

| No. | Objectives | Age | Developing the Games | Common Problems |
|-----|-----------|-----|---------------------|-----------------|
| 28 | Ball skills. Technique. Concentration. Coordination. | 18 | Number of cones, set up and players as in the previous game. The idea is similar but this time the player in possession runs around the course with 2 balls (on the ground) at the same time. This game is very difficult. | Leaving one of the balls behind. In this case the player should go back and collect it. |
| 29 | Running with the ball. Dribbling. Peripheral vision. Controlling the space around you. Coordination. Concentration. | 17-18 | Pitch square shaped with each side 2yds. There is a cone at each corner and one in the middle. There are 2 groups of 3 players with one ball per group standing at adjacent sides. On the signal the first player in each group sets off towards the central cone. The players run around the cone and then head towards the cone nearest to their starting point (which is not a cone either of the teams started from.) They run around the central cone again before heading back to their group to hand-over to the next player. The group that finishes first after each player has completed the circuit three times is the winner. The game restarts with the groups changing their starting position. | The players bump into each other. They go too slowly to avoid any collisions. Some forget where to turn. |

Fig 28

Fig 30

| No. | Objectives | Age | Developing the Games | Common Problems |
|-----|-----------|-----|---------------------|-----------------|
| 30 | Running with the ball. Dribbling. Speed off the mark. Changing direction. Explosive power. | 17 | 2 cones 6yds apart. 5-7 players and one ball at each. On the signal the first player in each group heads towards the cone opposite. Just as the players are about to meet in the middle they both put their feet on the ball, turn, head back and run around the cone where they started. Then they head back towards the cone opposite again, but just before they bump into the player coming the other way, they turn, head back and handover the ball to the next player in the group. This game should be played at a fast pace. There is a break after each player has completed 3 laps. | Some players go too quickly and lose control of the ball. Some bump into each other. Some never have any problems because they go too slowly. |
| 31 | Heading. Ball skills. Reflexes. Concentration. | 17 | Heading practice. This game involves 3 players (monkey in the middle). One player tries to head the ball to the other over the player in the middle who is trying to intercept. The player who receives the headed pass must control the ball in different ways: first, head the ball back first-time, then when he receives the next pass he has to keep the ball up with his head 2-5 times before returning the ball. If the player in the middle intercepts the ball or it bounces then he swaps with the player at fault. | Players who play 'one-touch' well are usually poor at keeping the ball up and vice versa. The player in the middle loses concentration. The players get too close or go too far away from each other. The player in the middle gets too close to the player who is about to receive the ball. |

| No. | Objectives | Age | Developing the Games | Common Problems |
|-----|-----------|-----|---------------------|-----------------|
| 32 | Heading. Ball skills. Controlling the body. Agility. | 17-18 | A group of players keeping a ball up in the air with their heads. When each player is ready he slowly gets down on his knees, still keeping the ball up. If this is successful then the player usually stands up again with little difficulty. The next stage is to kneel down and then from this position sit down, kneeling position again and then stand up. The ball should be kept up using the head at all times. As this is very difficult, only the older players usually manage to sit down successfully. | Players find this game difficult. Often, instead of progressing to higher levels of difficulty in stages, they start with the most complicated exercise (sitting down), of course fail and give up. |
| 33 | Heading. Ball skills. Concentration. Speed off the mark. Strength. Changing direction. | 17-18 | '3 v 3' in a game of 'head tennis'. Once the ball comes over the net to the other team's half, each player has to touch the ball at least once. Every time a player touches the ball he has to sprint to a flag 4yds behind his side of the court, run around it, then sprint back and rejoin the game (This is only to make the game more energetic). This is the same for each team and both teams have their own flag. Every so often the players swap positions in order to keep concentration levels high and to experience playing in different areas of the pitch. | Passing the ball back to the other side before all the players have had a touch. Players forget to run to the flag. Players do not sprint. The ball is kicked in play when it should be started with a header. The players carry on even after the ball bounces. |

| No. | Objectives | Age | Developing the Games | Common Problems |
|-----|-----------|-----|---------------------|-----------------|
| 34 | Heading. Ball skills. Agility. Controlling the space around you.<br><br>• | 17 | Pitch size 15 x 12yds. Goals 7 x 21'. 3 teams. 6 players in one goal (team 'A' and team 'C') and 3 players in the other (team 'B'). The 3 players in team 'A' set off towards the other goal heading the ball to one another. The player in the middle plays slightly behind the other two as he produces a diving header as he gets close to the opposition's goal. The defending team (in this case team 'B') can only stop a goal being scored using their heads. Then team 'A' stand in goal and team 'B' attack team 'C' in the opposite goal and so on. The players take turns playing in the middle and on the sides. The team that scores the most goals and concedes the least is the winner. | Passing the ball without moving forward. All the players do not have a touch of the ball. Some players do not attempt the diving header. These are the players who have not practiced on the 'suspended ball'. |

139

Fig 32

Fig 33

| No. | Objectives | Age | Developing the Games | Common Problems |
|---|---|---|---|---|
| 35 | Heading. Agility. Controlling the space around you. The ability to make runs and create space. | 17 | The same as the previous game except the team defending only has 2 players in goal. The third leaves the goal to try to intercept the ball (If he is successful the attack ends ). The attacking team passes the ball using their hands but has to score a headed-goal in 5 minutes. There is no particular order as to which of the 3 players tries the diving header first. The only rule is that each player should have an opportunity. The play is allowed to continue if the 5 minutes is up, but the coach will rule out any goal and let the team know how long they took. | 5 minutes is a long time but some teams still fail to make an attempt on goal. All the players do not have a touch. The same player always tries to score. Some never get a turn. |

Fig 36

| No. | Objectives | Age | Developing the Games | Common Problems |
|---|---|---|---|---|
| 36 | Jumping. Heading. Running with the ball using feints and dummies. The 'one-two'. | 17 | The players get into groups of three. They should all have similar heading ability. One of the players kicks the ball up high so that the other two can compete for it in the air. Something similar to the 'jump ball' in basket-ball. The player who delivers the ball watches the confrontation and quickly runs to recover the ball after it has been headed. Once he has the ball he teams up with the player who won the ball in the air to try to get past the third player by using feints and dummies or playing the 'one-two'. If the third player manages to intercept or win the ball he tries to beat the player who lost the ball with the help of the other player. The players change roles regularly. There are 2 winners: the player who wins the ball most in the air and the player who manages to beat his opponent most often. Make sure that the players jumping for the ball stand side by side and stretch the torso and neck as they jump. Beginners usually jump facing each other and if they collide this can cause nasty nose and teeth injuries. | Jumping facing each other is dangerous. Some jumps are illegal involving too much 'pushing' and 'shoving'. After heading the ball some players forget to continue playing. |

| No. | Objectives | Age | Developing the Games | Common Problems |
|---|---|---|---|---|
| 37 | Jumping. Heading. Anticipation. Speed. Dribbling using feints and dummies. Playing the 'one-two' and 'overlap'. | 18 | The same as the previous game but this time there are 4 players. The extra player stands close to the player kicking the ball for the other two who have to compete in the air. His job is to anticipate where the ball is likely to land after the header. He quickly runs to it and is supported by the player who made the header and a '2 v 2' confrontation takes place. The idea is to get past them using feints, dummies, the 'overlap' and the 'one-two'. If the defending pair wins the ball the teams swap roles and they become the attackers. The game only stops once a pair manages to beat their opponents by getting beyond them with the ball. All the players take turns in each role. | Some jumps are illegal, involving too much 'pushing' and 'shoving'. After heading the ball some players forget to continue playing. I stress that jumping facing each other can result in serious injury. |

Fig 37

Fig 38

| No. | Objectives | Age | Developing the Games | Common Problems |
|---|---|---|---|---|
| 38 | Positioning. Jumping. Heading. Concentration. Fast reflexes. | 18 | A 'round' played in an area 20 x 20yds. 3 attackers in the area and 4 attackers outside the area. There are also 4 defenders in the middle. A defender swaps with one of the outside attackers when the ball bounces (unless it bounces and is immediately kept up with a diving header). The attackers on the outside head the ball to each other but if defenders move out to impede this then the ball is passed to attackers in the middle. An attacker and defender should always compete for the ball in the air even if there is little chance of winning it. At least the opponent is 'put off' by the challenge and finds it difficult to control and direct his header. When a challenge takes place all the other players are watching and anticipating where the ball will go in order to get to it. The game is not stopped if a defender heads the ball if it does not consequently bounce. Remember never to challenge for the ball in the air from behind your opponent. | The strikers do not use their teammates in the middle. The attackers in the middle do not make space effectively. All the strikers 'freeze' when the defenders head a ball. This is when they should react quickly. The defenders wait for the attackers to make an error. They should try to force an error. |

| No. | Objectives | Age | Developing the Games | Common Problems |
|-----|------------|-----|----------------------|-----------------|
| 39 | Heading technique. Bravery in the challenge. Judging distance. Controlling the space around you. Strength in the jump. Playing in goal. | 17-18 | Pitch size 20 x 12yds. Regulation size goals. There is a '5 v 5' game taking place on various pitches. This is a 'soccer-heading' competition. The game involves strict marking. Throw-ins, corners and free kicks are all taken on the volley. After 15-20 minutes the winning teams play against each other and the losing teams do likewise. It is important for players to mark each other side by side and not stand behind as this can cause injury when jumping for the ball. Any player who follows this advice will greatly improve his ability to compete for the ball in the air. | If the ball approaches awkwardly, the players let it bounce or catch it. These errors need to be corrected before they become a habit. If the ball drops to the ground and a player wants to pick it up he runs the risk of getting hurt as another player is always tempted to kick it. The players do not produce diving headers even when they are unmarked. One player stands behind another when competing for the ball in the air. This should be corrected. |

Fig 39

| No. | Objectives | Age | Developing the Games | Common Problems |
|-----|-----------|-----|---------------------|-----------------|
| 40 | Heading technique. Bravery in the challenge. Judging distance. Controlling the space around you. Leg strength. Playing in goal. Most importantly, the player in the goal in the middle needs to be alert. | 17-18 | The same as the previous game but this time there are only two games going on at once. There are 3 goals. The third goal is in the middle and can be used by both games. The goalkeeper has to keep turning to observe the two games. If he gets the ball he immediately puts it back in play however he chooses. The other 2 goalkeepers can only do this by way of a jumping header. If a shot from one game goes wide the goalkeeper in the middle concentrates totally on the other game as the defenders go to collect the ball. The game is divided into two halves. Playing in goal in the middle is very tiring so it is up to the coach to swap goalkeepers as he sees fit. | If the ball approaches awkwardly the players let it bounce or catch it. These errors need to be corrected before they become a habit. If the ball drops to the ground and a player wants to pick it up he runs the risk of getting hurt as another player is always tempted to kick it. The players do not produce diving headers even when they are unmarked. One player stands behind another when competing for the ball in the air. This should be corrected. |
| 41 | Ball skills. Control. Passing. Concentration. | 18 | Pitch size 18 x 9yds. There is a net in the center separating the two halves, with a height of 4ft. This is a game of 'soccer tennis'. 2 players in each team. The game is not started in any particular way. Each player in the team must touch the ball alternately between 1-3 times before sending the ball back over the net. The ball must not bounce on your half of the pitch. A competition can be organized with all the players in the squad. | Some players stray onto the other side of the pitch and this causes problems. The players do not combine or they pass to each other too often. The ball is allowed to bounce, which defeats the object of the game. |

| No. | Objectives | Age | Developing the Games | Common Problems |
|-----|-----------|-----|---------------------|-----------------|
| 42 | Passing using the inside and outside of foot. Speed of execution. Concentration. | 17-18 | Positioned in a triangular formation (5yds apart) the players practice passing using first the inside then the outside of the foot. The passes are always played first time. Two balls are used at the same time which means the players have to concentrate and play quickly. The whole team can be split into threes to play this game. | It takes the players a long time to produce the skills at a good speed. Not using the specified area of the foot. Lack of concentration. |
| 43 | Long and short passing. Orientation. Speed of execution. Peripheral vision. Concentration. | 17-18 | Groups of 6 players run in a small area (perhaps start off with 10 x 10yds). This area increases as the players become familiar with the game until half the pitch is being used and long passes are needed. 3 balls per group. The players keep running while they make a series of passes. Player 'A' always passes to player 'B' who always passes to player 'C' etc... The last player (player 'F') passes to player 'A'. The fact that 3 balls are being used means that the players have to play more quickly and concentrate more. This is a good game for the whole team to play in groups. | Some players hold onto the ball too long, which means they often end up with two balls. Lack of concentration, which means that the player does not see a ball coming, or he does not spot the player he has to pass to quickly enough. |

146

**Fig 43**

Fig 44

| No. | Objectives | Age | Developing the Games | Common Problems |
|---|---|---|---|---|
| 44 | General technique. Speed. Peripheral vision. Multiple-observation. Concentration. | 17-18 | This game involves 10 players, 4 balls and 2 cones. The cones are 12yds apart with 3 players at each. The other 4 players stand two on each side opposite each other 10-12yds apart. The pairs have a ball each. One of the players receives a pass from the player opposite and controls it on the turn and ends up facing in the other direction. He then plays a back heel back to his teammate opposite. Most important is that these pairs are at either side of the cone-course as the other players run between them with the ball. A player from each cone (with a ball each) sets off towards the opposite cone and is faced with the problem of trying to go as fast as he can while avoiding the ball that is crossing his path(it is being back-heeled across the cone-course). Once the player reaches the opposite cone he has to head back and is faced with the same difficulties as the two balls are continually being passed to and fro. Then he gives the ball to the second player who runs the course and so on. All the players rotate in order to experience each role. Speed, technical proficiency and any passes that are intercepted by mistake are noted. | The control and touch lacks the necessary pace required. The players do not run with the ball as fast as they can and they do not look up. They either look up or go slowly or they keep their head down and so are easily hit by the balls being passed to and fro. The correct thing to do is change pace when approaching another ball and speed up again when in the clear. |

147

| No. | Objectives | Age | Developing the Games | Common Problems |
|-----|-----------|-----|---------------------|-----------------|
| 45 | Speed. Peripheral vision. Volleys. Multiple-observation. Concentration. Running with the ball. | 18 | The same as in the previous game but it is more difficult for the players running with the ball. Now the 'hitters' are 15yds away. They hold the ball in their hands and as the players run with the ball from cone to cone they volley the ball to each other trying to hit the players running from cone to cone. The players swap roles regularly. The winner is the player who got hit the least and who hit others the most. | Incorrect volley technique resulting in the ball going high and wide. Normally the players do not run as fast as they can with the ball as they concentrate more on trying to avoid the balls that cross their path. |

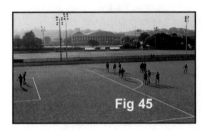

Fig 45

| No. | Objectives | Age | Developing the Games | Common Problems |
|-----|-----------|-----|---------------------|-----------------|
| 46 | Putting 'swerve' on the ball. Running with the ball. Dribbling. Peripheral vision. Multiple-observation. Concentration. | 18 | This is another game similar to the previous two. There are 8 cones. 4 cones form a square 10yds apart. 2 of the cones on one side of the square (let's say the left hand side) have two additional cones in line 1yd apart. There are 3 players (team 'A')with a ball each positioned at the top right hand cone and 3 players with a ball positioned at the left hand cone of the group of 3 in the bottom left hand corner (team 'B'). The first player in team 'A' sets off towards the 3 cones opposite, runs around them and then heads left towards the next 3 cones, runs around them and then heads across towards the cone opposite and finally back to the starting point. Team 'B' does the same, starting with the 3 cones first etc... A player from each team sets off at the same time. Meanwhile there are 2 pairs of players opposite each other. They have to put swerve on the ball and pass it to each other and try to hit the players as they run across between cones. The players are safe as they run down between the cones and can only be hit as they run across. The players swap roles regularly. | Hitting the middle of the ball and not putting curve on it. Some players stop, fearing getting hit with the ball. |

| No. | Objectives | Age | Developing the Games | Common Problems |
|---|---|---|---|---|
| 47 | Long passes. Orientation. Changing pace. Concentration. Imagination. Peripheral vision. Stamina. | 18 | This game involves virtually the whole pitch (stretching from the edge of one 18-yard box right up to the opposite goalmouth). There are 18 players and 9 balls. The game starts with the players on the ball jogging (in any direction) and looking up. When a player spots someone without a ball he calls out his name. The player without the ball gets into space and is passed the ball. The player who has just made the pass continues running, spots another player with a ball and calls for it. The player tries to control and move in one movement (on the turn) to save time and then he looks to pass to a player without a ball. So the game is about both the player on the ball looking to pass the ball and also involves the player without a ball calling for one. The shouts should be loud and clear. No specific number of players is needed as the game can be played with more or less players. If played correctly this is a tiring game (as long as the players continue to jog and move) and so should not last more than 20 minutes. The goalkeepers also take part (as outfield players) and they are allowed to alternate between using feet and hands. If they catch the ball they must not take | The coach has to make sure that the players do not stop or play at a slow pace. Name a player and pass before the player has had time to react. Some players are too shy to call out a name and so they continue running with the ball indefinitely. The player cannot 'give up' on any ball and has to chase after and control all the passes as if in a 'real' game. |

| No. | Objectives | Age | Developing the Games | Common Problems |
|-----|-----------|-----|---------------------|-----------------|
| 47 (cont) | Long passes. Orientation. Changing pace. Concentration. Imagination. Peripheral vision. Stamina. | 18 | more than 4 steps before passing the ball. The coach makes sure that the passes are always long (25-30 yards) and executed correctly. The coach asks the players to use their imagination and play balls as they would in a match. The player who receives the ball has to always control it and move in the same direction (as if attacking) even if it is easier (perhaps because of a poor pass) to move in the opposite direction. | |

**Fig 47**

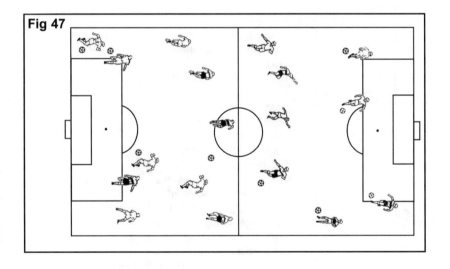

| No. | Objectives | Age | Developing the Games | Common Problems |
|---|---|---|---|---|
| 48 | Play 'the method' automatically. Speed of execution. Paying attention. Concentration. Stamina. | 17-18 | The whole pitch is used and the game is played end to end. The game involves perfecting passing and moves. The game can be played with any number of players but as an example let's say '9 v 9'. Marking is tight and the confrontations should involve players of similar ability. The team on the ball practices 'the method'. The player on the ball is supported on the wing by one player, there is another ready to play the 'one-two', another is waiting to exploit the space created by making himself available for the inside pass, while the player on the other wing can come inside and a player behind him can move up and exploit the space he leaves. When in possession each team repeatedly practices these moves. The game is played with one or two touches and always forward. Back and sideways passes are not allowed. To earn a point a team has to get to one end and back. The team with the most points wins. | Taking more than two touches. Passing sideways or back (ball goes to the opposition if this happens). Playing their 'own' way without thinking about playing 'the method'. Some players forget to mark. This defeats the object of the game. |

| No. | Objectives | Age | Developing the Games | Common Problems |
|-----|-----------|-----|---------------------|-----------------|
| 49 | Dribbling. Feints and dummies. Speed. Bursts of strength. Stamina. Shots on goal. | 17 | Two cones act as portable goalposts and are positioned 30yds away from the normal goal. The game involves 8 players: 1 in each goal, 4 playing '2 v 2' and 1 each on the flanks who act as 'neutrals'. The idea is for the attacking players to take advantage of the numerical superiority (i.e. with the help of the neutrals) and shoot as quickly as possible. The 'neutrals' are not allowed to shoot. | The 'neutral' players shoot. When the 'neutrals' get the ball the other players do not make themselves available. They should play the 'give' and 'go' etc. The defending team puts up little resistance. |
| 50 | Same as in the previous game. | 17 | Identical to the previous game except this time the 'neutral' players play 'one-touch' and the attackers have to play the 'one-two' and shoot immediately after they get the ball back even if ideally they would like to get closer to goal. | The 'neutrals' do not play 'one-touch'. Once the 'one-two' has been completed the player does not shoot immediately. The defenders drop back to the goal. This ruins the game. |

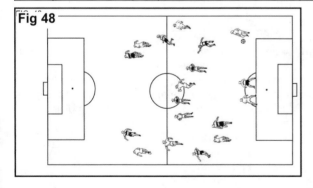

Fig 48

Fig 49

| No. | Objectives | Age | Developing the Games | Common Problems |
|-----|-----------|-----|---------------------|-----------------|
| 51 | Dribbling. Feints and dummies. Passing. Playing 'one-touch'. Explosive power. Speed. Stamina. Shots on goal. | 17 | Two cones act as portable goalposts and are positioned 30yds away from the normal goal. The game involves a '4 v 2' confrontation but the defending team has 2 of their players in goal (they are not allowed to use their hands). The attacking team must play one or two-touch and shoot as quickly and as often as they can. The goalkeepers rotate constantly. | The two defenders drop back to their goal instead of playing all over the pitch. The attackers pass the ball too much and forget to play feints and dummies. It is possible to beat a man and especially create a shooting opportunity by playing 'one-touch'. |
| 52 | Passing. Speed of execution. Explosive power. Speed. Stamina. Shots on goal. | 17 | Pitch size 25 x 15yds. 2 goals with a goalkeeper in each. The game involves '1 v1' situations with 2 'neutral' players who always support the attacking player. In other words '3 v 1', but the attackers must play 'one-touch' and shoot as much as possible. The 'neutral' players should be constantly involved in the play. | Too much passing. There should be less passing and more shooting. The ball is 'walked' into the goal. |
| 53 | Passing. Dribbling. Shots on goal. | 17-18 | Pitch size 30 x 30yds with 4 goals. There are 3 teams of 4 players where 1 player in each has to protect the goals. A team defends 2 goals and attacks the 2 opposite. The goalkeepers are changed on a regular basis. 4 players are used to facilitate the number of shots. | Too much passing. The players always want to get very close to the goal before shooting. Not shooting from distance or from difficult angles. |

| No. | Objectives | Age | Developing the Games | Common Problems |
|---|---|---|---|---|
| 54 | Being a 'real' soccer player. Passing. Dribbling. Feints and dummies. Improvisation. Shots on goal. | 17-18 | Pitch size 40yds square. 2 goals with a goalkeeper in each. There are 3 teams with 2 outfield players in each. Team 'A' attacks 'B', then team 'B' attacks 'C' and finally team 'C' attacks 'A'. As the main objective of the game is to improve shooting technique there is a line of cones 15yds from each goal. The tackling and dribbling only takes place in the 10yd-area between the cones. Once a player goes beyond the cones with the ball he has to shoot immediately (no shooting allowed unless beyond the cones). Once the shot has been taken the defenders get the ball and start an attack etc. The team who concedes the least amount of goals and scores the most is the winner. | The players find it difficult to produce creative soccer in such a small playing area. Shooting before going beyond the cones. |

**Fig 52**

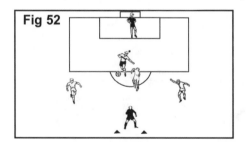

Fig 54

| No. | Objectives | Age | Developing the Games | Common Problems |
|---|---|---|---|---|
| 55 | Passing. Dribbling. Feints and dummies. The 'one-two'. Imagination. Shots on goal. | 17 | Pitch size 30 x 20yds. 2 regulation size goals with a goalkeeper in each. The game involves '2 v 2' with 4 'neutral' players, 1 positioned near each corner of the pitch. The 'neutrals' have to play 'one-touch'. Players can play the 'one-two' with any of the 'neutrals' but they have to combine with 1 of the 2 in the opposition's half before they shoot. The players swap roles regularly. The team who concedes the least amount of goals and scores the most is the winner | Some teams do not use the 'neutral' players. Some shoot before playing the 'one-two'. The team defending ruins the game by playing too deep. |

**Fig 55**

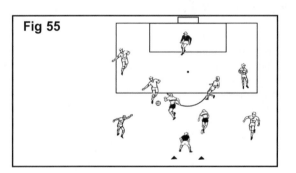

**Fig 56**

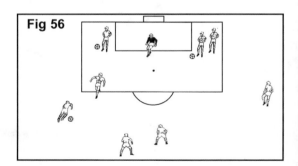

| No. | Objectives | Age | Developing the Games | Common Problems |
|---|---|---|---|---|
| 56 | Passing. Dribbling. Feints and dummies. Explosive power. Shots on goal. '1v 1' in attack and defense. | 17 | 2 goalkeepers and 8 out-field players. 4 players (the defenders) start off in the 6-yard box and the rest (attackers) stand 25yds away, spread out across the width of the pitch (2 on the wings and 2 in the middle). The play-ers are in pairs 'A', 'B', 'C' and 'D'(where the 2 'A' players are the left back and right winger and the 'B' players are the next 2 nearly opposite each other etc.). 'A' and 'C' play at the same time. Then 'B' and 'D' have a go. The game starts with a defender passing the ball to the player opposite, his partner, and then chasing after it as fast as he can. He tries to confront the player who has received the ball in a '1 v 1' before he gets to the 18-yard box. The player on the ball tries to get past his man and have a shot and the player who made the pass tries to win the ball and shoot himself. The ball can be won and lost several times but eventu-ally one of the players shoots. The players all swap roles and starting positions on the pitch. When the goals are tallied the coach should try to remember who played against whom and in what position | Once the players have passed the ball, some jog after it. They should sprint and try to get to the man before he reaches the 18-yard box. The player trying to win the ball does not make enough effort. The player on the ball also plays at a low inten-sity. |

| No. | Objectives | Age | Developing the Games | Common Problems |
|-----|-----------|-----|---------------------|-----------------|
| 57 | Passing. Dribbling. Feints and dummies. Explosive power. Imagination. Improvisation. Shots on goal. | 17 | Basically the same as the previous game but this time the attacker has a different task after he has finished his mission (getting beyond his man and shooting). He now goes to support the next attacker. The new attacker can choose to play the 'one-two' or dribble before he shoots. The supporting player runs towards the goal to take advantage of any rebound whether or not he was involved in the build-up. When the final scores are counted, rebounds are tallied separately. | Similar to the previous game. The attacker does not make himself available (in the 'light'). He also forgets to run towards the goal. |
| 58 | Long and short passes. Feints and dummies. Dribbling. Explosive power. Stamina. Imagination. Concentration. Mastering the '1 v 1' in attack and defense. Shots on goal. | 18 | The two previous games can be played in a similar way but with a distance of 40-45yds between the players. The player on the ball passes the ball long and high and sprints after it (this game is far more physically demanding than the previous two). The teammate/opponent passes the ball back on the volley using the inside of the foot and chases after it. The player who made the original pass (still running) plays the ball back again using the inside of the foot to his teammate/opponent who, without stopping, controls the ball and continues to try to beat his man and get a shot in on goal. The points system is similar to the previous games. | The same as in the previous two games. This game is very exhausting and as a result the players take it easy. It is up to the coach to see that the game is played at a good pace. |

| No. | Objectives | Age | Developing the Games | Common Problems |
|-----|-----------|-----|---------------------|-----------------|
| 59 | Running with the ball. Dribbling. Feints and dummies. Being a 'real' soccer player. Imagination. Improvisation. Concentration. Bursts of strength. Shots on goal. | 18 | Half the pitch using one goal. 3 cones are placed 5yds beyond the 18-yard box (2 in line with each post and one in line with the middle of the goal). Behind each cone are another 4 cones 2yds apart in a zigzag formation. Basically there are 3 cone obstacle courses. 3 groups of 3 players each with a ball lined up on the halfway line behind an obstacle course. There are another 2 pairs each standing near a corner of the 18-yard box, one pair per corner. There are 2 goalkeepers in the goal. The game is as follows: on the signal a player from each team sets off running with the ball through the cones. Once past the last cone the player must enter the 18-yard box before shooting. However, there are 2 players waiting to stop him. It is up to the player to improvise as best he can to get his shot off. | Running slowly with the ball on purpose so that all the other players are busy, which leads to an unchallenged shot. The coach should make sure this does not happen. Defending half-heartedly. Shooting from outside the area. It is difficult for the defenders to understand that whether they are successful or not they have no time to waste as another player is always about to arrive. |

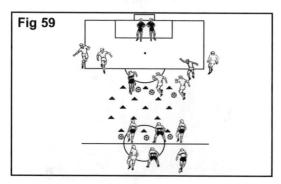

**Fig 59**

| No. | Objectives | Age | Developing the Games | Common Problems |
|-----|-----------|-----|----------------------|-----------------|
| 60 | Marking and making space. The 'one-two'. The 'overlap'. Dribbling. Feints and dummies. Shooting. Speed of execution. Stamina. | 17-18 | Pitch size 40 x 40yds. There is a goalkeeper in each goal and various '2 v 2' confrontations taking place (normally at least 4 pairs playing simultaneously). The players play freely but before shooting they have to perform the 'one-two', the 'doblada' or the 'auto-pass'. Playing '2 v 2' the 'one-two' is performed by passing the ball 'first time' between the opponents. The players need to be well-balanced, know how to play feints and dummies and be able to run backwards. The teams need to be evenly matched as man-to-man marking is employed. The defenders are not allowed to drop back as this limits the space. During the rest period the coach makes observations. After the break the game resumes with different pairings (still keeping the teams evenly matched). There is a note made of all the 'one-two's', 'dobladas' and goals scored by each pairing. | The players forget to mark and drop back. Shooting without playing 'the method'. When they are tired they give up and do not put in the extra effort required. As this is a tiring game the pulse rate should be taken during the breaks. If the pulse rate is not too high some players start playing again too quickly and if it is high the players become demoralized. |

Fig 60

| No. | Objectives | Age | Developing the Games | Common Problems |
|-----|-----------|-----|----------------------|-----------------|
| 61 | Running with the ball. Dribbling. Covering. Shots on goal. Speed. Explosive power. Astuteness in the challenge. Controlling the space around you. | 17-18 | There are 14-16 players and 7-8 balls on the edge of the 18-yard box. There is a cone 8 yards further on in line with the center spot and another 5 yards diagonally to the right. 2 goalkeepers alternate in goal. On the signal a player runs to the first cones and runs back in order to shoot. But at the same time as he sets off another player without a ball runs to the cone positioned diagonally. He runs around it to the right and pursues the player on the ball to try to win it so that he can shoot instead. The player on the ball can shoot from distance or shield the ball and dribble, but only once he has gone around the cone and is heading for goal. The players should be evenly matched and frequently changed. The players swap roles and run around the cone to the left. | The player without the ball tries to impede the player on the ball as he makes his run towards the cone. The player without the ball has to run as fast as he can to the other cone. The ball is not well protected by the body and if it is, the defender tends to push the player off the ball. |

| No. | Objectives | Age | Developing the Games | Common Problems |
|---|---|---|---|---|
| 62 | Passing. Dribbling. Speed of execution. Marking and making space. Playing in goal. Shots on goal. | 18 | A portable goal is positioned 20 yards opposite a regulation size one. There is a goalkeeper in each. The game involves evenly matched '2 v 2' confrontations. The game is one or two-touch and three touches are allowed only if immediately followed by a shot. The game involves playing the 'one-two', the 'doblada' etc. but the main objective is to shoot. A shot can be taken from anywhere. After 5 or 6 minutes another 4 players swap until the whole team has had a turn. This is a very intensive and tiring game. Each group of 4 players has 3-5 repetitions and the break in between each should involve light stretching activities. | The players concentrate on passing when the idea is to practice shooting. The marking is not tight. The players want to place the ball in the back of the net when the game requires power and urgency. |

Fig 62

| No. | Objectives | Age | Developing the Games | Common Problems |
|---|---|---|---|---|
| 63 | Passing. Dribbling. Marking. Making space. Concentration. Imagination. Shots on goal. | 17-18 | Pitch size is a circle with a radius of 20yds. 4 goals made from cones are placed around the circle. 3 teams of 4 players. One team acts as goalkeepers with 1 player in each of the 4 goals. The two remaining teams play against each other but split into two '2 v 2'. This takes place outside the circle but goals can only be scored from inside. No challenges can be made once a player has managed to get inside the circle. If a player challenges for the ball inside the circle then a 'foul' is awarded and the player who had the ball is able to take it outside the circle and proceed (unchallenged) towards any of the goals and shoot. All the teams rotate and have a turn in the goals. The team that scores the most goals and concedes the least is the winner. | The players dribble and pass but take relatively few shots. The player shoots as soon as he wins the ball no matter where he is. The goalkeepers follow one ball and ignore the other. |

| No. | Objectives | Age | Developing the Games | Common Problems |
|-----|-----------|-----|---------------------|-----------------|
| 64 | Making space. Control. 'Bicycle' kicks or 'semi-scissors'. | 18 | Pitch size 20 x 12yds. 3 teams of 3 players. 1 regulation size goal. Team 'A' attacks, throwing the ball to each other and carrying it in the hands. Team 'B' defends with 2 players in goal and the third trying to intercept the ball. Team 'C' is not involved at present and waits to take part. Attempts at goal can only be made with a 'bicycle' kick or 'semi-scissors'. After the allotted time 'C' attacks 'B' and so on. The team that scores the most goals and concedes the least is the winner. | The idea is to shoot at goal as quickly as possible but this does not happen. The players should shoot 'first-time' or control the ball with their head and then shoot immediately. The goalkeepers make little effort to save the ball. |

**164**

Fig 64

| No. | Objectives | Age | Developing the Games | Common Problems |
|-----|-----------|-----|---------------------|-----------------|
| 65 | Diving headers. 'Bicycle' kicks. 'Semi-scissors'. Explosive power, Speed, coordination and judging distance are all necessary in order to perform these skills properly. | 18 | Pitch size 40 x 25yds. 2 regulation size goals with a goalkeeper in each. The game is '2 v 2' with a 'neutral' player on each wing and 2 other players playing deep. Attempts at goal can only be made with a 'diving' header, 'bicycle' kick or 'semi-scissors' (high volley on the turn). There is one 'neutral' player on each wing and who always tries to make himself available by playing in 'the light'. The 'neutral' player keeps up with play even if it is taking place on the other wing as a change of direction is always possible or after using the 'deep' players near the goal they may be needed. The 'deep' players make themselves available to receive passes from the attackers or from the 'neutral' players on the wing. After a specified time the players rotate and swap roles. All the goals scored and any 'assists' that lead to goals are tallied. | The players have to attack and defend but they concentrate more on defense. It should be the other way around. The 'neutral players usually pass to the players involved in the '2 v 2' when they should make more use of the 'deep' players to 'unlock' the defense. Attempts on goal are not always made with one of the three specified techniques. There is no limit on touches but the 'deep' players should only need one or two-touches. Players take too many touches and do not make themselves available. |

165

Fig 66

| No. | Objectives | Age | Developing the Games | Common Problems |
|-----|-----------|-----|---------------------|-----------------|
| 66 | 'Acrobatic' attempts on goal. Running with the ball. Crossing. Speed. Explosive power. Judging distance. Making space. | 18 | 40 x 40yds. '3 v 3'. 2 regulation size goals. 3 players in the middle and 3 on each wing who alternatively support the attacking team. This is how the game works: Team 'A' attacks team 'B'. Team 'C' is not involved and waits somewhere away from the play. Team 'B' has two players in goal and one outfield player. Team 'A' has a goalkeeper and two outfield players. Team 'A' tries to get past the defender using the supporting players on the wing. Once the 'neutral' gets the ball he runs to the 'by-line' and crosses the ball. Meanwhile, the players in team 'A' run to get into position to meet the cross and the player in team 'B' runs with them to try to intercept the ball or at least make a challenge for it. Goals can only be scored with 'bicycle' kicks or high volleys on the turn. If the defender manages to intercept or the cross is poor the ball is passed to another 'neutral' and he crosses for the attackers to try again. Then team 'B' attacks 'C' and 'C' attacks 'A' and so on. The players rotate to experience each role. Keep track of: the team that scores the most goals, the team that concedes the least number of goals and the player whose crosses lead to the most goals. | The 'neutral' players on the wing do not run as fast as they can. The crosses are poor. The specified techniques for shooting at goal are ignored. The players do not play at full speed or intensity. If this happens the game loses its appeal. |

| No. | Objectives | Age | Developing the Games | Common Problems |
|-----|-----------|-----|---------------------|-----------------|
| 67 | Paying attention. Concentration. Peripheral vision. Ball skills. Playing 'one-touch'. Speed of execution. Coordination. Bursts of strength. Judging distance. | 18 | 1 goalkeeper in the regulation size goal. 6 players near a corner (not entering the 18-yard box) playing 'one-touch' in a '4 v 2' 'round'. There are 6 other players close together in the 18-yard box opposite the goal, each keeping a ball up. They each have a bib in their left hand (there are 2 red, 2 green and 2 yellow). While the 'round' continues these players concentrate on keeping their ball up. Suddenly two players pick up their ball and raise their green bib. On this signal 2 players in the 'round' (they are assigned a color before they begin) sprint towards the goal and the balls are thrown up so that they can try the 'bicycle kick' or 'semi-scissors'. They then return to the 'round' until another color is raised. After a while the players swap roles and the 'round' is played in the other corner of the pitch. Peripheral vision, shooting technique and goals are all noted. The first player to arrive shoots and the next waits until he has finished and then a ball is thrown up for him. The idea is also to try to be the first to shoot. | The players find it difficult to play 'one-touch' in the 'round'. They have to concentrate on the game and be aware of what colors are being shown. Some players find this very difficult and either concentrate totally on the game and ignore the bibs or vice versa. Sometimes the throw is very poor. If this happens another player throws the ball instead. |

**Fig 67**

| No. | Objectives | Age | Developing the Games | Common Problems |
|-----|-----------|-----|---------------------|-----------------|
| 68 | Multiple-observation. Total concentration. Peripheral vision. Explosive power. Judging distance. Coordination. Playing in goal. | 18 | An imaginary circle with a radius of 15yds. 6 players outside the circle throwing the ball to each other and 2 players inside the circle acting as goalkeepers. There are 2 balls in the game. The players throw the ball to each other either short or long. At any moment any player can suddenly play the 'bicycle' kick or the high volley on the turn, directing the ball towards the goalkeepers. The latter concentrate on trying to save the shots. Each player must attempt the prescribed techniques. | Too many passes and too few shots. Few long passes are made across the circle and even fewer shots, even though this is the best opportunity to execute the technique. Some goalkeepers lose concentration and even worse drop the ball. This is not a good sign. |

**168**

Fig 68

| No. | Objectives | Age | Developing the Games | Common Problems |
|-----|-----------|-----|---------------------|-----------------|
| 69 | Diving headers. 'Bicycle' kicks. High volley on the turn. Astuteness. Craft. Improvisation. Intelligence. Teamwork. | 18 | A goal is placed on the edge of the 18-yard box opposite the regulation size goalmouth. 1 goalkeeper in each goal. 4 other players are playing '2 v 2'. There are another 4 players, one at each goalpost. The game is played with the hands and attempts at goal can only be made by producing a 'bicycle' kick, high volley on the turn or in exceptional circumstances a diving header. The players are encouraged to use craft and intelligence. Apart from the classic move of passing to one of the players on the posts and running to receive the return, the game involves the following: **1.** Dummy to pass to one of the players on the posts and pass to the teammate instead. **2.**A player pretends to pass and then throws the ball up for himself to play the 'bicycle' kick. **3.** When close to the opponents goal, suddenly the ball is passed to one of the players next to the other goal and the passer runs to receive the return and plays the 'bicycle' kick. This move usually unsettles defenders and it is a good opportunity for the other teammate to get into space to receive the ball. After the allotted time the players swap roles. At the end of the game the goals and 'assists' are counted. | Sometimes the player on the ball fools the opposition with an unexpected pass, but unfortunately his teammate is also taken by surprise. Some players never try a shot. Monotonous play needs to be pointed out and addressed during the game. |

**169**

| No. | Objectives | Age | Developing the Games | Common Problems |
|-----|-----------|-----|---------------------|-----------------|
| 70 | Zonal defensive work. Changing the play. Discipline. Intelligence. Heading. Shots on goal. | 18 | Pitch size 30 x 20yds. A game of '4 v 4'. 4 goals. 2 next to each other and 2 more opposite these. Only 2 of the goals (opposite each other) have a goalkeeper, the other 2 goals are defended by the outfield players. Any type of goal (within the rules of normal soccer) is valid if scored in the goals with goalkeepers. In the other 2 goals only headed goals can be scored. The game is all about discipline, intelligence and creating chances. | In this game it is easy to spot players with poor positioning sense. Not changing and varying the play. Not shooting. |

Fig 70

Fig 71

| No. | Objectives | Age | Developing the Games | Common Problems |
|---|---|---|---|---|
| 71 | Running with the ball. Dribbling. Shots on goal. Explosive power. Speed. | 18 | Two false walls are positioned 10 yards from goal roughly in line with the goalposts. There is a line of 5 cones (each 2 yards apart) in a zigzag formation 5 yards further away from the goals and in between the two false walls. There is a player with a ball standing at the cone nearest the halfway line and another player with a ball on the next cone. On the signal the 2 players set off (one trying to stay ahead and the other trying to catch up) around the cones. When they get around the last cone they kick the ball against the false wall (the players split and use both false walls), collect the rebound and shoot. As they finish, 2 other players set off and do the same. There is a rest period and then the pair has another go but this time the positions are reversed and the other player has the advantage. There are 2 goalkeepers in the goal. They alternate or sometimes play at the same time. The coach is looking for a good shot and speed. It is very important to get your shot in first. | Some players go too quickly and collide with the cones. Generally the players are quick around the cones and slow to shoot. This needs to be addressed. |

| No. | Objectives | Age | Developing the Games | Common Problems |
|---|---|---|---|---|
| 72 | Running with the ball. Dribbling. Feints and dummies. Passing. Shooting. Explosive power. Speed. | 17-18 | Similar to the previous game but the players who have just shot immediately confront the player running with the ball near 'the wall'. Once past the cones the player can kick the ball against 'the wall' and collect the rebound or ignore the 'one-two' and try to dribble past his opponent before shooting. In this game speed, good shots and balls won are noted. | Some players go too quickly and collide with the cones. Generally the players are quick around the cones and slow to shoot. This needs to be addressed. Not many feints and dummies are played. |
| 73 | Running with the ball. Dribbling. Passing. Shooting. Explosive power. Speed. Coordination. | 17-18 | Similar to the previous games. This time the 2 players form a team and compete against the other pairs. The 2 players set off, one slightly in front of the other. The first player has the ball and his teammate follows. Once around the cones he kicks the ball against 'the wall' and runs around the other side. This acts as a perfect pass for his teammate who runs to take the rebound in his stride and passes it (preferably first-time) back to his teammate who shoots. Then they change roles. The pairs are timed and the quickest team wins. | Lack of timing and coordination between the runs and the passes. Shots are half-hearted. |

Fig 72

Fig 73

| No. | Objectives | Age | Developing the Games | Common Problems |
|-----|-----------|-----|---------------------|-----------------|
| 74 | Passing precision and power. Keeping calm. Concentration. | 17 | 8 balls are placed along the halfway line 5yds apart. There are 8 players with a ball each 15yds away from the halfway line on each side of the pitch. The idea is to kick the ball at a ball on the halfway line, trying to knock it into the opposition's side of the pitch. There is no specified way of kicking the ball but proper technique is required. If a ball is successfully hit and moved onto the opponent's half of the pitch then the player collects his ball, gets back in position and tries to hit another ball. After a certain time (perhaps 6 minutes) the number of balls in each half is counted. If the players quickly master the game or once it has been mastered, it can be played using the weaker foot. | Sometimes the balls being kicked collide. A perfectly struck pass may end in failure as the intended target is removed by another player's ball just beforehand. Whatever passing technique the player decides to use he should adopt the correct position and use his arms to balance etc. This is largely ignored and poor technique abounds. |

| No. | Objectives | Age | Developing the Games | Common Problems |
|---|---|---|---|---|
| 75 | Passing precision and power. Keeping calm. Concentration. | 17-18 | Pitch and number of players the same as above. Two teams of eight players. This time there are 16 balls one yard from the halfway line (8 either side of the halfway line) each on top of a cone. The idea is for the player to kick the ball off the cone and onto the other side of the pitch. The first team to successfully knock off all of the opposition's balls is the winner. If a player accidentally hits his own ball off the cone then this counts for the opposition and cannot be replaced. As in the previous game the kicking technique is up to the players but it must be correctly executed. | The players move to the side to avoid any possibility of hitting their own ball. They should shoot from directly behind their own cone. Shooting with the full instep is not a good technique to choose. Players should shoot either with the inside or outside of the foot for more accuracy. Accomplished players can even use the toe-poke with great success. |

| No. | Objectives | Age | Developing the Games | Common Problems |
|---|---|---|---|---|
| 76 | Precision and touch on the ball. 'Killing' the ball. Agility. Reflexes. Concentration. Multiple-observation. | 18 | The whole team can take part in this competition. 6 players per group. 2 players each with a ball and 5yds away there is a rectangular shape marked 4 yards wide and 5 yards long. There are 2 players inside the rectangle (they must stay inside this area). 2 others are another 5yds away. One of the players runs (they go alternately) with the ball, stops near the rectangle (he is not allowed to enter) and tries to kick the ball against one of the players in the area. The players in the rectangle try to avoid being hit as best they can and keep alert and on the move. However, whether they are touched or not the other 2 players opposite have to control the ball and turn at the same time. This is very difficult. The players swap roles and each gets a chance to take 20 shots at the players in the area. Points are awarded for hitting players, for avoiding being hit and for controlling the ball. | The players go into the area. They should choose accuracy over power in the shot. Some do not fall to the ground to avoid being hit. Poor body position when trying to control the ball on the turn. The players should stand sideways on not head on. |

| No. | Objectives | Age | Developing the Games | Common Problems |
|-----|-----------|-----|---------------------|-----------------|
| 77 | Marking. Making space. Volleys. Shielding the ball. Particularly the subtle and 'smart' use of arms. | 17-18 | Pitch size 20 x 12yds. 2 regulation size goals. '3 v 3' including a goalkeeper in each team. The game involves throwing the ball to each other and shooting on the volley (nearly always on the half turn). The defender should hassle as much as possible and the player shooting should make space for the shot using his body and arms to keep his position. When a player wants to take a shot he shouts out 'shot' and the defender cannot intercept the ball but uses his arms to impede the shot. The players should use as many tricks as possible. The throws should be short so that the shooter has to make space. The ball can also be thrown high over the players' heads. The shot must be taken before the ball hits the ground. | Not using the body or arms. Some players take the idea too far and hold, push and shove their opponent. Poor throwing. The same players always shoot. |

Fig 77

| No. | Objectives | Age | Developing the Games | Common Problems |
|---|---|---|---|---|
| 78 | Paying attention. Concentration. Peripheral vision. Reaction speed. Using the body, shoulders and arms. | 17-18 | A goalkeeper in goal and outside the 18-yard box a series of '1 v 1' confrontations take place. This is how the game works: 2 players stand shoulder to shoulder 10yds outside the 18-yard box facing the goal, behind them is a 'jet-ball' (if no 'jet-ball' available, the coach can stand behind). A ball is launched and as soon as the players see it they set after it with explosive speed off the mark, conscious of using their body, shoulder and arms to good advantage. The first player to reach the ball shoots immediately. The pairs interchange. The same pair never competes twice. | The players do not 'bend' the rules of the game enough. Some hold and push as if playing rugby. Players do not shoot immediately after they get to the ball. |

| No. | Objectives | Age | Developing the Games | Common Problems |
|---|---|---|---|---|
| 79 | Reaction speed. Explosive power. Running with the ball. Dribbling. Particularly Using the body, shoulders and arms. Playing in goal. | 18 | 2 players in a regulation size goal. 5yds outside the 18-yard box are 6 cones positioned in a zigzag formation with a distance of 2yds between each one. There is a player standing at each cone who acts as an obstruction. They stand firm with their legs shoulder width apart. 5yds away from the cone nearest the center circle are 3 more cones in a line with a distance of 3yds between each. There are 3 players with a ball each at these cones. On the signal these 3 players set off towards the first cone. They run between the cones, coping with the shoulder to shoulder challenges etc. of the players standing next to them until reaching the shooting area, where they shoot. Both goalkeepers do their best to save the ball. Once all the trios have had a turn the players are put into different teams and play different roles to avoid always competing against the same players. | The players shy away from the physical contact. Slow off the mark. Shooting before entering the 'strike' zone. The human obstacles move their feet. This is not allowed. |

Fig 79

| No. | Objectives | Age | Developing the Games | Common Problems |
|-----|-----------|-----|---------------------|-----------------|
| 80 | Running with the ball. Dribbling. Feints and dummies. Controlling the space around you. Explosive power. Speed. Using the body, shoulders and arms. | 18 | 4 cones are positioned to form a square with 3yd sides. 2 teams of 4 players compete. There are 2 players in each team at cones diagonally opposite each other. Only one ball is used. On the signal the player with the ball runs towards the cone on his right. There are 2 players waiting with their legs shoulder-width apart 1.5yds away from the cone. These players hassle, hold and shoulder the player on the ball but they are not allowed to move their feet. Once the player gets past the obstacles he runs to the next cone where he has no problem because his teammates are positioned there. He then runs to the next cone and gets the 'rough' treatment from the opposition. In reality these players stand one in front of the other so that the player on the ball faces them one at a time. The player then runs back to where he started. The other player sets off and does the same. Meanwhile the player who has just completed the course swaps with a teammate who is standing on the cone diagonally opposite. This continues until the whole team has completed the course. Once both teams have completed the course there is a break and then the game restarts in the other direction. | The players concentrate on the ball and run straight into the human 'obstacles'. Some leave the ball behind because they are worried about the physical contact. The 'obstacles' move their feet. This is not allowed. |

| No. | Objectives | Age | Developing the Games | Common Problems |
|-----|-----------|-----|---------------------|-----------------|
| 81 | Reflexes. Speed. Explosive power. Using the body, shoulders and arms. Shots on goal. | 18 | A goalkeeper stands in a regulation size goal. There is a group of players facing the goal 25yds away. On the signal 2 players trot side by side towards the goal. 1 player is carrying a ball. The idea is to suddenly throw the ball forward and set off to recover it. Then run into the area and shoot. However, the other player also wants to get the ball and shoot and so he uses his body, arms and shoulders to push and hassle in order to get it. Then the other pairs do the same. Once all the pairs have had a go they try again, but this time the other player carries the ball. If the game is continued the players need to swap partners. | Sometimes the pushing is so strong that the player falls over. He should not get annoyed if this happens. The players shoot from outside the area. The player with the ball should shield it and hold his ground. |
| 82 | Reflexes. Speed. Explosive power. Using the body, shoulders and arms. Shots on goal. | 18 | Similar to the previous game. The players line up on the edge of the 18-yard box and the 2 players competing jog towards the midfield, away from the goal. Suddenly the player carrying the ball throws it over his head, turns and sets off towards goal. The other player cannot push his opponent but he holds onto whatever he can (waist, shoulders, arms etc) in an attempt to win the ball. If his challenge is successful he tries to shoot himself but now the other player is making the challenge. All the players take a turn and then the partners are swapped. | Players lose their temper too easily when they are being held back. The player being challenged has to keep calm. Sometimes there is no need for physical contact but it is used in the challenge. The player making the challenge is not paying attention and reacts too slowly. |

| No. | Objectives | Age | Developing the Games | Common Problems |
|-----|-----------|-----|---------------------|-----------------|
| 83 | Speed. Explosive power. Running with the ball. Dribbling. Shots on goal. Using the body, shoulders and arms. | 18 | Regulation size goal with 2 goalkeepers. In the middle of the pitch 2 teams of 5 players facing the goal compete against each other to complete a cone obstacle course and finish with a shot. There are two parallel courses of 5 cones with the gap between the first two being 2yds and gradually increasing to 5yds between the last two. There is a player from the opposition standing 1.5yds from each cone. They stand firm (not allowed to move their feet) with their legs shoulder-width apart. Their job is to hold, push and hassle the opponent as he tries to run round the cones. On the signal a player from each team sets off and the first to complete the course earns a point. A point is also awarded if a goal is scored. The players swap roles. | Players find it difficult to deal with the pushing and holding. Some players standing at the cones make no effort. Some make too much, moving their feet or even chasing after the player on the ball. Shots are taken in the area when they should be taken immediately after passing the last cone. |

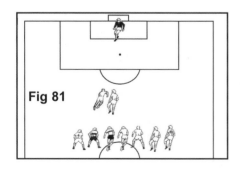

**Fig 81**

Fig 82

Fig 83

| No. | Objectives | Age | Developing the Games | Common Problems |
|-----|-----------|-----|---------------------|-----------------|
| 84 | Running with the ball. Shielding the ball. Craft. Astuteness. Peripheral vision. Winning the ball. | 17-18 | 3 cones 2 yards apart form a triangle. A player with a ball is jogging around the cones, conscious of the fact that a player is chasing after him a few yards back. When the player reaches him, he gets his body in front of the ball and shields it while still jogging. If the challenger cannot get to the ball he runs inside the next cone and faces the player in a '1 v 1'. The player on the ball can combat this by quickly turning and running in the opposite direction. The challenger can dummy to run inside the cone, anticipating the change of direction. The player on the ball wins a point if he keeps possession for 30 seconds. If he loses the ball before that no points are awarded. After the allotted time the player with the most points wins. A competition can be organized with all the players. | Players run with the opponent immediately behind them who find it easy to get to the ball between the legs. The player should keep the ball to the side furthest away from his opponent with his body in the way. Peripheral vision is not used to monitor the challenger's movements. The challenger does not use feints and dummies to outwit the player on the ball. |

| No. | Objectives | Age | Developing the Games | Common Problems |
|-----|-----------|-----|---------------------|-----------------|
| 85 | Passing. Dribbling. Shooting. Challenging for the ball. Using the body, shoulders and arms. | 17 | There are 4 goals, one on each side of half the pitch (including the regulation size goal). There is a goalkeeper in each goal. 4 groups of 3 players. Each group has a ball and they are playing '2 v 1'. Once the lone player manages to win the ball he runs towards one of the goals (not the nearest one) and shoots. The 2 players who have just lost the ball have to give chase and keep him from shooting. All 3 players (especially the player on the ball) should use their arms, shoulders and body to help them achieve their objectives. Whether the shot is successful or not the game starts again, but this time the shooter tries to keep the ball with a teammate and one of the others tries to win it off them. The groups are mixed and changed regularly. Shots, goals and winning the ball are highly valued in this game. | Some players make little attempt to win the ball and wait until the 2 players passing to each other make a mistake. This is not permitted. The player should feint and dummy to make space for himself when about to shoot, perhaps changing direction and shooting in a different goal than expected. |

**183**

Fig 85

| No. | Objectives | Age | Developing the Games | Common Problems |
|---|---|---|---|---|
| 86 | Positioning. Being a 'real' soccer player. Playing 'direct' soccer. Focused and peripheral vision. Winning the ball. Long and short passes. Changing the play. | 17-18 | A 'round' is played on a pitch 22 x 22yds. There are 4 players inside, 3 act as defenders and 1 acts as an attacker. There are 4 attackers outside (1 at each corner). The attacking players follow all the basics of soccer: they run backwards, play 'one-touch', look up and not at the ball, pass into the 'light' etc. All the players take turns playing as the attacker in the middle. The idea is for the 5 attackers to move and pass to each other. If the players outside cannot pass to each other it is up to the attacker in the middle to make himself available. Any attacker who makes a mistake becomes a defender. | The attacker inside the area does not play with intelligence and takes up poor positions. He should help the attackers on the outside by being very mobile and passing well. |
| 87 | Positioning. Being a 'real' soccer player. Playing 'one-two'. Focused and peripheral vision. Winning the ball. Long and short passes. Changing the play. | 17-18 | A 'round' with the same pitch size as above but this time there are 9 players (3 teams of 3). One of the teams defends from inside the area and the other 2 play as follows: 4 players outside the area (2 from each team) and 2 inside playing as 'pivots'. When a team loses the ball, one of the players plays as a defender. Otherwise the same as above. | The idea is to constantly change the game by playing a mixture of long and short passes. This does not happen often. The defenders make little effort, which defeats the object of the game. |

Fig 87

Fig 89

| No. | Objectives | Age | Developing the Games | Common Problems |
|---|---|---|---|---|
| 88 | Making space. Playing 'direct' soccer. Long, medium and short passes. Speed. Stamina. Teammate. | 17-18 | Pitch size 40 x 40yds. A 'round' involving 3 teams of 6 players. The teams wear different colors and so are easily recognizable. 2 of the teams play together and try to pass the ball to each other playing 'one-touch' while the third acts as a defense trying to intercept the ball. Once the ball is intercepted the team that lost the ball swaps with the defenders. | Monotonous game of short passes. Some players touch the ball more than once. |
| 89 | Reflexes. Speed. Explosive power. Speed off the mark. Changing direction. Running with the ball. Dribbling. Astuteness. | 18 | Pitch size 18 x 18yds. A 'round' with 4 sets of 2 players. The players have a ball each and stand one behind the other at each corner of the pitch. There are 2 other players in the game: the 'hunter' and the 'hare'. The 'hare' sets off with his ball and is chased by the 'hunter' who also has a ball. If the 'hunter' manages to touch the 'hare' then they swap roles. At any time the 'hare' can stop in front of any pair. When this happens the last player in the queue becomes the 'hunter' and the player who was chasing is now the 'hare'. From time to time the coach shouts "change" and the two players in the middle swap roles. In this way the coach keeps the game moving and the players working hard. | Not enough dummies. The 'hare' should pretend to stand in front of a pair only to run in the other direction. Clearly indicate the playing area or else the players end up chasing each other in a very confined space. This is an exhausting game, so if there are not enough breaks then it becomes a test of stamina. |

| No. | Objectives | Age | Developing the Games | Common Problems |
|-----|-----------|-----|---------------------|-----------------|
| 90 | Multiple-observation. Concentration. Playing 'direct' soccer. Alternating between Long and short passes. | 17-18 | 3 squares are marked, the 2 either side are 18 x 18yds and the one in the middle is 25 x 25. There are 6 players in each square. There is a ball in each of the outside squares. There is no ball in the middle square. This means that the 6 players in the middle square have to play as defenders and try to win a ball and to do this 3 go into one square and 3 in the other. The players in the outside squares try to make 5 'first-time' passes and on the sixth kick the ball over the middle square into the other area. If the pass is not made or possession is lost then the 6 players in the team become the defenders and 3 swap with the players in the other square etc. | The players do not always anticipate the arrival of the other ball. Not playing 'one-touch'. Not making space effectively and passing into the 'light'. |
| 91 | Playing 'direct' soccer. Playing moves learned in My Method. Changing pace. Concentration. Imagination. | 18 | 2 'rounds' 18 x 18yds played either side of the halfway line. The game is '4 v 2' (4 attackers and 2 defenders) and is 'one-touch'. There are 2 other players ('neutrals') in each half of the pitch between where the games are taking place and the 18-yard box. There is also a goalkeeper in each of the regulation size goals. When a defender wins the ball he passes it to the 2 players diagonally opposite. All the players in this 'round' run to where these players are (the other 'round' is not affected and continues). The attackers are | Some players find it difficult to suddenly change from being attackers to being defenders. The players forget to play 'the method' when attacking the goal. This game requires plenty of physical and mental effort but some players make little effort. |

| No. | Objectives | Age | Developing the Games | Common Problems |
|---|---|---|---|---|
| 91 (cont) | Playing 'direct' soccer. Playing moves learned in My Method. Changing pace. Concentration. Imagination. | 18 | now defenders and vice versa. The idea is for the 2 attackers to play the 'one-two', the 'doblada' and use the inside pass to create a shooting opportunity. They are helped by the 2 'neutral' players who are not allowed to shoot themselves. If the 4 defenders win the ball then they have to try to take it back to the where the 'round' started off. As they take the ball back the 2 attackers continually try to win it and if they do they take it back to where the 'neutrals' are. The 'round' either gets back to its original position because a goal has been scored or the defenders get the ball back themselves. Once the 'round' is back in position the game continues with the 4 players attacking and 2 defending. The 'neutrals' always stay in their half of the pitch. Both 'rounds' can obviously change halves at the same time. The players change roles regularly. | |

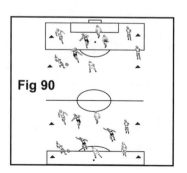

Fig 90

Fig 91

| No. | Objectives | Age | Developing the Games | Common Problems |
|---|---|---|---|---|
| 92 | Playing 'the method'. Speed of execution. Peripheral speed. Long passes. (Each well-executed long pass is worth a point). | 17 | Pitch size 75 x 60yds. '9-a-side' playing 'three-touch'. The formation is 3-3-2. The usual moves in 'the method' are used but essentially the players are looking to play long passes. Only a maximum of two consecutive short passes allowed. So every third pass must be a long one. Any team that ignores this rule gives away a penalty. | The players forget 'the method'. Too many touches. Always playing short passes. Instead of playing well-judged long passes the ball is wildly kicked upfield. |
| 93 | Playing 'the method'. Speed of execution. Peripheral vision. Playing a 'goal-scoring' pass. | 17 | Pitch size, number of players and touches as in the previous game. The important difference is that goals are only allowed after the ball has been 'cut back'. Therefore the players have to run down the wings and get to the 'dead ball' line to play a goal-scoring pass. A pass is worth a point and this converts to 3 points if a goal is scored. The team with the most points wins. | The players forget to play 'the method'. Too many touches. Not enough effort is made. |
| 94 | Playing 'the method'. (The 'one-two', the 'overlap', exploiting the space on front of goal, etc). Playing 'direct' soccer. Zonal marking. | 17 | A '7 v 7' is played on half a pitch. The formation is 3-2-1. There is also a 'neutral' player on each wing. The game is 'one-touch'. A second touch is only allowed if the first touch is to win the ball. | The players do not release the ball. The 'neutrals' are rarely used. Not enough shooting. The players forget to use 'the method'. |

| No. | Objectives | Age | Developing the Games | Common Problems |
|---|---|---|---|---|
| 95 | Playing 'the method'. Taking advantage of numerical superiority. Speed of execution. Zonal marking. | 17 | Similar to the previous game but now the 'neutral' players (still playing on the wings) play for one of the teams. So this team now has 8 outfield players and the game is '9 v 7'. The team with 6 outfield players plays with 3 defenders and 3 attackers with 2 of the forwards playing wide on the wings. There is no limit on touches for this team but the team with 9 plays a maximum of 'two-touch'. The game has two halves and in the second half the other team plays with the extra two players. | Too many touches. Not taking advantage of numerical superiority. Forgetting to play 'the method'. |

189

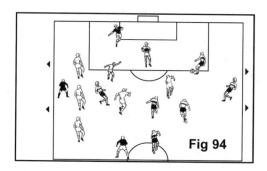

**Fig 94**

| No. | Objectives | Age | Developing the Games | Common Problems |
|---|---|---|---|---|
| 96 | Trying to get the players to realize that more players and less space is an advantage for the defense. The reverse is also true: few players and lots of space favors the strikers. (in a '2 v 2' situation the attackers win). | 17-18 | Pitch size is half the pitch plus an extra 20 yards where the other goal is positioned. The game is '9 v 9' and played in the following way: the team that defends the mobile goal plays with 6 defenders that lineup roughly around the halfway line and never go up to help the attack. The 2 forwards are 12yds from the goal area and are not allowed to drop back beyond this point. The other team has 6 attackers and 2 defenders. These defenders are allowed to move up and attack if the circumstances are right, in which case an attacker drops back and covers the position. After a certain time the two teams swap roles. | The team with 2 attackers often has the defenders attack as well. This is not allowed. The attackers also want to help out in defense. This is also not allowed as it defeats the object of the game. The attackers are often caught 'off-side'. |

Fig 97

Fig 98

| No. | Objectives | Age | Developing the Games | Common Problems |
|-----|-----------|-----|---------------------|-----------------|
| 97 | Perfecting 'the method'. Playing the 'long ball' game with angled passes. 'Passing and marking'. Being a 'real' soccer player. | 17-18 | Pitch size 90 x 60yds '9 v 9'. The line-up is as follows: 3 defenders (a 'sweeper' and 2 markers), 3 midfield players and 2 attackers that play very wide as out and out wingers. The game is three touch. There is a line across the middle of the pitch and 2 other lines marked at 25yds from each end of the pitch.. These lines are drawn to encourage long and angled passes. Any pass that goes over 2 of the lines is worth 1 point and 2 points if the 3 lines are crossed (as long as it is not intercepted by the opposition of course). The points scored for long passes are multiplied by the number of goals scored. The team with the most points at the end of the game wins. | The players become obsessed with playing the long ball and the game quickly deteriorates into a series of misjudged and wild kicks upfield. Long passes are not mixed with short ones. Forgetting to play 'the method'. The midfield players only attack and forget their defensive duties. Not enough shots at goal. The players do not cover and back up. |
| 98 | Defensive discipline: dropping back, changing roles, covering and zonal marking. Keeping possession. | 17-18 | Using half the pitch the players practice playing as a defensive unit. A goalkeeper, 4 defenders and 3 midfield players practice covering, dropping back, zonal play and collective discipline. They are faced by 8-10 attackers (the offense always has numerical superiority). If the defending team manages to win the ball they try to keep possession for 30 seconds before giving the ball back to the other team. Another attack starts and so on. | Lack of discipline in defense makes attacking easy. The coach should make the necessary positional changes and point out how the defending team should play to function as a unit. Long passes are not mixed with short ones. Forgetting to play 'the method'. The midfield players only attack and forget their defensive duties. Not enough shots at goal. The players do not cover and back up. |

| No. | Objectives | Age | Developing the Games | Common Problems |
|-----|-----------|-----|---------------------|-----------------|
| 99 | Taking advantage of numerical superiority.<br>Speed of execution.<br>Playing the game at the right pace. | 17-18 | Half the pitch. There is a goalkeeper in goal and 4 defenders stand near the center circle. They are faced by five offensive players (two wingers, two midfield players and a center forward). Starting from the half way line they have 15 seconds to shoot at goal. Whether they shoot or not the game starts again with another 5 attacking players against the same defense. After a certain time the defenders take a rest and are replaced by another defensive team. The shots and goals are noted and also which offensive team was attacking against which defense. | Problems occur because the attack is rushed or is too slow.<br>The players misjudge how long 15 seconds actually is (15 seconds either lasts an eternity or is over in a split second). |
| 100 | Taking advantage of numerical superiority.<br>Playing at a fast pace.<br>Speed of execution.<br>Shooting.<br>Dropping back.<br>Regaining possession. | 17-18 | Similar to the previous game except in this one there are 3 more defenders some 10 yards away from the others. On the coach's signal a swift attack begins. The defenders drop back to 'buy' some time while the other 3 defenders run as fast as they can to join the action. They take up their positions and give the strikers far less space to play in and less offensive options. The idea is for each team to achieve its objectives. | The attackers prefer to play controlled precise soccer rather than play at a fast pace which means they lose the advantage of numerical superiority.<br>Not enough shooting.<br>Defenders do not drop back or they drop back too slowly.<br>The 3 defenders do not try their best and as a consequence do not get involved in the play. |

| No. | Objectives | Age | Developing the Games | Common Problems |
|-----|-----------|-----|----------------------|-----------------|
| 101 | Playing 'the method'. Multiple-observation. Concentration. Analyzing the play. Peripheral vision. Visual memory. Tactical sense. | 17-18 | A '7 v 7' game using half the pitch. A maximum of two touches allowed. The players are warned beforehand that when the coach blows his whistle they have to stop and look down at the ground. He then chooses 2 players (one from each team) and asks them to tell him where all of his team-mates are located (without looking) and if the positioning is correct. 2 points are awarded for a correct answer and 1 point for a goal. | The players forget to play 'the method'. They take too many touches. They demonstrate a lack of tactical awareness, concentration and visual memory. |
| 102 | Being a 'real' soccer' player. Marking. Making space. The ability to change from defense into attack as quickly as possible and vice versa. | 17-18 | Pitch size 30 x 20yds. 4 players in each team. There are two goals at one end of the pitch with a goalkeeper in each while the other end of the pitch is a line denoted by 2 cones. A point is achieved by scoring in either of the 2 goals or by 'walking' the ball over the line opposite. The game involves disciplined positioning and rigid man-to-man marking. Each time a goal is scored the players swap positions and markers. | Not enough shooting even though there are 2 goals to aim at. Not crossing the line with the ball under control. When possession is lost the players take too long to change from attackers into defenders. |

193

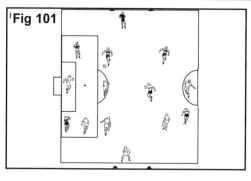

**Fig 101**

| No. | Objectives | Age | Developing the Games | Common Problems |
|---|---|---|---|---|
| 103 | Being a 'real' soccer' player. Marking. Making space. Perfecting the attacking movements of 'the method'. | 17-18 | A game of '5 v 5' using half the pitch. Plus a goalkeeper in the regulation size goal and a 'neutral' player with the ball on the half way line. Both teams line up with a formation as per 'the method': 2 wide players and 3 in the middle waiting to play the 'one-two, the doblada or exploit the space in front of goal. The 'neutral' player plays the ball to one of the teams and they immediately become the attackers and the other team the defenders. If possession is lost or the goalkeeper gets the ball then it is immediately passed to the 'neutral' player who starts the game and the ball is passed to the other team. | It is imperative that the attacking team practices the moves in 'the method'. The coach should intervene if he sees this is not happening. The 'neutral' player should move up the middle so that the goalkeeper or whoever can pass to him easily. However, he should not get in the way or become involved in the attack. |

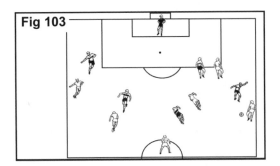

Fig 103

| No. | Objectives | Age | Developing the Games | Common Problems |
|---|---|---|---|---|
| 104 | Being able to 'control' the game. Being able to position the players well on the pitch, especially out wide. Changing the play. Controlling the play when attacking or defending down the flanks. Playing 'the method' in the central areas. | 17-18 | Pitch size 75 x 55yds. A game of '9 v 7'. The team with 7 play with 4 at the back and 2 in the middle close together. The team with 9 play 3-3-2. with the two attackers playing very wide. A move by the team with 9 players is only valid if it is touched by both the wingers. They can only play the ball 'first time' or with a maximum of two touches. The team with 7 players has no such restrictions. | The wingers do not play wide enough and if they do they are not given the ball. The midfield players do not exploit the space that opens up in front of goal. The team with 7 players has a negative attitude and expects to lose even though they have the advantage of unlimited touches. |

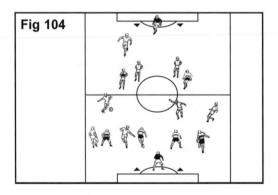

**Fig 104**

| No. | Objectives | Age | Developing the Games | Common Problems |
|---|---|---|---|---|
| 105 | Knowledge of the game. Being a 'real' soccer player. Analyzing the play. Focused and peripheral vision. Creative passing. Speed of execution. Quick thinking. | 18 | A game of '7 v 7' using half the pitch and playing a maximum of 'two-touch'. All the players are told that the main objective of the game is to develop concentration, observation skills and peripheral vision. If a player thinks he can get the ball and create a good move (even if the opposition has it) he indicates this to the coach by raising his left arm. If he gets the ball and starts the move (he intercepts the ball, immediately plays a long ball to a teammate who controls the ball and passes it 'first-time' to another player in the team on the other flank who controls it and shoots etc.) his team gets a point. If the move ends in a goal 4 points are awarded (normally 2 points for a goal). If the player who raised his arm does not get the ball the coach asks him what he was hoping to do with it. If the idea is good and demonstrates good vision then a point is awarded. The team with the most points at the end wins. A note is taken of all the moves, both good and bad. | The player who raises his arm gets the ball but fails to do anything constructive: he passes backwards instead of passing to a teammate in a potentially goal-scoring position. The players only have attacking ideas. This is admirable but they should be made aware that good defensive play can give the team possession from which they can mount a swift counterattack. |

| No. | Objectives | Age | Developing the Games | Common Problems |
|-----|-----------|-----|---------------------|-----------------|
| 106 | Focused and peripheral vision. Being able to 'read' and anticipate the play. Playing 'direct' soccer. Shooting Speed of execution. Timing interceptions. The 'give and go'. | 17-18 | Pitch size 30 x 25 with 2 regulation width goals (using cones as posts) and a half way line. The game is '6 v 6' with a goalkeeper in each goal. Of the other 5 players in the team, 3 must always stay in their own half and 2 must always be in the opposition's half. The game is 'one-touch'. A player must be in his own half to take a shot and a goal is only valid if a 'one-two' is played beforehand with a teammate in the opposition's half. If the attackers win the ball they have to pass it back to start the move as only the defenders can shoot. Once a defender passes the ball forward to an attacker it is returned to him or it goes to another defender who shoots. If the ball is passed back and the defender fails to shoot after the 'one-two' then it is given to the opposition. Throughout the game the players swap roles so that they all get a chance to shoot. | The players do not play 'one-touch'. The play is too slow. Players shoot when they should not and do not shoot when they should (as soon as they have played the 'one-two' with a forward). They do not shoot with the foot nearest the ball. Defenders take up poor positions, which means they do not take advantage of the numerical superiority. The 'one-two' is usually played with the defender who passed the ball when the one of the other two defenders might be in a better position to shoot. |

197

Fig 105

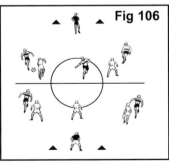

Fig 106

| No. | Objectives | Age | Developing the Games | Common Problems |
|---|---|---|---|---|
| 107 | Analyzing the play. Positioning. Speed of execution. Quick thinking. Defensive discipline. Attacking creativity. Changing the play. Each player should make several attempts on goal. | 17-18 | A game of '7 v 7' played in half the pitch. Each team defends three 5-yard goals that are 10 yards apart. Both teams play with 2 goalkeepers. The formation is 2-3-1-2. A maximum of two touches is allowed. The idea is to perfect 'the method' in attack and practice zonal marking in defense trying to protect the three goals. The goalkeepers are in the outside goals and play alternately in the middle one depending on the circumstances of the game. | The players only attack 1 or 2 of the goals. The defenders protect one goal very well but leave the other exposed and vulnerable. Playing more than 'two-touch'. The goalkeepers find it difficult to adapt and position themselves well. |

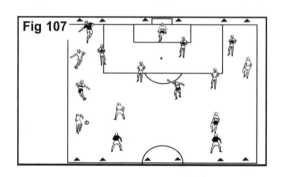

Fig 107

Fig 108

| No. | Objectives | Age | Developing the Games | Common Problems |
|-----|-----------|-----|----------------------|-----------------|
| 108 | Perfecting 'the method'. Speed of execution. Taking quick free kicks before the defense is organized. Multiple-observation. Concentration. | 17-18 | This is a game of '7 v 7' but played in a reduced area. Half the pitch is used playing width-ways from the edge of the 18-yard box to the half way line. There are 3 goals, one at each end and a regulation size goal on what is now the wing. Players position themselves and play to 'the method'. The game is played using the weaker foot with one or two-touches. The coach may blow his whistle at any time. When he does, this means that the fastest or most alert player picks up the ball, runs 5 yards towards the regulation size goal, places it on the ground and passes it to a teammate (if tactically astute) who has made some space for himself. There is no limit on touches during this move. Obviously the opposition does its best to impede the attack. If the move ends with a goal it is worth 2 points and 1 point if it ends with a shot. If the defending team win the ball before a shot is made then they continue playing as before (sideways and maximum 'two-touch' etc.) until the next time the coach blows his whistle. | Changing from 'two-touch' to any number of touches when the whistle blows confuses the players. There is always an alert player who gets to the ball first after the whistle blows, but his teammates do not bother to make space to receive a pass. Some of the opposition do not feel like running and do not chase the player who has picked up the ball. |

| No. | Objectives | Age | Developing the Games | Common Problems |
|-----|-----------|-----|----------------------|-----------------|
| 109 | The same as in the previous game. | 17-18 | Identical to the previous game but with one variation: when the coach blows his whistle, the player on the ball runs the 5 yards and takes a throw-in in order to attack the main goal. | Same as previous game plus: Some players obstruct the throw-in. The coach has to tell the players that this will earn a yellow card in a real match. If they continue a penalty is awarded to be taken at the regulation size goal. |
| 110 | Perfecting 'the method'. Analyzing the play. Speed of execution. Quick thinking. Appreciating the advantages of using the whole width of the pitch. | 18 | Full pitch. A game of '11 v 11'. Maximum 'two-touch' to make things more difficult for the attack. The players are allowed to play freely but the emphasis is on using the whole width of the pitch. As the game quickly develops and goal-scoring opportunities are frequent, the coach stops the play and asks the players to reflect on the efficiency of using the wings. The players readily agree with this and the coach asks why, if it is so productive to play down the wings, do the players persist in trying to 'bulldoze' their way through the middle during the match. | The pace of the game is too slow (both physically and mentally). Even though the width of the pitch is extended, the players (perhaps through habit) take a while to fully exploit the space. |

Fig 110

| No. | Objectives | Age | Developing the Games | Common Problems |
|-----|-----------|-----|---------------------|-----------------|
| 111 | Perfecting 'the method'. Focused and peripheral vision. Ball juggling. Changing the direction and pace of the game. The 'overlap'. | 18 | A goalkeeper, 'sweeper', and 3 defenders play against 4 attackers located near the half-way line. The strikers take up an unorthodox position as they all attack down the right wing (2 in front and the other 2 in support). 4 other players (each juggling a ball) are on the other wing in the other half of the pitch, apparently not involved in the play. The 4 attackers play the ball sideways and back to each other without trying to make a penetrative advance. Suddenly the coach signals (silently) to the players ball juggling. 2 of these players leave their ball behind and sprint to join the other 4 attackers. The players run and support as per 'the method'. The player on the ball should be aware that the others have joined in and may dummy or make a pass to one of these players and then continue running on the overlap. Each time a new move should be attempted. The players swap roles on a regular basis. | The attackers are often unaware that 2 new players have joined them and so any run is wasted. If this happens the coach may stop the game and point out the wasted opportunity. On other occasions a pass is made but it is poor. The defenders need to be very alert and work hard, especially when the 2 players join the move - but often they make little attempt to intervene. |

| No. | Objectives | Age | Developing the Games | Common Problems |
|-----|-----------|-----|---------------------|-----------------|
| 112 | Getting a 'feel' for the game. Playing with great intensity (Physically, technically, tactically and mentally). Controlling the space around you. Paying attention. Total concentration. Playing in goal. Stamina. | 17-18 | Two games are played simultaneously using only half the pitch. There is a regulation goal at one end and a goal of similar width marked by two cones at the other end. There is a goalkeeper in each goal. They play in both the games. There are 4 outfield players in each team. So there are 2 games of '4 v 4' (a total of 16 players). The game is maximum 'three-touch', with man-to-man marking, playing 'the method' and there is 'offside'. If the ball hits a player in the other game nothing happens - the game continues. A knockout tournament can be organized. | At first, the number of players and the lack of space is confusing and off-putting. The 'intelligent' player is able to use the congested pitch and the obstacles to his advantage. Players are caught 'offside' too often. As the game is very tiring the marking soon becomes lax. |
| 113 | Perfecting 'the method'. Playing as a unit. Paying attention. Concentration. Stamina. Changing pace. | 17-18 | Whole pitch. '11 v11' playing 4-3-3 and 'the method'. Apart from playing the normal moves in 'the method' a goal is worth 2 points if when it is scored all the players are in the same half of the pitch. A goal is worth 3 points if all the players in the scoring team are in the same half but one or more of the opposition is in the other half of the pitch. If an attack ends with a shot but no goal is scored, a penalty is awarded (but only if a player in the opposition was in the other half of the pitch when the ball was struck). The game is very physically demanding and the players have to play as a tight unit and move together. | The players are not fully focused at first (this soon improves as they are penalized by the points system and penalties). They forget to play 'the method'. The goalkeepers don't help by shouting advice to the rest of the team. |

| No. | Objectives | Age | Developing the Games | Common Problems |
|---|---|---|---|---|
| 114 | Perfecting 'the method'. Fast counter-attacks. Long passes. Paying attention. Concentration. Stamina. | 17-18 | An 11-a-side match. There is a line drawn 15 yards either side of the half way line. A team can only keep possession of the ball for a maximum of 2 seconds in this 30-yard area. If they keep the ball longer, it is handed over to the opposition who also play under the same restrictions. Despite this the game is about defense and attack and is played with 'two-touch'. | If only short passes are played there is no chance of a swift coun-terattack. This is also the case if the ball is wildly kicked upfield. The players do not play intelligently. The marking is poor. |
| 115 | Perfecting 'the method'. Focused and peripheral vision. Multiple-observation. Some players have a 'wild' imagination. | 18 | Another 11-a-side game but without the lines in the previous game. The only thing asked of the players is that they play 'the method'. The new ingredi-ent is that both teams wear the same full club strip (shirt, shorts and socks). Of course now the players have to use their peripheral vision and use their observation skills to distinguish their team-mates from the opposi-tion. This means they have to "watch the game more and the ball less". | At first a lot of passes are played to the opposi-tion. This improves as the game goes on. The players who lack concentration never get to grips with the game. Some players forget they are playing a 'prop-er' game and forget to shoot. |

Fig 112

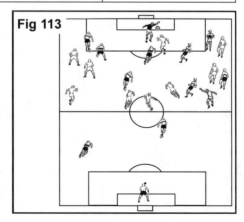

Fig 113

| No. | Objectives | Age | Developing the Games | Common Problems |
|---|---|---|---|---|
| 116 | Perfecting 'the method'. Playing in the opposition's half. Stopping counterattacks in the opposition's half. Playing as a unit. Economy of effort. | 17-18 | An 11-a-side game where one of the teams plays with a 'sweeper' and only one striker, trying to mount swift counterattacks. The other team plays 'the method' and tries to stop the counterattacks before they have a chance to develop. The game is stopped every 15 minutes to allow the coach to offer feedback to each team on progress and if necessary give advice and make changes. It is important for the attacking team to understand that if they make an effort after they lose the ball and close down the opposition before they have a chance to start their move then they will soon regain possession. If they 'drop off' and give the opposition time to create a move then it will take them a lot longer to regain the ball. Sometimes the ball is regained when it is too late: after a goal has been scored. | If the team is playing very offensively and lose the ball, they have to think about defending or else they run the risk of being severely punished on the counter attack. It is also very difficult to defend in the opposition's half if the team are not closing down the space and playing as a unit. |

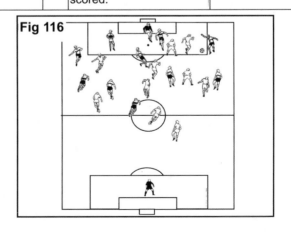

Fig 116

| No. | Objectives | Age | Developing the Games | Common Problems |
|-----|-----------|-----|----------------------|-----------------|
| 117 | Speed or stamina. Anticipation. Reflexes. Playing 'one-touch'. Concentration. | 17-18 | The whole squad or part of it split into groups of 4 players. 2 players with a ball each are 20 yards apart and the other 2 players are in the middle. The game starts with one of the players kicking the ball to the players in the middle. Both the players in the middle try to win the ball so that they can pass it back. As soon as the ball is passed back, the other ball is passed to the middle. The passes should be low, medium and high so that the players in the middle control them with feet, head, thigh, chest or by jumping and diving. The players alternate and experience each role. If the exercise is short but intensive with a long rest period then the focus is on speed. If the exercise is longer then the emphasis is on stamina. | This is a game that involves anticipation but if one of the players in the middle does not try then the game loses its appeal. Some players make no attempt to head the lofted passes. The passes into the middle do not vary - low, medium and high. |

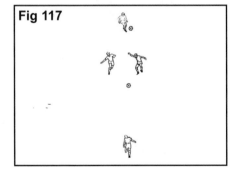

Fig 117

| No. | Objectives | Age | Developing the Games | Common Problems |
|---|---|---|---|---|
| 118 | Technical and tactical work. Soccer movements. 'Explosive' play. Particularly anaerobic stamina. | 18 | Pitch size 40 x 25. Regulation size goals with a goalkeeper and 5-6 balls in each. The game is '2 v 2' with other players on the wings acting as 'neutrals' who alternate roles with the players on the pitch after a set time. The game is played for 2 minutes with two sets of 3/6 repetitions. The rest period between the repetitions lasts until the pulse rate is down to 140. The recuperation period between sets lasts 5 minutes. The players are free to play as they wish and they can play the 'one-two' with any of the 'neutral' player on the wings. If the goalkeeper saves a shot he puts the ball back in play immediately. The same is true if a goal is scored or a shot goes wide, except when he throws one of the other balls in play. The game should produce short bursts of explosive play. | Sometimes the players make little effort and spoil the game. The recuperation and rest periods are vital and so pulse rates should be monitored closely. |

| No. | Objectives | Age | Developing the Games | Common Problems |
|-----|-----------|-----|---------------------|-----------------|
| 119 | Technical and tactical work. Especially anaerobic stamina. | 17-18 | A 9-a-side or 11-a-side match with suitable pitch size. The game lasts 20 minutes and this period is extended progressively. All the players (including the goalkeepers) are running at a steady rate keeping their pulse rate at a constant 150-160 beats per minute. They are not allowed to sprint after the ball. All the players monitor their own pulse rate by placing their hand on their heart and counting the beats for 6 seconds and multiplying this number by ten. Just because one player has a similar pulse rate to another does not mean that they are running at the same pace. Some are fitter than others and can run a lot faster without increasing their pulse rate beyond the specified number. However, the coach needs to monitor the players and if he thinks one is running too slowly or too quickly he should verify the pulse rate himself. | The players should not stop running. They should run a the right pace for them. Some players feel aggrieved if they are made to run faster than others. The coach should clearly explain why this is the case. |

| No. | Objectives | Age | Developing the Games | Common Problems |
|---|---|---|---|---|
| 120 | Speed. Explosive power or stamina. Anticipation. Control and passing. Reflexes. Concentration. | 17-18 | Pitch size is a rectangle 30 x 20. There are 3 players close together near the center of the playing area and 6 other players (with 2 balls) around it (2 each along the length and 1 at each end). On the signal 1 of the players around the perimeter kicks the ball to the 3 in the middle. Whoever gets to the ball first has to control it and pass it to a player outside the area playing 'two-touch' (not the same player who kicked the ball in). The other ball is then immediately kicked into the middle and so the game continues. Sometimes the players on the edge of the rectangle pass to each other before sending the ball into the middle to keep the 3 players on their toes. The passes into the middle are constantly varied and can be high, along the ground, hard or soft. The players are swapped constantly so that everybody gets a chance to play in the middle. The time spent in the middle depends on whether the exercise is based on speed, strength or stamina. | The 3 players in the middle need to work as hard as they can. If this is not the case the objectives of the game are lost. The players must play 'two-touch'. The pace of the game depends on the players outside. |

| No. | Objectives | Age | Developing the Games | Common Problems |
|-----|-----------|-----|---------------------|-----------------|
| 121 | Speed or stamina. Changing pace. Playing 'one-touch'. | 17-18 | A cone is positioned at 10 yds and a line is marked at 5 yards running parallel to a wall. The game is played with 2 players at a time and 1 ball. 1 of the players kicks the ball against the wall from just beyond the 5-yd line. He then sets off and runs around the cone. Meanwhile the other player kicks the rebound (the ball should bounce within the 5-yd line) and sets off around the cone. The first player now runs back and kicks the ball against the wall etc...The players have to run as fast as they can in order to return in time to collect the rebound after it has bounced only once. After a few minutes the pairs swap. The exercise can have speed or stamina as its focus. | The ball is not kicked hard enough and so the other player has little chance of getting the rebound. Not running quickly enough also means that the player does not get back to the ball in time. Whatever the emphasis of the exercise (speed or stamina) it is always exhausting and so the rest periods should be adequate. |

**Fig 120**

| No. | Objectives | Age | Developing the Games | Common Problems |
|---|---|---|---|---|
| 122 | Speed or stamina. Changing pace. Playing 'one-touch'. | 18 | A line is marked 5 yds running parallel to a wall. There are 2 cones placed 7 yds from the wall 4 yds apart. 2 players with a ball each are standing in between the 5-yd line and a cone. They both kick their ball against the wall and sprint around the other player's cone to collect the other player's rebound and so on... After a brief period another 2 players have a go. | The players enjoy this game so much that they expend too much energy playing it. The coach needs to monitor the physical condition of the players before and during the game. |
| 123 | Perfecting 'the method' and technique in general. Particularly improving stamina. | 18 | This is an 11-a-side game designed to increase stamina. The game is divided into 6 periods of 15 minutes that should be played with intensity and pace. This exercise is repeated later with less rest between periods and an even faster pace. For example: At first the breaks between periods are 4 minutes except the fourth one which lasts 12 minutes. Over the following 2-3 weeks the exercise is repeated with breaks lasting 3, 2 and 1 minute and 11, 10, 9, 8 etc. after the fourth period. In this way the players gradually become accustomed to playing at a good pace and intensity. | The objective of the exercise is only achieved if the players play at a good pace and give maximum effort. Some fail to do this and others play at a terrific pace but forget 'the method'. |

| No. | Objectives | Age | Developing the Games | Common Problems |
|-----|-----------|-----|---------------------|-----------------|
| 124 | Running with the ball. Touch. Particularly improving aerobic stamina. (This work is based on the ideas proposed by Bosco and Karvonen but tailored to suit the needs of the soccer player). Imagination. Concentration. | 18 | The players run freely throughout the pitch. This exercise is based on Bosco's method for improving stamina. The players run for 10, 20 and 30yds with breaks in between when they run in place to eliminate the lactic acid in the muscles. The amount of time spent on the relaxing runs increases in proportion to the length of the sprints 30, 60 and 100 seconds. The player runs with a ball and before sprinting kicks it forward and chases after. The speed of the run during the break between sprints is calculated based on Karvonen's theory as explained in the previous chapter. Lactic acid builds up during the sprints and the player has to get used to dealing with it and eliminating it just as he does during a match. The exercise lasts between 12 and 24 minutes. 1 x 12 minutes or 2 x 12 minutes with an 8-minute break between sets. | The players need to monitor their pulse rate. Some forget this important point. The players do not always have to run as fast as they can. Some players wait to copy what a teammate does. This is a mistake that needs to be rectified. Lack of imagination. During the more 'relaxing' runs the players should be imagining great moves that culminate in the sprint. |

211

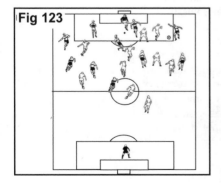

Fig 123

Fig 124

| No. | Objectives | Age | Developing the Games | Common Problems |
|-----|-----------|-----|----------------------|-----------------|
| 125 | Relaxation. Improving the imagination. The above ideas are applied when doing physically demanding work. | 18 | From this stage on it is a good idea for players to rehearse the skills and moves both physically and in the imagination. Good positive attitude and thought processes help confidence levels, reaction time and coordination. It also allows the player to perfect complex skills or moves in his mind before he tries them in reality. For example: if a player in a team is responsible for taking the 'free-kicks' and penalties then he should do the following: sit on a chair with a good backrest and relax. Once relaxed he should go through all the necessary movements needed to take a 'free-kick' faced by a wall or to take a penalty: position the ball, move backwards, hear the crowd, visualize the opposition, strike the ball perfectly, see it fly into the back of the net, then listen to the cheers from the crowd and experience the hugs from teammates. The player should repeat these images hundreds of times in the mind until they are engrained. Continue to do this in the changing rooms and then run out onto the pitch. Once the game starts the imagination and reality of playing the game merge and this has a positive impact on performance. | The player has to believe in these methods for them to work. The player will also fail to gain the true benefits if he is not able to totally relax before going through the moves in his mind. |

| No. | Objectives | Age | Developing the Games | Common Problems |
|-----|-----------|-----|---------------------|-----------------|
| 126 | Positive attitude. Trying to remove any unwanted negative thoughts. | 18 | It is perfectly normal for players to think about the moves they are going to make before they start a game. This can be very positive but unfortunately it can also be a negative influence. The player might be suffering from a lack of self-confidence and the fear of failure may lead him to visualize himself performing badly. This mental attitude may cause muscular stiffness and a general lack of concentration. The player should practice these moves and executions over and over until he has mastered them in order to regain his self-confidence and a positive attitude. Going through moves in the mind in a positive fashion helps utilize and exploit the mental capacity and potential to work for the player. In this way, the necessary signals to the nervous system are rehearsed even when going through the movements in the mind, which makes it a lot easier to produce the moves in practice. Go through moves in the mind before a game and take advantage of all the positive benefits this will have on your game. | Some players have very little self-confidence. They need to overcome this problem. The player should be fully relaxed before starting to use his imagination. Some players by-pass the relaxation stage and so never use the mind effectively. |

| No. | Objectives | Age | Developing the Games | Common Problems |
|-----|------------|-----|----------------------|-----------------|
| 127 | Observation and concentration skills. | 18 | In the previous level the players practiced focusing and concentration. They did this by using a grid 10 x 10 containing two-digit numbers ranging from 00-99. The idea was to look at the numbers for a certain period and then try to touch in order as many positions on the grid as possible in a set time (exercise number 123 for 16 year-olds). At this level, we present the added difficulty of distractions. While the player is concentrating on the location of the numbers on the grid he hears noises and is often spoken to and the lighting changes. The player has to concentrate totally on the grid and ignore all the distractions. | Interestingly, some players with good observation skills under normal circumstances do not do so well under these conditions. Other players are very good at ignoring the distractions. Nevertheless, this type of exercise is a good way to get all the players to improve their concentration skills and deal with distractions. |

| No. | Objectives | Age | Developing the Games | Common Problems |
|---|---|---|---|---|
| 128 | The ability to keep a positive attitude and high concentration levels under difficult circumstances. | 18 | Another useful way to exercise the mind is to practice not reacting and losing concentration when being distracted. The players do this exercise in pairs. One player relaxes and goes through some moves in his mind while the other player tries to distract him and get him to lose concentration. The player doing the distracting can do whatever he likes except touch the other player. The players swap roles when the first has finished. After they have both had a go the players give their concentration levels a mark from 0-5. This exercise should be continued for 6 consecutive days. A substantial improvement from the first to the last day is noted if the exercises are done correctly. Remember this type of exercise only works if the players are familiar with using their imagination. | Some players do not relax enough before they start and find it difficult to concentrate. If both players are not fully committed to what they are doing the exercise has no chance of success. This is also true if one player is committed and the other is not. However, if both players approach the exercise with the right attitude they gain tremendously from it. |

| No. | Objectives | Age | Developing the Games | Common Problems |
|-----|-----------|-----|---------------------|-----------------|
| 129 | Trying to improve the imagination and concentration levels of the players. The player tries to get to know and understand 'himself'. How the player reacts to adversity. | 18 | The players gather in a classroom and space themselves out as they sit at the desks. The coaches have prepared some information about soccer in general. The players have 5 minutes to read the information and 15-20 minutes to write their own ideas about what they have read. The players are encouraged to write exactly what they are feeling using their imagination and creativity without fear of failing. The players are told that the exercise is very informal and spontaneous and will not be scrutinized and marked. | Some players do not take the exercise seriously and gain little. |
| 130 | Keeping concentration levels high even when under pressure and the going is 'tough'. | 18 | The players gather in the classroom again to read about the system and 'the method'. After reading all the sheets they start to do the written exercises. The following takes place as the players continue to work through the sheets: the normal lighting changes to a very bright light for a few moments and then changes back again; suddenly a series of strange sounds is heard; then the normal peace and tranquility returns for a sustained period. Once again the lights are changed. After a short while the noises start again. There are a few moments of peace and quiet and the exercise finishes. The player should keep concentrating and not be distracted. | The strange noises and lighting provoke a reaction in the players. At first they seem confused and lose concentration. It is obvious when reading the finished written work that the players are distracted. Some of the answers make little sense. |

# *T**he Culmination: 19-30 years old*

By this stage any player who has followed 'the method' all the way through will have achieved a very high level of technical skill and excellent 'soccer' coordination. The player will now play at the correct pace using his energy effectively and with no unnecessary additional movements, allowing him to perform the technical skills while at the same time looking up and analyzing everything that is happening in the game.

In other words, the boy who started by simply 'pushing' the ball forward and chasing after it, needing all five senses just to keep the ball from 'escaping', has now developed into a player with a technical and tactical mastery where none of his 'six' senses is solely focused on the ball. The player has learned to keep his concentration levels high throughout the whole match and he is always ready to either play the ball or try to get possession of it by intervening with great speed and precision. He now runs with the ball on 'automatic pilot' with his mind and thinking power directed towards other considerations (the same thing happens when we drive a car). Once the player has reached this level his training routines differ from those in the previous stages of development. Now they are more difficult and performed at a faster pace.

As far as tactics are concerned, the player is fully aware that his actions depend on how the events unfold during the game. He has anticipation and the ability to make decisions and resolve any situation he is faced with on the field of play.

The ability to analyze the play (apart from motivation and concentration) depends on the player's vision and hearing along with the essential ingredient of a well-developed imagination. He has acquired an excellent knowledge of the game which helps him resolve all numerous and varied situations that occur during a match.

The decision making process during a game is characterized by the following:

- The decisions are nearly always very complex.

- The circumstances are always changing but even if a similar situation occurs the solution may be different, depending on the tactical motives.

- Individual and team resolutions are intrinsically linked to one another during the game.

- Any decision made by the player is affected by time constraints.

Once the analysis has been made it is very important that the player has both the inclination and the confidence to make the appropriate decision. Some players do this naturally and others struggle to take the initiative. Some players can only make good decisions that involve an element of risk and uncertainty when the team is winning. If the team is losing, these players often lack the confidence to make these difficult decisions.

Perception speed, anticipation and decision-making can all be improved during training. For this reason experience, continuity and progression play an important role. In general a senior player (with a wealth of experience) makes more correct decisions and a lot more quickly than a 19 year old. Even though the more mature player does not have the same physical speed as the younger player he makes up for it by processing the information on the field of play much faster. Thanks to all the games and practices, the more experienced player has developed his observational and analytical skills, which allow him to think more quickly and make decisions faster than when he was younger.

What I have just suggested has been proven in an objective study made by Schellenberger: He notes that the average decision-making time taken by senior players is 1.945 seconds, players aged 19-20 take 2.077 and youth players take 2.283 seconds. Of course there are always exceptions. Even at a young age Ivan De La Peña had the ability to think quickly.

Schellenberger also documents that the decision-making time spent by an outstanding player before shooting is 1.933 seconds, 1.948 seconds when dribbling and 2.651 when passing. The latter takes longer because the player has to get into position and direct the ball while at the same time taking into account the location of his teammates and opponents. The shot and dribble do not contain these extra elements and the player can concentrate solely on his own actions and movements.

A systematic practical and theoretical training program can greatly reduce decision-making times. The players at The School are taught how to understand, develop and improve their decision-making skills throughout the learning process. This stage is no different as the players are taught that:

**1.** If there is a chance to shoot at goal (assuming distance, angle and position of opposition permits) then shoot. This is the best option.

**2.** If there is no possibility of a shot at goal then play a pass to a teammate in the best position to receive the ball.

**3.** If it is impossible to shoot or pass then try to resolve the situation and make a better position by dribbling.

Some coaches think that these ideas are blatantly obvious and choose not to 'insult' the intelligence of the professional players by making any reference to them. I disagree. I know the players understand the theory, but I am also aware that when faced with the situation in a match, wrong decisions are made time after time. The coach should point out these errors and work on ways to develop the decision-making skills of his players. He should point out the various options, tell them which one is best and why, and what technical skills are needed to achieve the required result.

I coached Ivan De La Peña until he was 15 years old. The big flaw in his game was that when presented with the option to shoot or pass, his preference was always the latter, even if he had a perfect opportunity to score himself. I was unable to correct this flaw and he still has it today. Ivan is such a great team player that he prefers to pass to a teammate. I think he is better off shooting and scoring himself if given the opportunity. After all, a goal is a goal no matter who scores it. The day Ivan De La Peña corrects this flaw he will be a top goal scorer because he has a natural instinct for goal and an accurate and powerful shot. Unfortunately he rarely chooses to shoot and the goals he does score are 'passed' into the net.

## Special Training

Once the player reaches the age of 19, the training program follows the same rules and guidelines used for coaching professionals (with minor modifications for specific needs). Every activity in this program is perfectly organized and structured. One of the most important factors about the training once a player reaches this level is that the workload and the intensity of the activities need to be progressive.

The training sessions are divided into two separate phases so that the player can work individually and also work on his game playing with the whole team. This is done 3-4 times a week with a session in the morning and one in the afternoon. Each session lasts between 2-3 hours, depending on when the last game was and when the next one is to be played.

The morning session concentrates on physical and mental preparation and specific technical and tactical work. This work is done on an individual basis. After the morning session is finished it is always a good idea for the players to have lunch together in order to help develop and promote a good team spirit and camaraderie.

The afternoon session concentrates on preparing the players as part of the team when they practice and perfect the team system and tactics in preparation for the next opponent.

Obviously, if a team is playing on the weekend and in midweek then any player who is involved in both these games should have fewer and shorter low intensity training sessions.

Technique is practiced during all training sessions at this level, but not for long periods. The emphasis is now on quality, not quantity. This should not always take place at the beginning of the session. Sometimes it is beneficial to work on technique later when the players are tired. This is because during a match players have little time to rest and often have to perform complicated skills when they are tired or even totally exhausted. Perhaps this does not appear to make sense, but I can assure you that in my experience the player learns to produce skills automatically and is best able to 'program' the appropriate response in the central nervous system when he has to 'push' himself and make an extra effort. As long as the player is just 'tired' when he performs these skills, the exercise is perfectly safe and there is no risk of injury or long-term damage.

The young player needs to practice his technical skills constantly, whereas the professional player needs to take a short break from this type of training from time to time in order to avoid reinforcing bad habits and poor technique. A good time for this total break is during the pre-season and it should last at least 2 or 3 weeks.

The emphasis is on physical fitness during this period. This is because the player has developed and perfected the necessary technical skills and will not suddenly lose this ability overnight. After the break the player returns to the training ground full of enthusiasm and motivation.

During the individual technical training the player does a series of games and exercises that involve the following: speed of execution, changing direction, changing pace, mastering ball skills and the ability to run with the ball at speed. At the same time he is encouraged to be conscious of the decisions he is making and the speed at which he does things. The player makes use of apparatus such as the 'jet ball' and 'suspended ball' etc. and is able to experience a wide variety of games and exercises.

From the age of 10 the players at The School are given a real opportunity to gain an appreciation and understanding of the game and they are encouraged to play intelligent soccer and use their 'soccer brain' at all times. This knowledge of the game is developed with progression and continuity so that in the latter stages the player is not just concerned with his own play but gains an understanding of how to play as part of a team and against opposition.

This means that the player evolves and develops while taking the movements of his teammates and the opposition into account. No soccer player, irrespective of brilliant individual moves, will ever become a 'complete' player unless he plays as part of the team.

There is a desire to get the players to practice on a collective basis (they do in certain exercises at previous levels) but the age of 19-20 is still not the best time to get them to do this. Let me clear this point up. The phrase on a 'collective basis' is very much in fashion at the moment. It is true that the players all have to play as a unit and play for one another. But how can a player be expected to play as part of a team if he is unable to control his own body movements and has not mastered the necessary technical and tactical considerations? Some coaches ignore this and get the players to play as part of a team from a very young age, even before they have 'mastered' the game on an individual basis. The results of this misguided theory are all too familiar. All these players finish playing the game with the same technical faults and deficiencies as when they started out.

All the players at The School develop a real mastery and perfect the necessary technical skills on an individual basis, which allows them to 'grow' and express themselves as soccer players. This ability is the very thing that allows them to progress and play

# Artists or Office Workers?

Some soccer players go to training as if they are going to the office and they usually leave the ground as soon as they can. They do not allow the session to go on any longer than absolutely necessary as they have far better things to be getting on with.

These players know full well that the training sessions are morning and afternoon but they have a mental blockage as far as this is concerned. If the coach asks for these double sessions the players immediately start thinking to themselves who their replacement might be.

They do not appreciate that they belong to the entertainment world and as 'performers' they should not worry about clocking in and out. A few years ago the great actor-director Adolfo Marsillach said: "These days actors have a bank-clerk mentality: they work "9-5" and then leave saying "good bye, see you tomorrow". An actor is an artist and so his rehearsals should not have time restraints. He should only leave when the work for that day has been finished, never before, no matter what the time is".

I think that there are lots of players who should read these words, reflect upon them and put them into practice. Any player who has this mentality will soon see the benefits in his performance.

successfully as part of a team on a collective basis. In other words, at this stage the player is encouraged to start thinking about his own individual skills and how these skills fulfill an important role for the team. He has already reached an excellent level on an individual basis and soon these skills will serve him well as he becomes an important member of the team.

The player also has to progress from practicing moves freely without an opposition to trying to put these into practice (during training) against a strong and determined opponent. This is made all the more difficult because the opponent is fully aware of all the moves and systems practiced during training at The School. This encourages the player to improvise, use his cunning, tricks, intuition and most importantly play with great variety in order to 'outsmart' his rival. The only way to surprise an opponent is by playing with creativity: trying an unexpected move such as a back heel, making a believable feint, or having the confidence to try the unthinkable such as a fancy 'over head' kick. It is very important that the coach rewards this type of bold play, even if it ends in failure. It is all too easy to criticize when a risky and imaginative move goes wrong, but the essential thing is to 'have a go'.

The modern game is all about tight marking, confined space and high balls with very little 'one-touch' creativity. For this reason the training routines should be vigorous and played on small pitches where there is a distinct lack of space and maneuverability, leading to a lack of time on the ball and more pressure from the opposition. These are the typical situations the player encounters during a game. He is 'forced' to make decisions instinctively (without thinking) or else the chance goes and possession is lost. The degree of difficulty increases systematically as the player progresses at The School: more defenders are added and a greater speed of execution is required. Even the most simple techniques are done as quickly as possible and if possible with greater precision.

'The method' uses a series of complex 'rounds' during training to simulate the type of time and space restraints the player will face in a real match. This ability to play under pressure with little time and space is particularly important when playing in the 'danger' zones (in and near the penalty areas). A great many soccer players believe that 'rounds' are only useful for beginners or if they are used for adults they form part of a warm up exercise or recreational activity. These opinions are misguided as you will see when you read about the 'rounds' suggested in the games and exercise section for this level.

In order to overcome the feeling of helplessness the player experiences when he gets possession of the ball under these conditions (no time or space) I recommend that he practices all the exercises containing feints and dummies, especially those where the player is temporarily visually impaired. These exercises increase the player's hearing capabilities, his spatial awareness and his touch, all of which are invaluable attributes in the frenetic modern game.

Perhaps I should clarify that when I talk about collective play I am referring to two types: defensive and offensive. The evolution and development of these two facets of play has been very different and in my opinion this has had a negative affect on the game of soccer. Coaches have been keen to develop the defensive strategies using players with great qualities in this area of the pitch, but unfortunately the attacking qualities of the team have not made the same progress. Take a look at any bookshop selling soccer literature and you will see that the emphasis is almost exclusively on defensive play. There are very few books devoted to attacking play and how to score goals. For this reason 'the method' has a particular emphasis on attacking play.

**225**

## Knowing How to Defend

This does not mean that we forget about the attack. A good soccer player has to 'fight' to win the ball but there are various different ways to achieve this. A player with excellent ball skills and technique undoubtedly has control over his own body, which means he is able to compete for the ball and win it correctly.

Marking is very important in the professional game as the idea is to stop the opposition from playing. Having said that, the great teams have outstanding 'flair' players in attack who defend 'upfront' in an advanced position but do not chase back (a great striker hates having to chase after an opponent). This type of player is very astute when it comes to intercepting passes or stopping an opponent's dribble. They also collaborate well with each other, demonstrating discipline and order in defense and when they win the ball they pass it with speed and precision in order to mount a swift counter-attack.

No team is better at playing this way than the Brazilians. When anybody mentions Brazil it is always to talk about the legendary attacking players such as Pele, Garrincha, Didi, Zico, Romario, Bebeto, and Ronaldo but nobody remembers the defenders. These are all great players in their own right and they have the difficult task of stopping the formidable strikers with very little help (the 'sweeper' system is not played in Brazil). I was a professional soccer player and although I had weaknesses in my game I also had many strengths: visionary passing and excellent dribbling skills. When I used these qualities against a Brazilian team I was amazed to see that they anticipated the play and were not fooled by my dribbling skills (perhaps that says more about my game than theirs).

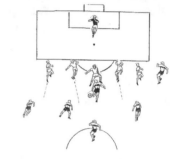

*This pass causes many of the Brazilian players to drop back rapidly and play as a collective defensive unit.*

Another incredible aspect of Brazilian team play is how the midfield players and the defenders play on a collective basis. For example, if the ball is passed beyond the midfield players to a striker behind them, they immediately realize that their current position has no relevance defensively. So, they immediately run back as fast as they can to help out the defense and put pressure on the attacking team. These players are now in a very good position. Now all the space has been filled and any potentially threatening pass will be intercepted. There is no danger (in theory) if the attacking team passes the ball back seeing that all the space is filled in front of them and they have nowhere to go.

The only way to learn and understand about defensive strategy during training is to develop an excellent understanding of the 'logic' of the game. If the game is played with great intensity then any errors may be compensated for by courage and determination. This is the right attitude during a match but during training the idea is to see the errors clearly so that they can be corrected.

Excellent communication is imperative when it comes to defending. It is far better to talk too much than too little in this area of the pitch. Defenders should be talking to each other all the time: "cover", "back", "man on", "out", "time" etc. These are vital messages that point out the movements of the opposition and indicate where a potential threat is coming from. The defenders constantly encourage each other and there is always a shout if someone is day dreaming or too impetuous. This constant flow of communication ensures that order and defensive discipline is maintained, helping the defense to play as an efficient unit.

There is a strange phenomenon in soccer. All players call for the ball and tell the player in possession what he should do with it when playing in attack but on the other hand the same players can play in defense and they suddenly have nothing to say. I repeat, communication is a vital and fundamental part of the game.

The idea of constant and efficient communication is discussed and developed throughout 'the method' at The School.

The method' is completed during this level with two very important concepts that every professional player should be familiar with: the 'off-side' rule and the tactic of 'pressing' the opposition.

Coaches and players think that these two tactical strategies go hand-in-hand as the 'pressing' game involves the defense pushing up and limiting the space the opposition has to play in with the security of the 'off-side' trap. This is perfectly true but the 'pressing' game can be played even more effectively with the defense pushing up diagonally (depending where the ball is) using a 'sweeper' at the back to counteract the long ball. As far as 'off-side' is concerned it can be played together with a 'pressing' game to limit the space the opposition has to play in or it can be played as appropriate depending on the circumstances during the game. This is the way it was played 20 years ago. Do not think that I am behind the times. Because the reality is that some players play the 'off-side' trap well and some play it poorly, whether or not the 'pressing' game or other tactical considerations are involved.

## Pressing

The tactic of 'pressing' is used when the opposition has the ball and the other team closes down the space in an attempt to win possession. The idea is basically a determined effort to stop the opposing team from achieving their objectives. This tactic is used to attack the ball and harass the opponent by not giving him a second to control it and do anything effective with it. It is then up to the team in possession to think of a strategy to overcome the 'attacking' defensive tactic.

The 'pressing' game is really a question of mental perception. The team doing the pressuring has to make the team on the ball feel as if they are under attack and being threatened so that all their effort goes into merely keeping possession rather than doing anything more damaging.

Before going into more detail about the 'pressing' game I would like to draw your attention to two important points:

1. If during the game a player is relatively near to an opponent on the ball and all he hears from his teammates, the coach or fans is: "Come on, pressure!" In reality this is merely a simple challenge or a way of stopping the rival's progress but it is not what I would call a 'pressing' game.

2. There is a very well-known saying in soccer: "Two against one, foul!" But this is not necessarily the case. If the confrontation is perfectly within the rules of the game there is no reason why it should automatically result in a foul. The fact is that the player on the ball can be challenged by two, four or more players without going against the rules of the game. Of course it is a totally different matter if the player on the ball is challenged by

three players and one grabs his shirt, another kicks his ankles and the third obstructs him, but any of these infringement would result in a free-kick if there was only one player making the challenge.

After clearing up the above I think it is a good time to give you my definition of the 'pressing' game: **A collective team movement in the direction of the ball, where two or three players actively challenge for possession**. For this reason there is a well-known saying that good coaches constantly tell their players: "Don't stand around watching your teammates putting on the pressure, get involved". If the correct 'pressing' movement is followed then two or three players should impede the progress of the player on the ball and another nucleus of players should mark the opposition nearby to prevent a short pass being played. In other words, this 'attacking' defensive tactic only works if everyone plays a role. If the players do not work as a collective unit the system breaks down. This defensive 'pressing' game is a risky tactic that only works if the players have a good understanding and play as a team. One weak link and the strategy is a waste of time and several players might be caught out of position.

Generally, people believe that the 'pressing' game can only be used by a team with players with great stamina and physical strength. This is a misconception. With this tactic there is no need for the incessant long runs up and down the pitch that take a lot out of the players. The basic requirements for the strategy are as follows:

**1.** A comprehensive knowledge of the game.

**2.** A correct mental attitude.

**3.** An extraordinary ability to concentrate.

**4.** And above all, tremendous coordination and understanding between the different areas of the pitch (the attack, midfield and defense).

The 'pressing' game is one of the best strategies a team can adopt. Any team that plays it must be brave and fully aware of the repercussions and the possible risk involved. However, there are mixed opinions as to whether this tactic should be employed throughout the whole game or whether it should be used sparingly depending on the circumstances in the match or only against certain teams etc.

I think it is a tactic that cannot be played the whole time. If this strategy is employed for every match throughout the whole season the emotional strain and the extraordinarily high concentration levels needed would sooner or later have a negative affect on the players.

Another reason not to use the same tactic during every match is that this makes it easier for the opposition to prepare and formulate their own tactics as they know what to expect. This preparation can take place on the training ground or simply in the minds of the players as they mentally get ready for what they are about to encounter in the match.

If the tactic is used sparingly the great advantages are that the players do not become as mentally exhausted and the opposition may not be prepared for the move and thus are taken by surprise.

In which matches should this tactic be used? Or when should it be used in a match? There is no simple answer to these questions. As with any other tactic there are numerous things to consider, such as:

1. If the team suffers from a lack of technique and genuine skill and the opposition is obviously superior in this regard then the 'pressing' game is a good defensive strategy that helps counteract the quality of the opponents.

2. However, if the opposition is obviously inferior the best idea is to play normally with the firm belief that superior technique and tactics will win the day. Nevertheless, the opposition (conscious of being the weaker team) will play defensively and

cautiously. So, under these circumstances the 'pressing' game with its ferocious hassling and pressurizing will make the opposition lose even more confidence and give away more ground, leaving them with no choice but to kick the ball wildly upfield so as not to lose it in dangerous areas of the pitch. The tactic is then to release the pressure slightly so that the opposition is allowed to 'relax' more in the hope that they will gain confidence (thinking they have weathered the storm) and play more offensively, leaving themselves vulnerable to a swift counterattack.

3. There are always matches where the going is tough and the situation is difficult: the team is losing and playing badly and action has to be taken. The coach can either change the formation, change players or play the 'pressing' game. He only chooses the latter if the team have practiced the tactic and are fully familiar with it. If this is not the case and the team is not fully conversant with the tactic and yet the coach decides to play it anyway, the chances of it being successful are virtually zero and the game will definitely be lost.

4. The 'pressing' game allows a team to totally change the rhythm and pace of the match at any moment. This tactic does not have to be employed just when a team is losing. For example, the opposition may be controlling the game and playing at a slow pace that suits them but not us. The score may be level but the opposition has the initiative in the match. This is an ideal moment to start playing the 'pressing' game. The match will change totally and the opposition will have less time on the ball and less space to play in. Suddenly they find the game is not so straightforward and they can no longer play at their own comfortable pace.

5. Another good time to play the 'pressing' game is after scoring a goal. The team that scored the goal is on a high, full of confidence and motivation whereas the opposition is confused, disappointed and with low self-confidence. Using this tactic at this particular time will leave the opposition with no time or space and desperate to relieve the pressure, which is often a time when teams make silly errors and leave them-

selves exposed. This is the time to keep the pressure on and go for the 'kill'.

When starting to teach the movements and rotations involved in the 'pressing' game it is necessary to give the defense a numerical advantage. Apart from this, the attack plays with other limitations: they have to touch the ball five times and constantly play horizontally across the width of the pitch (to give the defenders a chance). As the team gets used to playing the tactic the limitations are less and less, until finally it is like a normal game with the same number of players and no restrictions at all.

Once the players reach this level of understanding they have to mentally divide the pitch into three zones. This is because the 'pressing' game is only played in the defending third and attacking third of the pitch and not in the central zone. It is not a good idea to play the 'pressing' game in central areas. The opposition has too many options available in this part of the pitch. The player on the ball can pass it left, right or backwards or he can go himself. If the ball is near the wing then the tactic is used on that side of the pitch and in the middle. It is not used in the rest of the pitch. Of course the same is true when the ball moves to the other side. From these wide positions the player on the ball has very few options available to him.

Any defense that hopes to play the 'pressing' game effectively needs to take into account the following considerations:

**1.** At least two players have to challenge the opponent on the ball, working together to limit the time and space available.

**2.** At the same time the rest of the team near the area has to make a general movement in the direction of the ball to fill all the gaps and possible 'escape' routes (they always exist unless they are covered effectively). Of course, this means that a couple of the opposition's players will be left unmarked, but these will always be the furthest from the ball with little or no chance of getting it.

**3.** The 'pressing' game is most effective when a rival has the ball

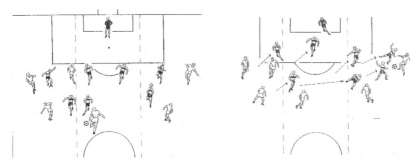

*The 'pressing' game is working.*

on or near the wings as it is easier to limit the space and thus his possibilities of making a pass (usually the only place he can pass is inside).

4. This marking strategy can be performed anywhere on the pitch, although it is extremely difficult to play in central areas of the pitch.

5. This tactic relies heavily on communication and playing as a tight well-organized unit. The players need to be close together in order to fill the gaps and limit the possibilities available to the opponent.

6. On the other hand, if the team does not play as a tight unit (especially when employing this tactic in the opposition's half) it is a great advantage for the opposition as it makes the counterattack an inviting proposition because many of the players are out of position.

7. Once the team wins the ball it should mount a swift counterattack. In other words the natural sequence of the 'pressing' game is as follows:

**a)** Pressure

**b)** Win possession

**c)** Counterattack

8. Just as with all modern-day systems, tactics and strategies,

the 'pressing' game requires the team to play as a well-ordered and disciplined unit, where the players have to play with intelligence and total concentration. This is sometimes too much for some players and they are not able to cope.
This tactic has to be played well or not at all.

Playing the total 'pressing' game involves the defense playing on the half-way line and obliging (almost with a 'siege-type' mentality) the opposition to play in their own half. The team plays as a tight unit filling all the space and putting pressure on the opposition. This tactic means that the game is played as far as possible from the team's own goal area. Nevertheless, it is worth repeating that this is easier said than done. The players (particularly the strikers) have to be able to change from one system to another instantly whether they have possession or not. If a team loses possession, there is always a short period of crisis as the team takes stock of the situation and regroups. If the players are able to adapt quickly to new situations this period of time is lessened.

Unfortunately, many players have negative thoughts and attitudes during this period:

- If the player loses the ball because of a poor pass or an inappropriate dribble he feels disheartened and disappointed. Some players try to explain what happened to a teammate and others may even fall to the floor holding their head in their hands if they feel the mistake was unforgivable.

- On other occasions the players blame one another and argue instead of concentrating on the job in hand, which is applying the pressure now that the opposition has the ball.

- Generally, strikers are a breed apart. They like to play their own game, they are lazy and they do not waste their energy chasing the opposition.

- Other players do not have the right mental attitude and are unable to 'fight' in a 'defensive' role once they lose the ball.

- Some players think of themselves as 'stars' and 'artists' and find the thought of chasing or pressuring the opposition belittling and disagreeable. After all, this is not what they are paid for. It is up to the 'workers' in the team to chase, tackle and generally get their kit dirty.

Having said all this, playing the 'pressing' game in the opposition's half also has many advantages:

1. The tactic unsettles the opposition and stifles their game. Sometimes the defenders are hassled into making elementary mistakes because they are not used to this type of pressure.

2. If a team has practiced a well-rehearsed counterattack in training, they have to improvise and change their plans because they are not allowed any time on the ball to develop the play. The player on the ball (especially) and his teammates nearby are put under tremendous pressure, which means he desperately looks for ways to continue the move and keep possession. On numerous occasions the only option he comes up with is to kick the ball wildly up-field with a 'hit and hope' attitude.

3. The team doing the pressuring upsets and breaks the opposition's rhythm. They dictate the pace of the game. Furthermore, the players who are used to playing the 'pressing' game have also developed a better 'fighting spirit' and improved powers of concentration as a consequence. These qualities will unsettle and trouble even the most technically gifted teams if their attitude is not right.

4. The great advantage of putting pressure on the opposition in their own half is that as soon as possession is won a chance to score quickly follows because of the proximity to the goal.

It is worth mentioning again that I am not recommending that this all out attack and total pressure should be played throughout the whole match. I think it is best to use this tactic at certain times during a match. Sometimes it is a good idea to slow the pace of the game, drop back and invite the opposition to attack in order to mount swift counterattacks.

# The Pressing Game and the Goalkeeper

Some teams play the 'pressing' game from halfway inside their own area to halfway inside the opposition's area. In this way the opposition can advance with the ball up to this area without being pressured or challenged by the attackers. This apparent freedom ends as soon as the ball enters the 'pressing zone'. Once in this zone all the team plays the 'pressing' game. The defenders position themselves some 30 yards from goal to limit the space the opposition has to play in with the security that if an attackers is standing behind them he is 'off-side'.

The fact that the defense is so far forward means that the goalkeeper stands on the edge of his area ready to intercept the long ball. The opposition often become frustrated under such pressure and decide to kick the ball into the wide open space behind the defense for the attackers to chase. Under these circumstances the goalkeeper acts as a 'sweeper' and even runs out of his area if necessary to intercept these passes.

Many coaches believe it is dangerous for the goalkeeper to play so far off his line as he may be caught out of position by a 'lob' or a long shot. This is only possible if the 'pressing' game is not being played properly. If the player on the ball is being harassed by two or three opponents then he has enough trouble trying to keep possession, let alone try a fantastic shot. However, if the team does not advance as a tight unit and the player on the ball is not put under pressure and he has enough time and space then (if he has the vision and technical ability) he can try a long shot and may score. But as I have said before, the 'pressing' game only works if it is played well.

This type of 'pressing' game was used by the Brazilian team in the 1994 World Cup. They were able to win the competition thanks to their perfect 'pressing zone." Because the Brazilian team is a naturally gifted offensive unit always able to score goals, the onus was put on defensive play and the struggle to win possession so that a new attack could commence. Once the opposition reached the midfield area they were harassed and

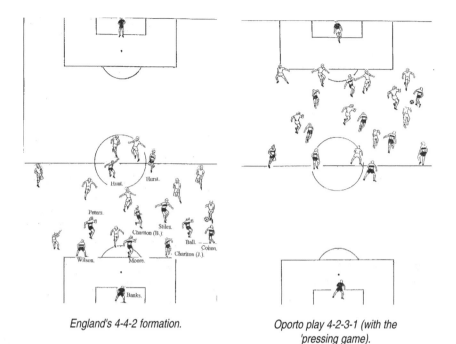

England's 4-4-2 formation.

Oporto play 4-2-3-1 (with the 'pressing game).

pressured, eventually losing possession and allowing Brazil to mount one swift counterattack after another.

This was a master stroke by the coaches, Parreira and Zagalo, who asked the Brazilian team to change its style and way of playing and even left out the more technically gifted players. The idea was to change the tactics so that the team would have more space and freedom when in possession and would expend less physical effort throughout the matches. The Brazilian coaches demonstrated once again that players have to play with a plan and tactical discipline (especially defensive discipline).

The tactic of dropping back and having a solid defense between the half way line and the team's own goal in order to mount counterattacks from this area was a tactic introduced by the English. This system and the 'Great' Bobby Charlton helped England win the 1966 World Cup. However, the Portuguese and especially Oporto have been able to advance and perfect this style, thanks to their wonderful technique, 'feel' for the game and well-disciplined 'pressing zone'.

They play numerous players in a restricted area and they 'know' how to fill every gap (they used to play with a 4-4-1-1 system but now they prefer a 4-2-3-1 formation) leaving the opposing strikers with literally nowhere to go. There is no strict man-to-man marking but as soon as a rival has the ball in this area he is faced by at least two or three players stopping him from any progress.

It is well-known that the most effective attacks are played down the wings. To counter this there is also an opinion that if a team plays the ball on the flanks the idea is to keep the player wide and 'trap' him, not giving him the possibility to come inside. These two opinions appear to be contradictory. Of course attacks are best played down the wings and if a player is forced out wide and allowed to advance then there is a possibility that he might get to the edge of the area and play a dangerous cross. However, it is also true that a well-organized defense can 'trap' the opponent on the wing leaving him few options.

The Portuguese never leave an opponent in a 'one-to-one' situation on the wing. The idea is to stop any progress by having two or three players harass and pressure the player on the ball. The English prefer to play with a specific defender (left back or right back) to stop the opposition on the flanks. He gets between his opponent and the touchline 'inviting' the attacker to try to outrun him (this is very difficult) or take the ball infield where other defenders are waiting as part of the 'pressing' game tactic. These defenders push forward as a unit  and play the 'offside' trap which is also a common defensive tactic used in the English game. This tactic was used repeatedly by Venables and helped his Barcelona side win the Spanish league in 1984

In 1957, the extraordinary coach Scopelli explained how to stop the legendary Gento, who was gaining a reputation as the best winger in the world. "It is a mistake to allow him to run freely down the wing as his blistering pace allows him to exploit the wide-open space, get to the edge of the penalty area and play what has now become known as a 'killer'  pass". (The ball pulled back from the touchline).

Scopelli goes on to say: "The thing to do with Gento is stop him running down the wing and force him inside where there is little space and lots of players and he cannot use his speed. The more he advances and gets nearer the goal the more defenders he will come across and he will have very little chance to do anything with the ball".

# How to Counteract the Pressing Game

Everybody talks about how the 'pressing' game is a great tactic to destroy the attacking possibilities of the opposition but nobody has put forward any ideas how to combat this strategy. For every strategy there is a counter strategy and the 'pressing' game is no exception. Teams I have coached (professional and youth) have successfully scored goals playing against this type of system. As I have mentioned several times already, obviously the secret is not to 'hit and hope' by kicking the ball wildly upfield. If this was the only possibility then there would be no point paying the professional players and coaches vast sums of money to do something that any coach or player at any level could come up with.

Here are some of the strategies I have used in the past to counteract the 'pressing' game. They are all equally effective and are in no particular order. The important thing to remember is that whichever tactic is chosen has to be played correctly and it should always suit the current circumstances in the game. Basically, if it works, use it!

**1.** Players with great dribbling ability ( and only these) should try to go alone. If the player successfully breaks free of the 'stranglehold' leaving the majority of the opposition behind, then he will have plenty of space ahead of him and his team will have a numerical advantage in attack. If this happens the player on the ball should be aware that the opposition will try to resolve the situation by playing the 'off-side' trap.

The best thing to do under these circumstances is to continue running with the ball as the opposition move up to set the trap. If successful, his teammates should run forward (staying behind the ball) to support so that when the player on the ball is challenged by the goalkeeper he may pass it to one of them, giving that player the simple task of kicking it into the empty goal.

2. Another good way to combat the 'pressing' game is playing the ball 'first-time'. The idea is to pass and immediately run upfield into space, ready to receive the return ball. But remember, the players in the opposition will apply the pressure as soon as he receives the ball in an attempt to win possession. If the player on the ball is technically and tactically astute he will play it 'first-time', leaving the opposition 'stranded' with no possibility of getting to him or to the ball. The opposition soon loses heart and confidence (chasing shadows) if the attackers are able to repeat this type of move consistently.

3. When on the wing, the team plays three or four short passes to 'suck in' the opposition. At this precise moment the ball is passed back to a central defender or the 'sweeper' who changes the direction of play by kicking the ball to a teammate (perhaps a midfield player or winger who has sprinted into position)on the other side of the pitch. Remember that this player is unmarked and in plenty of space as the 'pressing' game is all about 'filling' the area near the ball and other parts of the pitch are left unguarded.

4. Something similar happens when a player (a striker or midfield player) has the ball near the opposition's penalty area. On seeing that two or three players are about to put pressure on him and close him down, he turns and runs with the ball in the direction of his own goal. The whole team has a role to play in this move and acts as a tight unit. The central defenders move out wide and one of them is given the ball. Meanwhile the wingers run back so as not to be 'off-side' and to cover for the defenders who are moving forward. These defenders are the wing backs who must time their run perfectly. The central defender plays the ball 'first-time', changing the direction of play and placing it in the path of the on-coming wing back on the opposite side of the pitch. If he gets the ball the other defender (who moves up with him) takes up the center

forward's position. With any luck the move will end with a great goal-scoring opportunity.

I must clear up two essential points as far as this move is concerned:

**a)** The striker making the pass has to run towards his half of the pitch before he does so or else his teammates will not have time to think, let alone move.

**b)** I know from experience that this 'strange' tactic has a very negative psychological effect on the opposition. It confuses them and makes them lose confidence and become static (which is the antithesis of the 'pressing' game). Imagine what happens if this move ends with a goal?

**5.** Sometimes the defenders all come up to try to limit the space their opponents have to play in. Under these circumstances there are always collisions and the ball often rebounds or is deflected for a throw-in. If the team is fully prepared, this type of situation can result in a goal: a player runs to retrieve the ball and takes the throw-in quickly, while other players sprint to get behind the defenders. If one of them gets the ball (he is not 'off-side' as this is impossible from a throw-in), he finds himself in the clear with only the goalkeeper to beat.

Finally, it is worth repeating yet again that there is no point in playing the 'pressing' game if the team does not have a good understanding and play with intelligence as a well-disciplined unit. The same is true if trying to combat this tactic. Just as with any other skill this can only be learned and perfected with constant repetition and practice during training. One last point to reflect upon: these ideas (defensive and offensive) together with hard work and thoughtful planning offer no guarantees of success. But this is true of any defensive or offensive strategy. Fortunately, (this is what makes the game 'Great') nothing in soccer is that simple and straightforward.

# The Offside Rule

A brief history of the 'off-side' rule. In 1862 when 'official' soccer began, J C Thring introduced 10 rules and regulations into the game. One of these rules was taken from the game of Rugby: any player who receives the ball from a more advanced position up the pitch is deemed 'off-side'. This rule is still in existence today but has been modified so that a player is not deemed 'offside' in the following circumstances:

- If the player is in his own half of the pitch

- If there are at least two members of the opposition between him and the goal or if he is in 'line' with them.

- If the player receives the ball directly from an opponent.

- If the ball is received directly from a throw-in, goal-kick, corner or 'drop' ball.

A player who is caught 'off-side' should never be penalized unless he is interfering with play or gains an advantage from his position.

The 'off-side' rule adds a touch of 'science' to the game as it makes players think and play as a unit. If it did not exist there would be no need for any systems, tactics or strategies as the ball would just be kicked from one goalmouth to another with little finesse. The skill and creativity would disappear from the game. Players would 'goal-hang' and crowd the penalty box, crashing into and colliding with the goalkeeper.

Essentially, 'off-side' only occurs because of a lack of understanding and timing between the player on the ball making the pass and the player making the run. At the beginning of the century a popular tactic was to play with a 'flat' back four with all the defenders in a 'line' parallel to the goal. The idea was to disorient the opposition, looking to catch them 'off-side' and keep them as far away from the goal as possible. In 1925 the rule had to be amended because it was so effective the strikers were unable to beat the 'trap'. The change facilitated better soccer and a 'free-flowing' game with plenty of goals and emotion.

# The Disadvantages of the Offside Rule

Since its inception, playing the 'off-side' rule has enjoyed periods of popularity but never on a consistent basis. However, over recent years, playing with a 'flat' back four to catch the opposition 'off-side' has become commonplace. Some coaches and players feel a real sense of pride and satisfaction every time they catch a forward 'off-side'. Some think this makes them superior in some way as if they are more intelligent, more cunning and in some cases, even more handsome. This self-congratulation does not allow them to see the disadvantages of playing this tactic:

1. The main difficulty with playing this tactic is that if it goes wrong (and it does) the team is left exposed at the back with no cover. If one of the defenders does not move forward with the others, or moves up after the pass has been made, or the linesman does not flag for 'offside' then the forward is left with the goal at his mercy.

2. It is also true that the attackers can beat the 'off-side' trap by playing intelligently, skillfully and with a good understanding and sense of timing. Each time they do, a goal is scored. On the other hand if the defense plays in a 'step' formation diagonally across the pitch then if a ball goes beyond the first player there is always another available to resolve the situation. The same is true if a player manages to dribble past a defender. In other words, this defensive line up makes it very difficult for the striker to get near the goal. All too frequently when playing with a 'flat' back four the opposite is true.

3. It is fair to suggest that players used to employing this tactic begin to rely on it and become too complacent and consequently lose their fighting spirit, which is a vital quality for any defender.

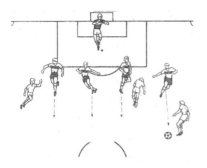 

*The rest of the defense comes out in unison (in a 'line') as they support the defender who runs out to challenge for the ball.*

*Now they maintain the 'line' covering the player who makes the challenge.*

**4.** Another very important disadvantage of playing 'off-side' is that it nullifies the possibility of a swift counterattack. Imagine a team with the necessary ability to produce swift counterattacks but they never do because they play 'off-side' and win a free kick. By the time the ball has been retrieved, placed in the correct position and the free-kick taken, the opposition will be ready and well-organized and there is no chance of taking them by surprise.

Having said this, I do not agree with the coaches and commentators who say that playing 'off-side' is anti-soccer. They believe it is immoral and unsporting as its objective is purely to stop the other team from making any offensive progress. I do think that stopping a team by kicking and holding them is unsporting. However, playing the 'off-side' rule which is based on intelligence, timing and teamwork in order to stifle the opposition is a perfectly legitimate tactic which any team is free to try.

Let me make it clear that I am not a great fan of playing the 'off-side' rule on a regular basis but I do respect it and think it merits consideration. This is why 'the method' makes reference to it right from the first level to the last. This level concentrates on how to play specific set moves and tactics and how to overcome them. In order to understand and overcome the problems generated by the 'off-side' rule both in defense and in attack, the player must go through the following stages:

- A player practices on his own (individual tactics).

- Two or more players practice together (group tactics).

- Whole team practice (working as a team).

By this level the players practice the 'off-side' rule on a team basis.

These are the basic principles of the practice routines:

**1.** The defenders (four or five) all play in a 'line' the same distance away from the goal and parallel to it. The idea is to set the 'off-side' trap, unsettle the strikers and keep them as far away as possible from the goal.

**2.** The defense may also play in 'line' with the defender covering for the one who goes to challenge for the ball. This formation is more flexible and in my opinion more sensible.

**245**

**3.** Both cases use zonal marking and the midfield players and the strikers need to put pressure on the opposition when they have possession in the central area of the pitch.

In the first principle, when their own team has the ball, the defense plays in a 'line'. If possession is lost then the defense keep the same formation and sometimes moves two yards forward. The defense never drops back. If an opponent advances with the ball the defender responsible for that zone moves forward to challenge (forcing his opponent to play the ball) and as he does the other defenders also move forward as one and hold the 'line' level with this player's position. No opponent can position himself beyond this 'line' because if he does he will be caught 'off-side'.

*If the defense plays in a 'line' in an advanced position then the goalkeeper needs to 'fill' the space intelligently.*

In the second principle, a defender goes to challenge for the ball and another moves up to cover him while the rest of the defense hold the 'line' level with the player doing the covering. This tactic is known as playing in a 'line' and covering. This tactic also makes use of the 'off-side' trap but with less emphasis on it.

In the third principle, if the player on the ball is not being challenged and one of the defenders in the 'line' spots another opponent invading his zone, then he immediately turns and sprints back to his goal. If he does not do this then the ball could easily be passed beyond him into the path of the on-coming attacker who is running at pace and has the advantage as the defender has to turn and start running. Obviously, if the player on the ball is being challenged or has his back to goal then the defense hold the 'line' and let the other advancing attacker run into an 'off-side' position.

If the defensive 'line' is far up the field then it is up to the goalkeeper to play intelligently on the edge of his area prepared to intercept any long balls as if playing as a 'sweeper'. In other words, the goalkeeper needs to keep at the perfect distance behind his defenders. If he is too close he is not able to cover and fill the gaps and he is exposed to danger. If he is too far away a striker may break forward and exploit the space getting to the ball before the goalkeeper and consequently threaten the goal.

When the defense takes up this formation the 'key' to the success of the tactic is the positioning and anticipation of the goalkeeper. Any ball that gets beyond the defenders has to be intercepted by the goalkeeper from either inside or outside his area.

## How to Combat the Offside Trap

Obviously the players need to learn how to play against the 'off-side' trap. This level allows the players to practice and perfect the necessary strategies to counteract this tactic. There are various ways to combat the 'off-side' trap but all the strategies involve a well-disciplined and coordinated team effort. Any team that does not possess this cohesion will be caught 'off-side' time after time. How many times have we seen two smart, quick-thinking and intelligent strikers beat the 'off-side' trap only to hear the whistle blow as a third striker with less vision and concentration is caught day-dreaming.

Here are some strategies for breaking the 'off-side' trap:

**1.** Some players are so concerned about not being caught 'off-side' that they lose all their creativity and concentration. Believe it or not, some players consciously take up innocuous positions and do not get involved in the play to avoid the 'shame' of being caught 'off-side'. In order to confront this tactic the players need to be mentally strong and have the attitude that of course they will be caught 'off-side' from time to time but they have to keep trying as every time they succeed they could and should score.

**2.** It is very common in the modern game for the defense to push up as far as possible and leave a huge space between them and the goal. If both teams play the same tactics (and they often do) then the actual playing area is reduced to a 25-30-yard space in the middle of the pitch. It is very difficult to play soccer under these conditions with so many players around the ball. Everyone tries hard to break free from the melee but in reality the attackers are left with few clear offensive possibilities. But at the same time it also means that as the opposing defenders come forward to try to catch their rivals 'off-side', any striker paying attention with good anticipation skills can use his intuition to position himself in the best position to take advantage of the rebounds and deflections (in such a tight space with so many player they always occur) that leave him in the clear. The striker should also be encouraged and optimistic when he sees the opposition running forward with the ball because if he makes a challenge and wins the ball he is also in the clear. The sad reality is that there are very few astute and intelligent strikers able to use their ingenuity and guile to break the 'off-side' trap.

3. It is a very good tactic to run down one flank and then pass a deep diagonal ball over and beyond the 'line' of defenders to the other side of the pitch. Before the pass is made a defender or midfield player has to make a sprint from deep and time his move to perfection. This leaves the defense static and with the ball behind them, forcing them to turn and give chase as quickly as possible (but it is a lost cause as they are already beaten).

4. Another way to beat the 'off-side' trap is for a player to go on an individual run, but this also relies on good team work. The player on the ball runs slowly towards the defensive 'line'. Meanwhile two attackers blatantly run into an 'off-side' position and shout for the ball. The player in possession dummies as if to play a pass to one of his teammates. As the defenders relax and are ready to appeal, the player suddenly kicks the ball forward and goes alone. The defenders are taken by surprise, expecting to regain possession thanks to their 'cunning' defensive ploy. The player who makes the run can either shoot at goal himself or pass to one of his teammates who have kept up with the play and are now in a correct position to receive the ball.

5. The defensive 'line' can also be breached by playing an effective 'one-two': once again a player runs with the ball towards the defenders. The forwards do not run away from their teammate but instead stay fairly close to him. Suddenly, the player on the ball passes it to a teammate and starts his run beyond the defenders, hoping to receive a 'first-time' pass back. Apart from the timing and the technique involved, the key to this move is the proximity of the forwards. If the pass is long then this gives the defenders time to react and resolve the problem. If the players are too close (apart from the fact that the pass will be intercepted) by the time the ball is returned the player is in an 'off-side' position. If the distance is correct the forward will beat the static defenders with ease.

6. If a forward receives the ball in the clear he should never wait to listen for the referee's whistle. Instead, he should run as fast as he can towards the opposition's goal while conscious of any movements made by his teammates.

**7.** Avoiding the 'off-side' trap is all about the run made and the pass delivered. The training sessions should concentrate on players running with the ball and observing the runs made by their teammates. If a player sees that a forward has moved too late or too quickly and is in an 'off-side' position he should pass the ball sideways to another teammate to give the forward enough time to get back on-side.

In recent years Milan has been a very successful team with a style of play based on the 'pressing' game and supported by the 'off-side' trap. The game in Italy has always been played using a 'catenaccio' (a 'sweeper') but Liedholm introduced the zonal system with a combination of the 'pressing' game and the 'off-side' trap and soon all the teams in Italy were playing this way. As often happens, due to Milan's success, Arrigo Sacchi was seen as the inventor of the system by many people. When the team was at its best, Sacchi analyzed 'his' system for the 'Gazzeta Dello Sport':

- "The system was practiced and perfected on the training ground against other teams in the club before trying it in an official match. Even after using the system for three years in the league I was still asking the players to correct their mistakes and practice more during training".

- "It is vitally important that the players in the team (especially the defenders) are intelligent and possess an excellent tactical understanding and awareness because if one player makes a mistake this can spark a chain reaction in the rest of the team".

- "The system relies on a deep understanding and total cooperation between the various parts of the team so that they are able to support each other and expend less energy, which is extremely important throughout the long season".

- "I don't understand why some coaches dislike the system. Any team that hopes to beat us needs to possess very intelligent players, not just on an individual basis but also (particularly important) on a collective basis. In other words we play as a team and to have any chance of beating us the opposition must play as a tight unit as well. This is the plain truth; the reality of the situation. Any other reasons that are given are simply excuses for a defeat".

Finally, to finish off this topic it is worth highlighting the fundamentals again: this system just like the 'pressing' game or any other is based on individual and collective play both in defense and in attack. This necessitates a carefully planned and well organized training program that deals with both the practical and the theoretical considerations. The coaches should work hard and never relax thinking their work is done. They should never look for scapegoats for any failures among the players: when a musician in an orchestra plays a wrong note it is totally his own fault. But if all the musicians play a wrong note the blame lies with the conductor. The same is true in soccer. If one player plays poorly then perhaps he is having a bad day, but if the whole team performs badly then we know who to blame...

**250**

# Playing and Resting

A training program is made up of many different things, all of which are aimed at producing better players and although I keep mentioning the importance of repetition (and it is important), do not forget that the best way to improve as a soccer player is by actually playing: the games and small-sided games during training, the friendly matches and the official matches. Actually playing the game is the vital complimentary ingredient to any exercise and training program and it is the only way to improve.

The games take a high priority in the training program and planning and the coach should make a note of every game each player participates in, the type of game (training, friendly, official etc.) and how many minutes he plays. At the same time the coach should make a note of the player's work-rate, physical and mental effort, technical performance and tactical knowledge.

At this stage it is important for the players to participate in at least one official match per week, either with the 'first' team or in the reserves. If the player does not compete on a regular basis he will never be 'match-fit' and worse still he will never realize his full potential. Once the player reaches the age of 24-25 and even though he is not in the 'first' team playing every week it is not absolutely necessary for him to compete in a match on such a regular basis. Instead, this break may act as a well-earned rest which allows him to recover physically and especially mentally.

If a team plays three important games per week (league and cup) always using the same players, sooner or later as the weeks pass these players will become exhausted physically and mentally. In the end the players will be over-worked and over-stressed, leading to poor performances, especially in the most crucial games. This has a negative impact on the fans, leaving them disappointed and disillusioned. This phenomenon is likely to affect the younger players and the over 30s in particular. The coach should be aware that this is a potential problem and that he should do everything he can to make sure the players get enough rest whenever they need it.

I am convinced that any player who has followed 'the method' right the way through to the professional ranks will be capable of playing fast, sensible but with an emphasis on creative and attractive soccer. These days, some teams base their tactics on continuous and speedy attacks with no let-up, never looking to change the pace of the game. The teams that play at such a fast pace (too quick to play the game properly) do not put together any moves, instead they play like 'headless chickens' limited by their own mediocrity, they produce a constant flow of ill-conceived and poorly judged passes and runs. The number of balls that go astray and passes that miss the target is in direct proportion with the speed they play at. If they slowed down and varied the pace from time to time, the game would contain far fewer mistakes and would be more attractive to watch.

This idea of playing at such a fast pace throughout the ninety minutes was first seen by the Ajax team of the 1970's with Cruyff, Keizer, Neeskens, Rep etc. This team played at a tremendous pace and used this tactic to get the better of their opponents. However, although this strategy managed to subdue the opposition at times, it proved counter-productive and often stopped Ajax from playing an attractive and intelligent game. Kovacs, the team's coach, later admitted that he tried to get the team to 'slow down' and play with the same style but at a more relaxing pace but with little success.

Just as a slow player or a player who is too quick for his own good are easily dealt with by the opposition, the same is true when a team always plays at the same pace with no variety or imagination.

These are the teams I have enjoyed watching over the years:

- The 1950 Hungarian team with Puskas, Bolzik, Kocsis and Higdekuti.

- The Madrid team during the glory years with Di Stefano, Gento, Kopa and Del Sol.

- The Brazilian team with Pele, Garrincha, Didi Gerson and the 1982 Brazilian team with Zico, Socrates, Junior and Cerezo (this team did not win the tournament but they showed their class).

- The Barcelona team with Cruyff, Koeman, Laudrup, Stoichkov, Bakero and Guardiola.

All of the above teams played at their own pace, making short sideways passes when confronted by a well-organized defense. The pace of the game was slow and relaxed. However, as soon as a slight gap appeared in the defensive 'wall', suddenly everybody started sprinting and the ball was played at 'lightning' speed producing panic and confusion in the defense and thus opening up even bigger gaps for the team to exploit. These changes in pace were dramatic and explosive, allowing these teams to control games with great success.

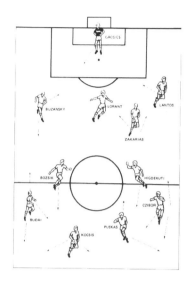

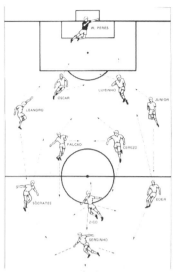

*The 1950 Hungarian team was a soccer-playing 'machine'.*

*Zico's fantastic 1982 Brazilian team. Notice the 4-2-3-1 formation that many coaches today claim as their own tactic.*

**253**

*The Santos team Pele played for was another brilliant outfit. In the photo we see Coutinho, Pele, Zito, Gilmar, Mauro etc.*

# Attack or Counter-Attack?

I mention my favorite teams to give some background as to how and why I formed my predominantly offensive philosophy which led to me formulating 'the method'. These are the ten most important offensive concepts in 'the method':

1. In reality, building an attack is a lot more difficult than mounting a swift counterattack, as the opposition is organized and in position. Building an attack also has far more positional and strategic possibilities than a counterattack. Even after so many years the most popular form of attack is still the 'Brazilian Method'. Strangely, many people in South America believe this way of playing was started by teams from Argentina and Uruguay whereas the Europeans give the credit to Austria and Hungary. The idea is that if necessary the attack should be very slow, patient and relaxed with the team content to keep possession with apparently little ambition. However, the team is merely waiting for a chance to exploit any weakness in the opposition's defense and once this occurs they suddenly change the pace of the game dramatically and pass the ball quickly and accurately.

2. When the team is playing at this slow pace, looking for a gap, it is vital that the attackers do not get too close to the opposition's goal or else there will never be any space to exploit. This is because if they move and position themselves near the edge of the penalty box, the defenders will mark and organize themselves accordingly, filling all the available space.

3. During an attack a player should rarely take four steps in the same direction. If a gap does not appear and there is no chance of a pass then the player should be intelligent and mature enough to move away and look to make space elsewhere. If this also fails then the player returns to his previous position and tries again etc. This constant mobility is fundamental as it unsettles the opposition and keeps them on their toes. This constant movement causes defenders to be 'dragged' around the pitch, perhaps towards one wing only for

a diagonal ball to be played to the other, leaving a player in space in front of goal.

4. The best way to 'unlock' a well-organized and disciplined defense is to play the 'one-two' and the 'overlap' on the wings. If a player can produce an in-swinging or out-swinging cross (by putting 'swerve' on the ball using the inside or outside of the foot) from the wing this is very unsettling for any defense, however organized. If the ball is struck with pace the advantage is with the on-coming forwards who unlike the defenders are facing the goal.

5. The only way to achieve real attacking success is to have the necessary ability and technique to be able to use the ball effectively despite the lack of time and space. The attacks usually involve 4-6 players playing at 'breakneck' speed (I am not referring to the final stages of the move) so it is essential that they all communicate and collaborate effectively.

6. In this section I am referring to the attack and the difficulties involved in initiating and creating offensive play. In my opinion the best way to arrive at the opposition's goal with a clear advantage is via a swift counterattack. The ability to quickly turn defense into attack is a top priority in the modern game. The best teams in the 1994 World Cup scored 60% of their goals after winning the ball from the opposition. Once the ball was won the speed of the counterattack did not give the opposition time to get back into position and re-organize. These counterattacks usually started from the defensive or midfield areas and took no more than three to five passes on average.

7. The counterattack is such an important tactic that it should be well-rehearsed in training so that when the ball is won the move is so quick that the opposition do not have a chance to react. In order to achieve this rapid response time the player who wins the ball needs to be aware that if he touches it three times (if more, this is a disaster!) any advantage disappears and the chance has gone. The same problem arises if the player on the balls lacks the necessary technical and tactical skills, or if his teammates are too far from the play or they

make a poor run. Unlike a normal attack where precision is the most important element, the essential factor in the counter-attack is speed. For this reason, the number of touches taken is in direct proportion to the effectiveness of the move.

**8.** Any player who hopes to attack or counterattack effectively needs the following attributes: an excellent combination of creativity, peripheral vision, spatial awareness, timing and technical skills. If the player also has an excellent positional sense and a good 'soccer-brain' and is able to play at speed then he is well-equipped to resolve any situation that occurs during a game.

**9.** Do not make the move 'too creative' and complicated as the best moves in soccer are the simple and direct ones. If I had to summarize what I mean in one phrase I would say: "Try to position yourself in the zone where your teammate has the ball (at the back, in midfield or up front), and you are faced by only one opponent. It seems quite simple but in reality it is not and the players need to be able to play well on a collective basis: one goes away from his teammate on the ball (perhaps to 'drag' a defender away in what is called a 'dispersion' tactic) while the other runs to the side of his teammate on the ball and close to the opponent who is trying to win it. This is a fundamental idea in attacking strategy.

**10.** Quick speed of execution is another pre-requisite to good attacking play. Any player with this ability has a real advan-tage when it comes to initiating and creating attacking moves. Research into the subject has highlighted the fact that speed of execution and performance are directly related. In other words, players with this ability perform far better than players who do not have it.

*Bakero was not quick but he always lost his marker, he was not tall but always did well in the air, he did not have a good shot but managed to score lots of goalsÖ What was his secret? He understood the 'logic' of the game. He could see how a move was likely to develop and so he anticipated quicker than the opposition. This is how he managed to win so many trophies.*

## Natural Ability vs Soccer 'Intelligence'

Continuing the theme of the attack I would like to make reference to some important considerations that I feel are of interest to coaches and players alike:

**a)** It is very important that coaches accept players with the ability to create and 'make things happen' even if this is not done using a 'classic' style.

**b)** At the same time, if the coach is fully convinced that the player is able to produce difficult skills (shooting from distance, slide rule passes, playing 'one-touch') then he should give him his full support and backing. He should encourage him to 'create' without worrying about making a mistake or letting anyone down. When the move goes horribly wrong, keep the player's confidence high and encourage him to try again and again.

**c)** For his part, the player should be fully aware of his strengths and weaknesses and should always try to play to his strengths during a match and reach his full potential. However, the worst thing that can happen is for a player to play beyond his own capabilities. I am not just referring to attackers as some defenders do not keep the game simple by playing to their strengths.

**d)** Who has ever seen Hugo Sanchez or Bakero go on a dribble? No one, because they always got into space, received the ball, passed or made an attempt on goal. These players did with 'one-touch' what other players did with three or four. They were brilliant at making space and getting behind defenders and they instinctively knew how to be in the right place at the right time especially when close to the opposition's goal.

**e)** Of all the defenders I have had the privilege of coaching, Migueli was probably the best. But he only succeeded because he accepted his own limitations and based his game on a tenacious and uncanny aptitude for stopping the opposition. If he had tried to play a creative role similar to that played by Schuster, then he would have disappeared into mediocrity.

**f)** Another example is Guardiola and Redondo. The Argentinean is a formidable player, strong and determined with an excellent technique and if given enough space he is a good dribbler of the ball. But he does not make the most of his qualities. Too often he battles his way through and perhaps he makes it to the edge of the opposition's box but this does not help his team as invariably he holds on to the ball too long (he did this less with Capello) and gives the opposition plenty of time to get into position. Guardiola on the other hand is perhaps not as naturally gifted as Redondo but he has a tremendous 'soccer-brain' and always knows what to do with the ball. Before he receives it he generally has two options in his mind and he always chooses the best one. Because of his intelligence he is able to take up perfect positions and does not have to rely on making a hard challenge to win the ball. If a player does not have to compete on a physical level with the opposition then it does not matter if he is 'slight' like Guardiola or 'strong' like Redondo. In other words, Guardiola is the less gifted player on paper but makes the most of the qualities he has and plays to his strengths, whereas Redondo is a formidable player on paper but he fails to fulfill his potential.

**g)** The players should realize that they all play important but diverse roles during a match. A player who carries out a less glamorous role and perhaps 'grafts' for 90 minutes should console himself with the fact that he is playing an invaluable role for the team. The 'stars' of the team should reflect on the words by the 'Great' Benito Diaz: "Nobody can appreciate the sweat and toil of the bricklayers more than the architects". By the same token nobody should appreciate the efforts made by the rest of the team more than the main beneficiaries, the 'stars' (unless they are totally egotistical and conceited).

**h)** The 'stars' and talented creative players are generally the most difficult to control and coach. It is up to the coach to appreciate the player's talent and to convince him that he should use it for the benefit of the team.

**i)** Despite what I have just said, however talented a player might be there is one thing he certainly will not have learned due to his inexperience and that is when best to make his contribution. Just as an actor in the theater needs to make his entrance on cue so too does the soccer player. Sometimes a player is too willing to show how good he is and intervenes when he should not or perhaps is over-elaborate and instead of helping the team causes unnecessary problems. The player should be patient and only participate when the time is right. Perhaps he takes part less but when he does it is with more success. He produces quality, not quantity.

There is no question that if two equally balanced sides with a similar game-plan and similar technical and physical characteristics play each other, the winner will be the team which has more players with a good 'soccer-brain'. These players are able to analyze and adapt to any situation as it occurs throughout a game.

## Why Players Analyze

Having read the above it makes sense that the players find out as much as they can about the opposition before the game. Of course, the same thing is done by the coach in order to analyze the main factors that are likely to influence the outcome of the game:

- The system of play used by both teams.

- Strengths and weaknesses of their own players or of players in the opposition.

- The condition of the pitch (dry, wet, snow, ice etc.).

- The crowd, the referee and linesmen.

- Specific things that take place during the match (injuries, substitutions, a sending off. Difficult to predict, I know, but nothing is ruled out).

Once the game starts, the coach controls the overall style and play of the team but the players on the pitch can help out by using their initiative to resolve tactical problems as they arise during the match. Any player who is not good tactically and relies on stamina and brute strength has a limited future in the modern. game. The winning team will have players able to analyze and adapt accordingly thanks to their tactical understanding, knowledge and 'soccer-brain'.

Here are some examples of common tactical dilemmas that any player has to deal with during a game:

**1.** Each player needs to be fully familiar with the strengths and weaknesses of the players around him.

**2.** He should be familiar with the strengths and weaknesses of the player he is marking.

**3.** He should be aware of and monitor the physical and mental condition of the opposition throughout the game.

**4.** He should be aware of which players in the opposition have been 'booked' in order to exploit the situation.

**5.** The player should be aware of the situations in the game when his team has numerical advantage or numerical inferiority in order to use his 'soccer-brain' to try to repeat the former and also try to stop the latter from reoccurring.

**6.** The player should take note of how strict the referee is and how he applies the rules (especially number 11 (the 'offside' rule) and number 12 (fouls and dissent).

**7.** The player also needs to think in order to resolve certain situations as they occur on the field of play . The coach once had exclusive responsibility for such considerations but now the player himself needs to find a solution for certain questions as they arise: the opposition is running the midfield. Why? What can we do to change the situation?

**8.** The opposition is playing very deep and there is no way of getting through, especially as they are also dominant in the air. What should we do? Try speculative long shots? Perhaps try changing the direction of play to see if that unsettles them?

**9.** The opposition has worked out that one of our midfield players is not strong defensively and so is attacking incessantly trying to exploit this situation. What can be done on the pitch to resolve this problem?

**a)** Force the player to defend (even though this is not his strength)?

**b)** Let him continue attacking freely and creatively and use other players in the team to fill the space he leaves?

**10.** Our best striker is being marked out of the game. What should we do?

**a)** Support him a lot more to give him more options when in a '1 v 1' with his marker?

**b)** Direct the play away from this area as possession is always being lost?

**c)** Change his position as he not proving effective against such a well-disciplined marker?

Up to this point in time the clubs have been responsible for signing new players. Ideally, these signings should be made for the following reasons: the player will make the team better and more competitive and he will fit in nicely at the club. The style of soccer played at the club suits the player and he will fill a position that is not well covered at present. Unfortunately, this is what usually happens : the president visits the representative to sign a fast attacker and ends up coming away with a technically gifted midfield player. The club has no need for another midfield player but the representative assures the president that he is something special and that if he does not sign him his 'arch enemy' and main rival will.

In the future it will not just be the clubs looking for the best player. But the players themselves will want to sign, not for the club that pays more (all the top players earn a fortune anyway) but for the club where the following circumstances do not exist:

**1.** The club and the player play different styles and he would not fit into this system.

**2.** The club and the player agree on the style of play but the new signing does not best compliment the more senior players in the team. If the new player has outstanding vision and intelligence and he is able to play wonderful passes all over the pitch, but his work-rate is not his strength then he needs team-mates who are able to run and take advantage of his creativity. The older players will be unable to take advantage of his talents and they will not be happy with this situation.

**3.** The player needs to check before he signs that the club does not have a player of similar characteristics who is 'in form' because if this is the case then he may spend a lot of time on the bench.

# Understanding Strategy

What I mean by strategy is the pre-rehearsed game-plan and lineup that the player adopts when the game starts or resumes after an interruption. So the strategy is used for throw-ins, corners, goal-kicks, free-kicks, penalties and drop-ball situations. Obviously, the strategy can be defensive or offensive.

This book would be incomplete if I did not dedicate a chapter to this topic so that the players have an opportunity of becoming outstanding players as far as this most important facet of the game is concerned. A game is stopped on numerous occasions for lots of different reasons (throw-ins alone make up a sixth of the playing time) so it makes sense to get them to practice a relevant strategy to prepare themselves for these stoppages during training.

During the 1994 World Cup 40% of the goals resulted from a foul, corner, throw-in or penalty. Also, it is significant that Athlético de Madrid won the league title in 1996 after scoring 49% of their goals from these 'dead ball' situations. They scored 75 goals, 37 of which came from these situations. This is how the goals were distributed:

263

- Penalties, 11 goals (14.5%)

- Corners, 11 goals (14.5%)

- Throw-ins, 6 goals (8%)

- Direct free-kicks, 5 goals (7%)

- Indirect free-kicks, 4 goals (5%)

This was achieved despite the fact that these situations are not given a high priority during training. Some coaches do not practice these strategies because the players do not enjoy the monotonous and repetitive nature of the exercises. It is difficult to understand this attitude as the players are professionals who work for the club and for the coach and not the other way around. Rehearsing in the theater or for a film or any team sport is always monotonous, repetitive and hard going at times but...

As I have already mentioned, the tactical evolution of the game means that players with greater intelligence and a good 'soccer-brain', able to improvise and use their initiative, are more likely to do well. The player who daydreams and lacks concentration is a serious weak-link in any team and the opposition will never be taken by surprise by a strategic move (the reverse may happen however) if he is unable to think-quickly and act decisively. These days more than ever, soccer players need to be alert and ready to react to any situation during a match for the benefit of the team.

In conclusion, it is always important for a team to gain any advantage it can and the use of 'set' moves from 'dead ball' situations can be the decisive factor that turns the match in their favor. These strategies should not be thought of as mere formations or organizational systems put into practice every time there is a stop in play, but instead as potentially match-winning situations.

Any team has the possibility of gaining an advantage from a 'dead-ball' situation from anywhere on the pitch and these often lead to goal-scoring opportunities. If the team waits for the 'specialist' to arrive, time is wasted. The opposition is allowed to get into position and this rules out the surprise factor. All the players at The School are constantly reminded about the need for urgency and quick-thinking at dead-ball situations.

Nevertheless, despite the need for speed, it is very important to have dead-ball 'specialists' in the team ready to take the 'free kick', corner, penalty or throw-in (the latter is seen less and less these days). It is imperative to have at least one 'free kick' specialist in the team and if possible two or three who can produce wonderful curling or powerful shots from any area within striking distance. Apart from the goal that may result, the craft and sheer beauty of the little 'work of art' is always a special moment in any game. As the free kick is about to be taken the whole ground takes on a mystical atmosphere: the 'specialist' prepares to show his quality, his teammates are hoping he can produce what he does in training, the opposition hope the technique goes wrong and the crowd are full or emotion and expectancy.

Even though it was 40 years ago I can still remember a match I played for Racing against Barcelona with the 'Great' Kubala who took free kicks with majestic style and brilliance even when confronted by a 'wall'. When he first arrived in Spain he scored lots of goals from free kicks, putting both power and swerve on the ball. The ball invariably went over or around the 'wall' and ended up in the net with the goalkeeper on the other side of the goal.

I remember Kubala had a free kick on the edge of the area in that game. As he placed the ball the crowd went strangely quiet with keen expectation as he stood next to it and observed the goalkeeper (normally players stand back from the ball in order to take a run-up and gain momentum). The goalkeeper was well aware of his talent and kept as alert as possible and nervously patrolled his goal-line ready to jump and or dive. The 'claret and blue' player deliberately took an extremely long time to take the kick and the goalkeeper's muscles were becoming stiff because of the tension. By the time the kick was taken the goalkeeper could not even manage a jump and could do nothing but watch the ball fly into the net. Immediately the crowd leapt to its feet and the ground was filled with a cacophony of cheers and applause. This atmosphere was impressive and overwhelming and it seemed almost as if the crowd was bearing down on us and 'stamping' us underfoot (I am sure the Barcelona players had different sensations and emotions).

Without doubt, the Brazilians are the 'crème de la crème' when it comes to free kicks. They have such a prodigious talent that they are able to score by playing the ball right through the middle of the 'wall' (this is extremely difficult as there are so many players in the way) thanks to a piece of individual genius. No matter what the technique, the opposition knows that if they commit a foul near their area there is a strong possibility that the ensuing free kick will result in a goal. These goals are not a result of intricate moves formulated in the 'laboratory'. They are direct shots on goal and the Brazilians shoot from close range and from distances that are unthinkable for 'mere mortals'. Of course each team has at least three players who are genuine 'dead-ball' specialists. Brazil has taken part in every World Cup and has scored goals from free kicks in each tournament. The first of these goal-scorers was the legendary Leonidas, and others followed such as Ademir, Didi, Pele, Garrincha, Rivelinho, Dirceu, Nelinho, Zico, Eder, Bebeto and the list goes on...

But Brazil is not the only country in the world that produces wonderful 'dead-ball' specialists. Argentina has produced players such as Maradona (a prodigious goal-scorer) whose shots swerved and dipped as if by 'magic' and Scotta who struck the ball with so much power that it almost broke the net. Then there was the Peruvian player Cubillas who kicked the ball with such a 'super-human' technique with the outside of his right foot that it swerved so violently it left a 'smoke trail' as it entered the goal.

There have also been great European 'free kick' specialists such as Kubala, Eusebio, Bobby Charlton, Puskas, Luis Aragones and Platini to name but a few. I have already made reference to wonderful talents of Kubala and Puskas. Eusebio had a terrific shot whereas Bobby Charlton and Pele had the added advantage of being able to shoot just as brilliantly with both feet (although the former was not as technically gifted as the Brazilian). Of all the European players, Platini came as close as anybody to playing like a 'Brazilian'. His control over the ball was so complete that he was able to bend free kicks around the 'wall' to the left, to the right or above or right through the middle. Luis Aragones was a wonderful 'dead ball' specialist thanks to his 'soccer brain' and his vision. When he was about to take a 'free kick' he would move the ball back a few yards. Usually players try to get closer to the goal so when Aragones made his move the opposition in the 'wall' looked on and did nothing about it, thinking he was doing them a favor. This was a mistake on their part. A goal is 2.44 meters high and the 'wall' usually blocks 1.80 meters. In other words, leaving a target of 64 centimeters for the player taking the free kick to aim at. If the ball is moved back just one meter this means that the 'wall' blocks 1.60 meters and therefore gives the shooter a target of 84 centimeters.

# Pele and the 'Dry Leaf'

Pele's free kicks were both spectacular and used an economy of effort. This is what Menotti ( a former teammate of his) had to say about his free kicks: "I have seen him score lots of fantastic goals. He used to stand next to the ball and then 'caress' the ball with the inside or outside of his right or left foot. It was impressive to watch".

In 1982 in Barcelona I had the chance to ask Pele the secret of his free kick technique and that of the Brazilians in general. This is what he had to say: "The truth is that the ability is handed down from generation to generation by watching and learning from all the 'great' players Brazil has had over the years. Hard work and dedication is the other vital ingredient and like many of my teammates I stayed behind after training practicing taking shots at goal until I perfected the technique. As a boy I was a big fan of Didi and I tried to emulate his awe-inspiring technique by practicing and then practicing some more. When I started playing for the National team I began to develop my own 'special' way of taking free kicks. I was never able to produce his 'Folha seca' (literally means 'the dry leaf' - a ball that is kicked high and then dips suddenly taking the goalkeeper totally by surprise) but perhaps I kick the ball with more power".

We cannot leave out Koeman and Ivan de la Peña from this list of European 'dead ball' specialists. The Dutch player's free kicks were always struck with great power and precision and often ended up in the back of the goal. Barcelona won its first and only European Cup thanks to the fact that his free kick was able to 'power' its way through the 'wall'. There is no doubt that the brilliant Laudrup and company and the many goals scored by Stoichkov owed a lot to Koeman even though he was not directly involved in the majority of the moves. This is because the opposition were always worried about making a challenge or interception near their own goal in case they gave away a free kick conscious of the fact that Koeman was on the pitch. This was a real advantage for all his teammates.

As far as Ivan is concerned I think he has the potential to become one of the all-time 'Greats' at 'dead ball' situations and that his name would not look out of place alongside the others I have just mentioned. He has a fantastic right foot and has the uncanny ability of to be able to place the ball with power and precision wherever he chooses. All that is needed is for his teammates (the free kick specialists) to let him take a few and not be so greedy. This is history repeating itself as Pele and Maradona had the exact same problem with their teammates when they started out in the game.

## Koeman's Free Kicks

When Koeman was playing for Barcelona I had the opportunity to talk to various first division referees, separately, on different occasions and was amazed at their attitude towards the Catalan players.

Each referee told me the same: "I could have given a foul in Barcelona's favor but I played the advantage and let play continue. I was amazed to receive an immediate protest from the claret and blue players. Of course, I explained that I had played advantage but they told me, "We do not want you to play advantage, we want the free kick". The referees went on to say: "We can't win, if we blow for a foul the players want to play the advantage and vice versa."

However this was not the case with the Barça players as they always wanted the free kick to be taken by Koeman. But the referees never quite understood this concept.

It is a shame that England (the country that introduced the game to the rest of the world) has not been able to develop and progress as far in this facet of the game. Apart from notable exceptions such as Bobby Charlton, Glen Hoddle and now David Beckham, this country is not renowned for producing brilliant dead ball specialists. Perhaps because of this they have tried all forms of imaginative ways of taking free kicks such as the one used by Carr and Hunt. Carr 'took' the free kick by placing the ball between his feet and jumping, thus 'flicking' the ball up in the air. Hunt stood close by and

*Laudrup and Koeman, both excellent players and 'long ball' specialists. They complimented each other: Laudrup won lots of free kicks thanks to his fantastic dribbling ability and Koeman scored from the resulting 'dead ball' situation usually with a 'pile driver'.*

269

hit the ball on the volley which often got beyond the 'wall' resulting in a goal. There was a protest made to FIFA ( I am talking over 30 years ago) and the organization decided that free kicks could only be taken using one foot. This law is still in effect today and it would be nice if somebody in FIFA would change this rule and others like it as at present the odds are stacked against the attack and are very much in favor of the defense.

All of the players I have just mentioned have one thing in common. They practiced for hour after hour shooting at goal from every conceivable angle They all started from a very young age and (most importantly) practiced more than ever when they reached the highest level in the game. Platini took full advantage of the soccer equipment at Nancy. He stayed behind after every training session to practice repeatedly taking free-kicks confronted by a 'wall' of 'plastic' players. This piece of training equipment is commonplace nowadays and now every player in every club is able to practice taking free kicks when faced by a 'wall'.

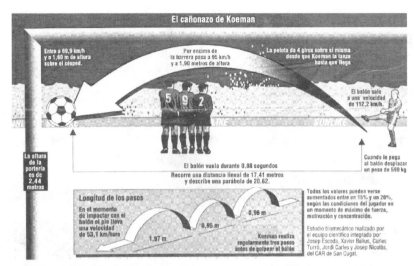

Entra a 69,9 km/h y a 1,60 m de altura sobre el césped.

Por encima de la barrera pasa a 95 km/h y a 1,90 metros de altura

La pelota da 4 giros sobre sí misma desde que Koeman la lanza hasta que llega

El balón sale a una velocidad de 112,2 km/h.

La altura de la portería es de 2,44 metros

El balón vuela durante 0,88 segundos
Recorre una distancia lineal de 17,41 metros y describe una parábola de 20,62.

Cuando le pega al balón desplazar un peso de 590 kg

Longitud de los pasos

En el momento de impactar con el balón el pie lleva una velocidad de 53,1 km/hora

0,96 m
0,95 m
1,97 m

Koeman realiza regularmente tres pasos antes de golpear el balón

Todos los valores pueden verse aumentados entre un 15% y un 20%, según las condiciones del jugador en un momento de máximo de fuerza, motivación y concentración.

Estudio biomecánico realizado por el equipo científico integrado por Josep Escoda, Xavier Balius, Carles Turró, Jordi Carles y Josep Nicolás, del CAR de San Cugat.

*Koeman's 'pile driver' - The Catalan Television program 'Atac i Gol' presented these 3-Dimensional images of Koeman's free kick. The research was carried out by Car of Sant Cugat. The picture comes from the newspaper 'El Pais'.*

**270**

If a player wants to become a 'Great' free kick specialist he should practice 40-60 kicks a day, every day of every month of every year. But before he does, he should make sure that he has mastered the very difficult technique of putting curl and dip on the ball. This technique is rarely used by the majority of professionals, not because they do not want to but because they do not have the necessary ability to produce the effect.

Here is some advice on how to produce the technique using the inside and the outside of the foot:

**1.** The end of the boot must be placed under the ball and the contact is made at the start and outside of the big toe, causing the ball to take a swerving trajectory. This technique means that the ball does not travel with tremendous pace and power. So, in order for this technique to be effective the player must practice generating as much speed and power as possible without losing accuracy.

**2.** If the player prefers using the outside of his foot (Physical characteristics have a lot to do with this as the 'bow-legged' prefer to use the inside of the foot and the 'knock-kneed' the outside of the foot) he should approach the ball as if moving slightly to the side of it. If the right foot is used then the approach should be from the left of the intended direction of the ball. If the left foot is used the opposite is true. Regardless of which part of the foot is being used, the inside or the outside, the back-lift should be as full as possible right through from the hip and knee while the arms are used for balance. If striking the ball with the outside of the foot, the point of contact is made along the length of the little toe.

The power is generated from the hip and the foot points inwards as much as the ankle will allow. The foot is kept pointing downwards and the body is inclined from the hip as the ball is struck. Just as when shooting with the inside of the foot, the important consideration is to master the technique first and then work on producing power. Any player who achieves this will make life very difficult for goalkeepers.

3. The next stage is a bit more complicated. It involves judging the height, speed, distance and the amount of swerve the shot requires. The 'chanfle' shot ( This is a word used in Argentina for putting swerve on the ball using the inside or outside of the foot) involves kicking the ball over the third or fourth player in the 'wall', which is not easy. Any player who masters all of the above and can swerve and dip shots over or around any 'wall' will be an invaluable 'dead ball' specialist in any team.

*The 'chanfle' shot*

# The Olympic Goal

Years ago a team that won a corner was virtually assured of scoring a goal from it but these days it is just another 'dead ball' situation. A lot of the blame for this lies with the coaches and players who lack creativity, imagination and are not able or willing to try something new and improvisational. Instead of trying a surprising and innovative move the player invariably takes no chances physically or mentally and merely crosses the ball to the near or far post.

There are lots of different ways to take a corner kick. The fact that not many diverse and interesting moves are seen means that the players are not able to take advantage of the situation and punish the opposition at this moment of potential vulnerability. Corners can be taken short or kicked a medium distance, hit low or medium height or long to the far post, directed straight at goal, in-swinging, out-swinging etc. This is why I find it difficult to understand what Menotti means when he says that corners should not be taken with the 'wrong' foot (the right foot from the right corner and the left from the left) as this gives the advantage to the defenders. At first glance this opinion seems to make perfect sense, but very few things are straightforward in soccer. Let me remind the Argentinean coach that many goals have been scored over the years using the 'chanfle' technique and the 'wrong' foot. The Uruguayan team were Olympic champions in 1924 in France and on their return the Argentineans offered to play them in a homage to the victorious team. The Argentineans won 1-0 and the goal was scored by Onzari from a corner using his 'wrong' foot. This was the first time that this type of goal had been scored and the Argentineans called it the Olympic goal. Since then there have been many players who have scored from corners: Roig was a two-footed Celta player in the 1940's who scored goals from either side using the wrong foot. Pepe, playing for Santos and a teammate of Pele's (and come to think of it, Menotti's as well) also scored lots of goals from corners. Other players such as Kubala, Matthews, Landaburu, Schuster, Platini, Ginola, Pantic and Ivan de la Peña were, and in some cases still are, masters at taking corners. Remember, a player cannot be 'offside' from a corner and can stand on the goal-line. With so many players crowded into a small space it is often very difficult for the goalkeeper to get to the ball effectively. This was one of the successful ploys used by A. Madrid during the 1995-96 season.

Finally I will remind any player who wants to master this technique that the key to success is total dedication and practice. The player needs to practice each of the many possibilities and see which one suits him best because some will come more naturally than others. It is strange fact, but usually the free kick specialist is also excellent at taking corners and an impressive penalty taker. This makes sense because the three disciplines all require similar qualities: reliability, concentration, power and accuracy.

Another technique that is often ignored in the modern game is the throw-in. This technique is often a very dangerous 'dead-ball' situation if taken quickly. Years ago a misguided coach came up with the idea that only the wingers could take the throw-ins. This

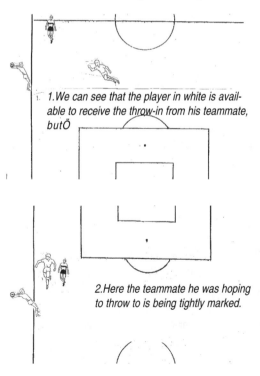

1. We can see that the player in white is available to receive the throw-in from his teammate, butÖ

2. Here the teammate he was hoping to throw to is being tightly marked.

was where I got the idea for turning this seemly innocuous move into a very successful move that I began during my playing days and later practiced with beginners and professionals alike as a coach. A forward collects the ball that has gone out of play for a throw-in. A teammate is in space some distance away and he runs towards the thrower asking to be thrown the ball. By the time he gets close enough to the thrower and is given the ball he is being marked and so the surprise factor has been lost.

The idea I advocate is that any player in the team can take the throw and take advantage of the speed element. What I am proposing does not mean that there is no need for a 'specialist', as the more possibilities and options a team has at its disposal the better. If a throw cannot be taken quickly or the opposition are marking tightly then a 'specialist' can turn the 'dead ball' situation into a virtual corner by throwing with power and precision right to the danger area with no fear of 'offside'. Juanmi plays for Elche and has the ability to throw the ball to the far post which often causes panic and chaos in the penalty box and results in a goal.

*Juanmi, known at Elche as 'the last of the Mohicans'.*

I recommend that players practice the throw-in technique by playing games, using apparatus and medicine balls of different weights. These should be performed on the run because the ball travels much further than when adopting a standing throw-in technique.

Even better, try copying Changez Khan's technique that was made famous throughout the world thanks to the media interest.

Khan played for Stafford Rangers, an English fourth division semi-professional team. His claim to fame was that he could launch the ball 60 yards from a throw-in. He did this by taking a run-up, producing a 'death-defying' summersault, landing on two feet (in accordance with the rules) and launching the ball thanks to the impetus this spectacular acrobatic jump generated.

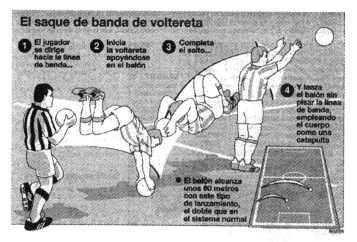

*Kahn's innovative throw-in technique made headlines around the world. This is how 'El Pais' covered the story via Reuters.*

The acrobatic throw-in.

1. The player heads towards the touchline...
2. He starts the somersault balancing on the ball.
3. He finishes the acrobatic move.
4. He throws the ball without stepping on the touchline, using his body as a catapult.
The throw reaches a distance of 60 yards using this technique - twice the average distance using the orthodox style.

At first, the referees were divided as to the legality of such an unusual move. So much so that when such a throw-in rebounded off a post and was kicked into the back of the net the referee disallowed the goal for 'unsporting conduct'.

But there was a problem, Kahn needed plenty of space adjacent to the pitch in order to generate the speed for his technique but most of the pitches in England were close to the crowd and did not provide the necessary width he needed. This was even the case in his home ground. Earlier I mentioned how Koeman's mere presence on the pitch made the opposition nervous about giving away free kicks near their own goal. Well, the team playing against Stafford Rangers were given different instructions: "Don't kick the ball out for a throw anywhere near the tunnel and the changing rooms because Kahn will take it".

Later the 'The College of Referees' approached FIFA for a definitive answer as to the legality of such a throw-in. The throw-in was considered to be perfectly legal as it did not contravene any of the rules and regulations of the game.

# The Penalty Kick: Kubala, Pele and Koeman

The penalty kick is without doubt the most emotive part of the game. It is an event that keeps the fans on the edge of their seats. This is because while there is a good probability that a goal will be scored, there is always the possibility that the chance will be squandered.

There are many ways to take a penalty and these different styles depend largely on the individual characteristics of the players who take them. Some players try to 'break' the back of the net and others prefer to play a 'slide-rule' pass into the corner of the goal. The technique used depends on the strengths and weaknesses of the penalty taker.

Having said that, the best penalty takers in the history of the game (as far as penalties taken, penalties scored), Kubala, Pele and Koeman, all used a virtually identical technique: they all stood a long way back from the ball (Kubala not quite as far) and ran towards it facing the left post ( to the right of the player). The approach to the ball was followed by a temporary pause or adjustment (Pele's famous 'Paradinha') and they made a clean strike to their right, towards the post they were facing with the inside of the ankle. This was their 'trade mark' penalty kick but if they saw that the goalkeeper was making a move in that direction then they made a quarter-turn and shot to their left using the inside of the instep.

Pele's movement as he was about to strike the ball was a contentious issue. Many people felt it was illegal because the penalty taker was not allowed to 'dummy' the kick as a way of fooling the goalkeeper. After close scrutiny (watching examples

*Pele and his famous 'Paradinha'.*
Notice his sheer 'class'. He was such a 'maestro' that when he took a penalty his teammates and the opposition took the outcome for granted. ¡What's the point of running for a possible rebound when a goal is inevitable?¡ ( Pele seen here in a France v Brazil game).

on film) the conclusion was that it was not a 'dummy' but an adjustment to his run-up and so his technique was seen as perfectly correct and within the rules. It is perfectly acceptable for a player to take a long or short run-up or he can have no run-up at all choosing to stand next to the ball (I do not recommend this) and the movement can be continuous or disjointed.

Of course there are other ways to take a penalty kick but statistics show that they are not as effective as the one I have just mentioned. Di Stefano, Gento, Neeskens, Kempes and Hugo Sanchez used the full instep to generate as much power as possible. They often kicked the ball straight towards the middle of the goal confident that goalkeepers would dive to one side or the other in anticipation.

I think that the mental strength, character and temperament of a player are essential factors in determining his penalty-taking technique. Taking a penalty when the team is winning 4-0 is relatively simple and straightforward but taking one in the last minute of an important match with the score level requires a cool head and nerves of steel.

Rinus Michels, a coach for so many years at Ajax, Barcelona and the Dutch team, never made his players practice taking penalty kicks because he believed it was impossible to simulate the tension and atmosphere present during a real match. This is an extreme view and using the same argument all training sessions would be a waste of time. Nevertheless I can see the point he was trying to make: it is one thing taking a penalty during the relaxed atmosphere of a training session and totally different when compared to taking one in an important match where the pressure is immense and the responsibility on the player to score makes him nervous and anxious not to fail.

The self-confidence of the player is usually the difference between success and failure and this is often determined by how well he is playing during the game. I was responsible for taking numerous penalty kicks during my playing days and I sometimes thought to myself: "This is all I need. I'm already having a poor game and things will get even worse if I miss." It is imperative that the penalty taker is on top form on the day. This is why as a coach I choose three penalty takers before a match and I tell them that I will decide who takes the kick depending on who I think is playing the best at the time.

I strongly recommend that you try to emulate the technique used by Kubala, Pele and Koeman: changing the pace of the run-up and watching out for any movement made by the goalkeeper that may help you decide where to place the ball. This technique is all about repetition so if you practice and work hard you will become good at it. But do not forget that just as important as the technique is mental toughness and excellent concentration levels.

I would like to point out (to players and coaches alike) that when a penalty is about to be taken the goalkeeper must stand on his line, but not necessarily in the middle. He can position himself next to one of the posts if he likes.

I explain this to the players and I encourage the goalkeeper to stand slightly to one side of the goal, leaving the other more 'exposed'. This is especially the position I encourage if the penalty is important and the player taking it will have a heavy weight of

# Venables and Luis

What I mentioned about how players should adapt to the circumstances of the game might sound obvious, but unfortunately professional soccer players are creatures of habit and show little aptitude for innovative and creative ideas.

In 1983 the English coach Terry Venables came to Barcelona and won the league title thanks largely to his tight defensive unit that played the 'pressing' game and goals achieved from 'set pieces'.

This was one of the 'set pieces' used with great affect to score lots of goals: two players would stand near the ball when a 'free kick' was given near a corner in the opposition's half. Four or five players would take up a position in the box (one behind the other) all ready to attack the ball and try to score. The player at the front was Alexanco. This is how the moved works: one of the players near the ball runs towards it. At the same time Alexanco turns and runs to the back of the queue of players. As this happens, the rest of the Barcelona players in the area run to the near post and take their markers with them as it seems these players are causing the threat. In fact, the ball was crossed deep to the far post to the now unmarked Alexanco who often scored from these situations.

Barcelona used this technique to score two goals against Athletico Madrid. Luis Aragones (a smart coach) spotted the move and decided that it was a good tactic for his team to use, especially as there were two tall defenders in the side (Ruiz and Arteche). He explained it to the team and they practiced the move and managed to score several goals using the tactic.

On the return match with Barcelona, Luis remembered the two goals his team conceded and asked his team to watch out for the move this time around. One player was even asked not to take the bait and stay back waiting for Alexanco to make his run.

The strange thing was that after only a couple of minutes Alexanco scored! Sometimes even though you know a move is likely to happen it is still difficult to defend against.

*This Venables 'set play' involves Alexanco trying to get behind his marker as the first player approaches the ball.*

responsibility on his shoulders and will be nervous. So as he spots the 'strange' position of the goalkeeper, all sorts of things will go through his mind: "If I hit the ball as hard as I can I cannot be accurate enough to place it in that 'gap', or should I take it quickly? Perhaps I should call his bluff and shoot in his direction but what if he does not move?" Usually all these problems are too much for a player and they invariably do not score from the penalty kick.

Often, the ball is directed to the opposite side of the goal to where the goalkeeper is standing (sometimes it is kicked so far away from the goalkeeper that it misses the target completely). However, the confident and composed player will usually opt to kick the ball to the side of the goal where the goalkeeper is standing, after first 'feinting' to 'rifle' the ball to the opposite side.

This brings to mind three positive memories for me. In 1965 the Racing under 13's became Spanish champions by beating Real Sociedad on penalties. We took our five first (in those days one team took five and then the other team their five) and managed to score three goals. Our goalkeeper took up his position slightly to one side of the goal as the Real Sociedad players prepared to take their penalties. The first one headed straight for the 'gap' at a slow pace and chest-high and was easily saved. I noticed the 'brains' of the team was about to take the second one and so I made an appropriate signal to the goalkeeper. He 'feinted' to play the ball in one direction and then shot as hard as he could towards the 'gap' and surprise, surprise, the ball was saved by the goalkeeper. The third player took a long run-up and hit the ball as hard as he could. The ball missed the target and almost struck the referee who was some way away from the goal.

The second memory concerns a first division match between Celta (my team) and Real Sociedad (the fact that this recollection involves the same team is pure coincidence). We were winning 1-0 when part-way through the second half they were awarded a penalty. The goalkeeper (Hortas) took up his position slightly to one side of the goal and the penalty taker (Lopez Ufarte) stepped up to take the 'spot' kick. He 'dummied' to kick the ball towards the 'gap' and Hortas 'feinted' a move in this direction also, only to immediately dive the other way and save the ball.

The third experience took place in 1995. The School went to Toulouse to take part in the 'Violettes' tournament. The under 15's reached the final and the game went to penalties. We went first (now the five kicks are taken alternately) and both teams were successful with their first four penalties. We scored the last kick and then the French goalkeeper stepped up to take the fifth penalty for his team. Our goalkeeper was not familiar with the above technique (there are 1000 players at the school and only so many hours in a day to learn more important aspects of the game) but I could see that the opposition's goalkeeper was slightly demoralized because he had not saved any penalties, the score was 5-4 in the final, he was playing at home and he was under immense pressure to score. I told our goalkeeper to position himself slightly to one side of the goal. The French goalkeeper was looking down at the floor as he made his approach from a long way out. He looked up as he got near the ball and noticed the position of the goalkeeper and he stopped. Looking confused, he said to the referee, "The goalkeeper is in the wrong position." The referee replied that the goalkeeper's position was perfectly correct and that he had to take the penalty. By this time the French player had lost his nerve completely and his shot was so weak that our goalkeeper had to come off his line to reach the ball.

## Getting in Top Shape

Stamina, speed and explosive power are essential qualities for a soccer player, but the main emphasis of 'the method' is not to try to develop these to their full potential. This is simply because it takes too much time, exhausts the players and most importantly it gives the players less opportunity to improve technique and tactical skills in 'small-sided' games and matches. Remember, the best time to learn the skills and techniques of the game is from a very young age, whereas the best time to put more emphasis on physical fitness is when the players are adults.

All the players are 'soccer players' by the time they reach this advanced level and so now is the perfect time to concentrate more on the physical fitness aspect of the game in order to help them produce the technical and tactical skills throughout the entire 90 minutes.

However, when embarking on purely physical fitness work there are various things that the players and coaches need to bear in mind:

1. There are two basic types of muscle fiber: those that contract slowly ('red' ones) and those that contract quickly ('white' ones). In general the percentage of each is largely down to each player's own genetic makeup. The majority of soccer players tend to have a greater amount of fibers that contract quickly. However, when it comes to planning the training workload the coach needs to be familiar with the individual characteristics of each of his players as there are always a few exceptions in each team.

The 'red' fibers are more resistant and recover quickly from an intensive training session. On the other hand, if the exercises are based on speed and strength they are less effective and the recovery time is longer. For their part, the 'sprinters' (white fibers) are not designed for intense and prolonged sessions and take a long time to recover from these.

2. As we can see, there will be different responses to the same training session. For some players it will be ideal, others will struggle and some will find it difficult to cope. For example, if referring to a training session that concentrates on aerobic stamina, the 'sprinters' (those with more 'white' fibers) should not do the exercises with the same intensity as the 'long distance runners' (those with more 'red' fibers) as they will soon tire and the exercise will turn into an anaerobic one.

3. Conversely, if the exercise is a 'specific' stamina activity for soccer, the 'long distance runners' should be careful not to try to perform extremely quick explosive movements on a repeated basis. They also need longer rest periods during this type of exercise than the 'sprinters'. If this difference is not taken into account and all the players do the same exercise and have the same rest periods then only the 'sprinters' will get the full benefit and achieve the required objectives.

4. In summary, when carrying out stamina or speed training it is very important to know which of the players are naturally 'fast' with not much stamina and which players have more natural 'stamina' but lack explosive speed. The ideal is to meet the needs of the individual players. A team can usually be split up

into four or five groups of similar type players with each group doing different exercises that suit their physical characteristics. It is also very important to get feedback from the players to see if they think they are working at optimum capacity and taking the necessary recovery periods. An experienced senior player will know his strengths and weaknesses very well and he will be able to pace his activities expertly knowing when to do the 'sprints' and when and how long to rest in order to gain the full benefits from the training sessions.

5. It is a good idea to carry out stamina work as part of a game from time to time as this is the most complete training the players can do and it has the added advantage of preparing them for the 'real' matches. I say from time to time, because if stamina training is only done in this way the players may become 'conditioned' and may not be able to produce the same amount of effort under other circumstances. These games also put a tremendous strain on the players (bones, cartilage and tendons) which could easily result in an injury and the concentration levels are intense and so there is a strong possibility of over-exhaustion.

6. There are very few specific exercises and activities that concentrate exclusively on improving basic stamina. So the soccer player achieves a good level of aerobic and anaerobic stamina in a variety of different ways: during the competitive games throughout the season, exercises involving a ball and activities during the pre-season without a ball.

Resistance training can be done at the beginning of the session, in the middle or at the end. If the stamina work is carried out at the beginning it should be kept short because there is a risk that the players will be too exhausted to gain the full benefits of the rest of the session and in some cases they will not be able to continue under any circumstances. It is a good idea for any team that trains on a regular basis to do the stamina work halfway through each session. A team that trains on an occasional basis can incorporate the work alongside the technical and tactical considerations. Each training session should end with a relaxation period as this helps the recovery process.

This relaxation period with the pulse rate at 140 does not help to speed up the recovery process. But it does help to improve basic stamina levels (especially during the pre-season). It also helps the body to recover from the physical strain and keeps the player in generally good physical condition once he reaches the age of thirty. This period can also be used as part of the resistance work but the last 10 minutes has to take the form of a 'cool down' period.

## ◢ Great Player Needs Great Acceleration

Any run produces a curve made up of two parts. One indicates the speed off the mark and the other indicates the speed of the overall run itself. There does not have to be a correlation between these two factors as the explosive speed off the mark may be followed by a slow run, or the player can start slowly and gradually pick up speed. For this reason the coach should concentrate on explosive speed off the mark and overall speed of a

run over a certain distance as two separate considerations that require totally different training activities.

The most important physical characteristic a player needs is good acceleration. In other words, speed over a short distance. This makes sense because a player rarely has to run 40-50 yards when playing a game of soccer. Usually a player has to get into position quickly to jump, challenge, shoot, or come out of defense. It is also important to stop and change direction suddenly and land properly after a jump.

To give you an idea of the importance of acceleration speed the Italians Bosco and Margaria

*Ronaldo's two great strengths: his 'eye' for goal and his acceleration!*

both carried out separate research on the speed and acceleration of first, second and third division players (players in Serie A, B and C). They both came to the conclusion that although the speed of the players is similar in Serie A and C and slightly less in B, when it comes to acceleration and explosive speed off the mark the players in the first division are far superior.

This research along with my own experience leaves me in no doubt that players should monitor and develop their acceleration speed from this level right up until the end of their career. One way to check acceleration and monitor its development is by carrying out the following test:

1. The player gets an idea of his reaction and acceleration speed by running a distance of 15 yards from a standing start.

2. The player gets an idea of his potential speed by covering the same distance from a running start.

3. The player makes a note of the difference between the two times. This is a crucially important number and so the calculations should be as precise as possible.

These different disciplines should be trained for separately. However, there are a number of considerations that the player should be conscious of when trying to develop either speed off the mark or overall speed:

a) The time involved should be kept short (3-5 seconds) and the intensity should reach 95-100% of capacity. If the exercises are done at a medium pace this offers no benefits as they do not produce the necessary anaerobic activity. This can only be achieved by running at top speed. The players should be reminded that the idea is not merely to do the runs and technical activities correctly; the idea here is to go as fast as possible.

b) If the player is tired he can not produce his top speed because he lacks the necessary coordination skills as The Central Nervous System tries to cope with the strain. For this reason these exercises should be performed after the warm-up and stretching exercises.

**c)** If the player feels tired at any stage during this type of exercise he should take the necessary rest his body needs to recover. The player should take an 'active' but relaxing break from the exercise by going for a walk, jogging and stretching but if the tiredness persists he should not continue the exercise. If he continues under these circumstances, the activity reverts to a stamina-based exercise and he risks causing a muscle or tendon-related injury.

**d)** This type of exercise is only effective if the player is fully rested, he works 'flat-out' and the appropriate rest periods are taken. Just as with the stamina exercises, the frequency and length of the rest periods should meet the specific needs of each player. During resistance training it is appropriate to divide the team into small groups of players of similar ability. This is not possible with speed and acceleration training. This type of activity needs to be carried out on a strictly individual basis.

287

**e)** The length of the training and the amount of repetitions involved depends on the individual players. In general, 2-4 sets of 6-8 repetitions is usually enough. There should be a rest period of 2-4 minutes between each run and the break between sets should last about 10 minutes, during which time the player should carry out simple technical ball skills.

**f)** In summary, the only way to achieve the aims and objectives of these exercises is to do them properly and follow the correct procedure. There are no shortcuts! Any exercise of this type that is too long, with few breaks and of low intensity is a waste of time. Liesen suggests that the timing and the length of the breaks should be left up to the players as they know exactly how their body is coping with the exercises. Monitoring the pulse rate (which is particularly useful during stamina training) is not recommended during these exercises. If the player does the exercise, takes a short rest and then checks his pulse rate, the likelihood is that it will be satisfactory, but this does not indicate the high build-up of lactic acid in the muscles. The only way to get these levels back to normal is by taking a long rest.

There are lots of different ways to train to improve these two aspects and of course this includes games and exercises:

1. I think that it is a mistake to take long runs in order to improve speed because this creates a build-up of lactic acid in the muscles due to the effort and it neither helps develop acceleration nor sprint resistance. What it does help develop is improved stamina for a long run, which is of little interest to the soccer player. The best way to train for speed is over a distance of 15-25 yards, with various changes in direction and 2-3 interventions with a ball (pass or shot).

2. Acceleration on the other hand is best improved by running even shorter distances (5 -10 yards) with a standing start and preferably involving simulating match-like situations: movements in a confined space, twists and turns, sudden and dramatic changes in direction. All these movements should be done as fast as possible and they should always be performed with a ball.

3. As I have mentioned before this attribute is a natural ability. People are either born able to run quickly or not. Nevertheless there are some psychological factors that have an influence on the ability to run quickly. Speed can be generated by three main factors: natural ability, motivation and determination.

These three factors are fundamental. If they are present and used to the full the player will be able to generate more speed and accelerate more quickly. If the 'spark' is not present then the necessary chemicals and hormones are not released into the body and it is impossible to reach full potential. It is just the same as when adrenaline is released into the body in the 'fight or flight' situation. The body is motivated and prepared and performs on a higher level (albeit temporarily) thanks to the injection of 'energy'.

**4.** No player should do any intensive speed or acceleration training within a 48 hour period of a match (before or after). However, it is advisable to do a brief set of acceleration exercises the day before the match in order to 'wake' the players up and give them that final 'burst of energy'.

## Explosive Power

Training for explosive power is as you might imagine a demanding and strenuous activity that takes a lot out of the players. The intense concentration and effort involved means that the players become very tired and are unable to carry out activities that require precision and effort over the next few days. Obviously this type of training is not done before a match as the performance of the players is likely to be affected negatively and there is a serious danger of picking up an injury.

Nevertheless, it is very important for the professional soccer player to train every day so here is some advice for coaches and players alike:

- Training exercises involving explosive power should simulate as much as possible situations that occur in the game. If the player carries out a 'pure' explosive power exercise totally unrelated to soccer then he will improve his strength, but this will not be in the context of the game and so will not help his performance on the pitch.

- It is vital that these training exercises are performed as fast as possible and with total commitment. Anything less is a waste of time and will not produce the required objectives. For this reason the exercises should be carried out after the individual and general warm-up routines when the player is still fresh.

- As the training is so intense it should consist of 4-6 sets with 5-10 repetitions in each. The periods between each repetition should last between 2 ½ and 4 minutes and the player should keep active and perhaps do some stretching exercises. The rest periods between the sets should be approximately between 6-8 minutes depending on the players involved.

- Because these exercises are so intensive and demanding on the players they do not follow the usual rules of progression usually found in a training routine (starting off gently and then progressively requiring more and more effort). In this case the most difficult and exhausting parts should be carried out first.

- These types of exercises should not be performed by a player who has just recovered or is in the process of recovering from an injury. The player should be fully recovered and in top shape before attempting them. If at any time any player experiences pain or discomfort during the exercises he should refrain from doing them until he is in perfect condition.

Once the players have reached the age of 19 and if they have practiced 'the method' for many years they will have enviable technical skill and tactical awareness. However, some of the other qualities required in the game will not yet be as fully developed. Reporters, analysts, directors and coaches should all make allowances for the fact that at this young age the players are not fully developed physically and lack maturity. Furthermore it is up to the coach to help the players 'grow' and develop in these areas. Of course, there are always exceptions and there have been some very talented young players in the game such as Di Stefano, Gento, Suárez, Luis Aragonés, Netzer, Hugo Sánchez, Caminero and the German Muller etc. But even these players went through a difficult time at first and were accused of a lack of maturity, poor decision making, having low self-confidence, suffering from nerves, being afraid to take risks, lacking authority and presence, not taking responsibility and not coping well with stress. Once they overcame these difficulties they all performed at an exceptionally high level and excelled in the game. Players still face the same problems today. It is up to the players to strive to overcome these difficulties (a lot depends on the bravery or cowardice of the coaches to pick them) if they want to succeed in the game.

Obviously, any player who wants to make it to the very top in the game needs to have talent but also a great deal of will-power, determination and enough dedication to be able to work hard on a consistent basis.

## Psychological Considerations

What are the main psychological factors that affect players? The truth is, there are many: worrying about being picked for the team, lacking confidence in one's ability, experiencing a bad run and successive defeats, feeling the heavy weight of responsibility of being favorites, worrying about the physical presence or aggression of the opposition, worrying about refereeing decisions, feeling pressure to stand out, worrying about television coverage, trying to impress the coaches from the 'big' clubs, having the usual problems in the squad (problems between the young and senior players, for example), worrying about completing the contract and not being offered a new one at the present club or any other club.

There are also other factors not directly involved with the game that have an impact on the players: negative articles in the press, family problems, problems with studies, sexual difficulties, the birth of a child that upsets the routine (perhaps keeping the player awake at night), worrying about injuries and the future...

The coach has the difficult task of trying to get the player to overcome or at least deal with all this stress. He should therefore incorporate specific sports related psychological techniques into the training program. These exercises allow the player to improve relationships, relax more, become more motivated, achieve greater imagination and concentration and help with emotions and feelings.

Unfortunately, some coaches are fully aware that one of more of their players is experiencing difficulties in this area (even the player knows something is wrong), but he is powerless to come up with an effective solution to the problem. There are a number of exercises after this section that deal with the techniques necessary to help the player produce his best on a consistent basis without ups and downs. Never forget that if two players are evenly matched then the one that succeeds is the one who can quickly compensate and deal with the constant changes in the game (either good or bad). When two players are evenly matched then keeping relaxed, concentrating, persevering and a tremendous self-belief are fundamental pre-requisites for success. I have seen many players over the years who had the potential to be 'greats' in the game but performed inconsistently because of a lack of concentration and the fact that they did not want to put in the necessary effort and hard work to succeed.

Any player who wants to improve his concentration has to learn to ignore irrelevant factors and concentrate fully and totally on the game. An excellent way to help the player achieve this is by using Sauron's technique of 'expanding the mind'

This technique allows the player to discover different ways to focus his mind. To do this, he might think of a certain place and then completely change the dimensions in his mind going from one size to another. This is a wonderful exercise for soccer players.

It is always essential in soccer (but especially at the highest level) for there to be a good relationship between the coach and the player. The player should never feel that the coach is treating him with disdain or ignoring him. On the contrary, he should feel that the coach is always interested and concerned in trying to perfect his game. They should work closely together and discuss and organize the training and agree on the game-plan. At this level the following is sound advice: "Teach the player to train himself." In this way the coach can organize individual training sessions and leave the players to work on improving their own particular strengths and weaknesses. As far as psychological factors are concerned, this type of training gives the coach a wonderful opportunity to chat with the players on a one-to-one basis and build up a rapport. He is able to target each player individually and focus on his psychological requirements.

Nevertheless, there are a number of reasons why this close one-to-one relationship between the coach and the player is not very common:

1. The coach has to pick the team for the next match which can cause difficulties. This is especially true if the player is not in the team or has been dropped as he may feel victimized and not appreciated. Those that are picked for the team steer clear from a close relationship with the coach for fear of being branded 'teacher's pet.'

2. Under these circumstances it is very difficult for the coach to get close to the players in order to fully understand their feelings and 'psychological' state. It is not easy to find out about any personal problems that might be affecting the player's performance as these may be of a very sensitive and intimate nature. Any 'interference' by the coach might be seen as a 'threat' to the player's soccer career with the possibility that he might be dropped from the team (for his own good, of course).

3. Even though the coach and the player have a lot in common when it comes to the 'love' of the game and both may have years of experience, there is usually a big difference in tactical knowledge and understanding. The coach has a wealth of experience from his playing days and can see the whole game as it unfolds but the player is in the best position to decide on the appropriate tactics at the right time. In other words which move is best to play at any time during the game. These two viewpoints often cause the coach and player to have different opinions and interpretations. But these situations are made even worse if the coach was only a mediocre player or never played the game at all. If this is the case, the player will not respect his opinions.

4. The way the coach treats his players is very important. A new coach will use 'positive reinforcement'. This is a wonderful way to keep a good and friendly atmosphere at the club. Of course, sometimes he needs to 'criticize' and be firm. He has to walk a thin line between encouraging and discouraging the player with positive criticism. The coach needs to have a lot of

tact with the players, especially the 'flair' players and individuals who do the unexpected and often 'stray' from the agreed game-plan which takes the opposition by surprise (and confuses teammates). The rest of the team do not appreciate this type of player and will only accept him if he is particularly gifted.

I think it is a positive benefit for all concerned (especially for the club paying the wages) to see a better and closer relationship between the coach and the players. In order for there to be any chance of this happening with any success the coach needs to improve his knowledge and understanding and the players need to stop thinking of themselves as 'stars' who have nothing to learn about the game (or about human relationships).

Finally, here are two pieces of advice if you are playing as a professional in the game that will help you in your work and with your personal relationships:

1. You can consider yourself a soccer 'great' only when you perform well against good opposition, match after match and season after season. In order to achieve this you need: a great 'soccer brain' in order to fully appreciate and understand the game, eyes in the back of your head, wonderful creativity and imagination to surprise the opposition, excellent technique, great physical attributes (especially coordination and acceleration) and a strong and determined mental attitude. (how do you rate yourself? The complete player? Then continue to point number two).

2. Always remember and repeat Socrate's famous words (I am referring to the Greek philosopher not the Brazilian player here) that are still as fresh and relevant today as when he uttered them: "I only know that I know nothing."

# Cruyff and His Teammates

The following anecdote refers to the tolerance or intolerance some players have towards 'great' players.

When Cruyff started playing at Barça the Catalan club was bottom of the league but slowly but surely got higher and higher until eventually they won it.

Meanwhile, Cruyff's wife was in Amsterdam expecting their son, Jordi. Cruyff went to be with her after every game and returned to Barcelona every Thursday afternoon. He only trained with the rest of his teammates on Fridays and Saturdays. Despite this 'special treatment' he was idolized by his teammates and the team was very united.

The following year the whole family was in Barcelona and Cruyff usually trained every day but on occasion he was allowed to save his strength and have a rest. Gradually this news filtered down to his various teammates and they were very upset (they never said anything to his face) that they had to train hard while Cruyff was able to 'take it easy' and relax.

Why the sudden change in attitude? This was simply because the team was performing badly and Cruyff was not playing at his best.

**295**

*The Barça team coached by Michels was bottom of the league in 1983. Then Cruyff arrived at the club and the team ended up winning the league playing exceptional soccer.*

# Games for
# 19-30 Year Olds

| No. | Objectives | Age | Developing the Games | Common Problems |
|---|---|---|---|---|
| 1 | Control. Passing. Peripheral and focused vision. Paying attention. Concentration. Thinking. Speed of execution. | 18-20 | Using half a pitch 18 players (including goalkeepers) with a ball each are put into pairs. On the signal the players pass their ball to their partner who controls the ball and with the second touch passes it back. The players constantly move around and are always approximately 20-25 yds apart. Both the players in the pairing make sure they pass the ball to each other at the same time. The games last 5-7 minutes. It is repeated after a few days so that the players can see the progress they have made. | At first the players find this game very difficult but soon overcome the initial problems. They play the obligatory 'two-touch' sometimes. Some players need extra encouragement because they never get the idea and need to be shown what to do. |

| No. | Objectives | Age | Developing the Games | Common Problems |
|---|---|---|---|---|
| 2 | Ball control. Positioning. Concentration. Quick reflexes. Speed of execution. Feints and dummies. | 19-30 | Pitch size 18 x 18y. '4 v 2' playing a 'round' (the playing area stays roughly 18 x 18y but moves from place to place as the players move). The idea is for the 4 attackers to throw the ball to each other while the 2 defenders try to intercept. These are the differences from similar 'rounds' at earlier levels: 1.Control the ball, run with it in the hand and then pass it using the weaker foot. 2.Control and pass (not letting the ball bounce) without picking the ball up. 3.Pass the ball 'first-time'. 4.The defenders should hold and hassle the attackers in order to put them off. If the defenders touch the ball but it does not bounce the game continues. If an attacker kicks the ball as it bounces the game continues. However, if it bounces the attacker who made the mistake swaps with a defender. All the players should work hard and try their best. | The ball is not played into the 'light'. The attackers make little attempt to reach 'difficult' balls. The attackers only try to control the ball when a defender is nowhere near. The players in the middle do not make enough effort. The defenders do not hassle and hold onto the attackers enough. |

Fig 2

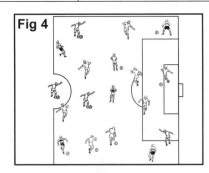

Fig 4

| No. | Objectives | Age | Developing the Games | Common Problems |
|-----|-----------|-----|---------------------|-----------------|
| 3 | Ball control. Positioning. Concentration. Thinking. Speed of execution. Unpredictable passing. | 19-30 | A similar 'round to the previous game with 6 players, except this time one of the attackers is in the middle with the 2 defenders. The 3 attackers on the outside work hard to cover all the ground to make sure all the space is utilized effectively. The attacker in the middle needs to be very mobile, always looking to make space to receive the ball. This is a difficult and tiring position and so all the players rotate on a regular basis. The passes should be unpredictable. | The same as above. The attackers do not disguise the passes and so they are easily intercepted. |
| 4 | Long passes. Control and turn. Speed of execution. Peripheral vision. Concentration. Aerobic stamina. | 19-30 | 18 players and 9 balls in half the pitch. All the players are jogging freely (half with a ball and half without a ball). The idea of the game is to practice long passes. A player on the ball calls out the name of a player without a ball (or vice versa), he acknowledges, and a long pass is played. The player who receives the ball has to control it on the turn and move off in the opposite direction from where the pass was made. The game continues in this way until the coach feels the players have done enough. Each player should play accurate long passes and also execute the control on the turn correctly. | The control on the turn is never correct if the player receiving the pass does not position his ankle (of his standing leg) in line with where the ball is coming from just before he makes contact with it. Sometimes the player does not have enough time to acknowledge the 'call' and so is not ready to receive the pass. |

| No. | Objectives | Age | Developing the Games | Common Problems |
|---|---|---|---|---|
| 5 | Speed. Explosive power. Running with the ball. Shooting. Running backwards. Playing in goal. | 19-30 | 2 goalkeepers alternate in a regulation size goal. 18 players are put into pairs and are expected to produce explosive power. 2 players stand 5 yds beyond the 18-yard box with their backs to goal. On the signal they sprint (running backwards as fast as they can) to the edge of the 18-yard box. Then they sprint (running forwards) towards the halfway line to try to claim the ball that the coach placed there earlier. The player who gets to the ball first does not pass it back to the coach until the other player arrives. Once the pass has been made the 2 players sprint (running backwards) back to their original starting position 5 yds beyond the 18-yard box. Once there, they sprint (running forwards) waiting for the pass from the coach. The fastest player is given the ball. He can either play the 'one-two' with the coach or control the ball on the turn as he heads towards the goal. Whichever option he chooses, he must shoot at goal immediately. | The players need to sprint as fast as they can to produce the explosive power. Some players do not try hard enough. Others cheat by turning round when they should be running backwards. |

Fig 5

| No. | Objectives | Age | Developing the Games | Common Problems |
|---|---|---|---|---|
| 6 | Speed. Explosive power. Running with the ball. Shooting. Running backwards. Playing in goal. | 19-30 | 2 goalkeepers alternate in a regulation size goal. This game is played by 2 teams of 4 players. The 2 teams stand 5 yds apart, 30 yds from the goal. Each team lines up behind an obstacle course of 4 cones positioned in a zigzag formation. The 4 cones are 2 yds apart with the first one 4 yds away from the players. Both the courses have a ball at the second cone. On the signal the first player in each team runs backwards around the cones as fast as he can (without a ball). Once they reach the second cone they collect the ball and turn, run around the remaining 2 cones and shoot before entering the 18-yard box. The player that does this the quickest in each pairing earns 2 points and 2 points are also awarded for each goal. All the players follow the same routine. The team with the most points at the end is the winner. | Even at this level some players are not good at running backwards and fall over. Running backwards and then forwards is very tiring on the legs and so stretching exercises are recommended. Some players lose coordination and balance after running backwards and consequently find it difficult to control the ball effectively at the second cone. |

| No. | Objectives | Age | Developing the Games | Common Problems |
|---|---|---|---|---|
| 7 | Running with the ball. Dribbling. Feints and dummies. Peripheral vision. Changing pace. Explosive power. Paying atten-tion. Concentration. Craft. Being astute. | 19-21 | 3 playing areas 20 x 20y. 18 players each with a ball. There are 6 players in each square. 2 players try to 'tag' the other 4. The latter have to keep the ball under control at all times and avoid being 'tagged'. To make things more complicated, the 'chasers' are not carrying 'bibs'. This means that the players being chased have to be particularly vig-ilant. The 'chaser' can pretend to go one way to lull the player being chased into a false sense of security, only to turn suddenly and 'tag' him. The 'chasers' should also change pace and direc-tion as often as possible. Once a player is 'tagged' he swaps roles with the 'chaser'. | The 'chaser' often con-centrates on a particular player when he should constantly move from one to the other. The 'chaser' often leaves his ball behind when he is about to 'tag'. This is not allowed. Some players do not participate and merely stand to the sides. This is not allowed as no player should ever stop running. |
| 8 | Running with the ball. Dribbling. Feints and dummies. Peripheral vision. Changing pace. Explosive power. Paying atten-tion. Concentration. Multi-tasking. Being astute. Craft. Improvisation. | 22-30 | The same as the previous game except: it is played using half the pitch and all 18 play in the same game (12 are being chased and 6 are trying to 'tag'). This game requires better peripheral vision, greater concentration and more physical effort than the previous one. Any player who plays with craft, the ability to improvise and move intelligently does well in this game. However, the game is very tiring and so ade-quate rest periods are required. The coach observes and will ask a player to work harder or 'slow down' as required. | The 'chaser' often con-centrates on a particular player when he should constantly move from one to another. The 'chaser' often leaves his ball behind when he is about to 'tag'. This is not allowed. Some players do not participate and merely stand as far away from the action as possible. This is not allowed as all the players should be constantly on the move. |

| No. | Objectives | Age | Developing the Games | Common Problems |
|---|---|---|---|---|
| 9 | Passing. Changing pace. Quick reflexes. Paying attention. Concentration. Multi-tasking. Peripheral vision. Explosive power. | 19-30 | Pitch size 25 x 25yds. 8 players. 6 players pass 2 balls to each other playing one or 'two-touch'. The 2 other players try to 'tag'. However, a player cannot be 'tagged' when in possession of the ball. If being chased it is a good idea to call for a ball in order to receive it and gain immunity. If a player is 'tagged' he swaps roles with the 'chaser.' The 'chasers' should not touch the ball. | Some players stand to the sides and do not participate. Some try to 'tag' a player in possession of the ball. This is not allowed. Some stand next to a player waiting to 'tag' him as soon as he passes the ball. This is not allowed. |

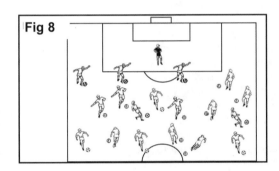

Fig 8

Fig 9

| No. | Objectives | Age | Developing the Games | Common Problems |
|---|---|---|---|---|
| 10 | In defense: Paying attention. Concentration. Quick reflexes. Rapid interventions. Working as a unit. In attack: Ball control. Peripheral vision. Speed off the mark. Explosive power. Dribbling. Feints and dummies. Shooting. The presence of mind to take advantage of the opportunities that arise. | 19-30 | 2 goalkeepers alternate (sometimes play in goal at the same time) in a regulation size goal. This game involves 9 players (excluding the goalkeepers), 3 players (defenders) are positioned a few yds beyond the 18-yard box opposite the goalmouth. The defenders observe 6 players(the attackers) performing ball-juggling skills (3 near the left wing and 3 near the right, each with a ball). The coach signals to the attackers with his fingers (so that the defenders do not see) and these players (could be 2 from the left side and 3 from the right side etc.) run towards goal and try to score. No matter how many attackers are involved or from which side of the pitch they approach, the defenders always have to be well organized and play as a unit in order to prevent goals. Once an attacker has made it into the 18-yard box he cannot be challenged by the defenders. The 3 groups swap positions and roles frequently. The coach makes a note of the goals scored by each team. | Some players lack concentration and defend poorly. Some defenders continue to challenge for the ball even though they have been beaten and the attacker is in the 18-yard box. The defenders should challenge one attacker and immediately look to see if another attacker is approaching. If only one attacker is involved the defenders should play the 'pressing' game but they do not. The attackers find it difficult to perform the ball-juggling skills and look for the coach's signal at the same time. |

| No. | Objectives | Age | Developing the Games | Common Problems |
|-----|-----------|-----|---------------------|-----------------|
| 11 | Perception. Peripheral vision. Change of pace and ideas. Paying attention. Concentration. Multi-tasking. Intelligence and improvisation. Stamina. | 22-30 | Pitch size 30 x 30yds. 12 players. 2 teams of 6 players (with 1 ball per team). The idea is for the 5 players in each team to go from one end of the pitch to the other as many times as possible (getting 'tagged' as little as possible) passing the ball playing one or 'two-touch'. There is a 'chaser' in each team trying to tag his teammates. He cannot tag a player in possession of the ball. If he manages to 'tag' he swaps roles with the player. This game is difficult because there are 2 teams on the pitch at the same time and because the 'chasers' cause panic and confusion. The players need to play intelligently and pass the ball to a player if he is about to be 'tagged'. The 'chaser' is not allowed to touch the ball. | The players find this game very difficult and therefore make lots of mistakes. The players should show more determination, keep trying and never give up. The 'chasers' often touch the ball. This is not allowed and should be corrected. |

Fig 10

Fig 11

| No. | Objectives | Age | Developing the Games | Common Problems |
|-----|-----------|-----|---------------------|-----------------|
| 12 | Marking. Making space. Having a 'feel' for the game. Being a 'real' soccer player. Perfecting 'the method'. Producing quality soccer. | 19-30 | Using half the pitch (playing from wing to wing). 12 players, 2 teams of 6 with 1 ball in the game. The idea is to play a passing game moving the ball from one end of the pitch to the other. The moves practiced in the game are as follows: the 'one-two, the 'doblada', the 'inside' pass, the 'overlap', the 'auto-pass' (when confronted, kick the ball to one side and run to the other to collect it), kick the ball over the opposition's head and run to collect it and the 'nutmeg' (kicking the ball between the opposition's legs to pass to a teammate or collect the ball). Each one of these moves earns a point for the team. The team with the most points at the end wins. | The players use the 'auto-pass' too often. This move should only be attempted when appropriate. The players forget to play the moves in 'the method.' The players pass back and sideways too often. |
| 13 | Running with the ball. Peripheral vision. Paying attention. Concentration. Producing quality passing and touch on the ball. | 19-30 | 2 players are 25 yds apart. There are 2 poles halfway between the 2 players 2 yds apart. The players put 'swerve' on the ball as they pass it to each other using the inside or the outside of the foot. The idea is for the ball to curl around the outside of one of the poles and arrive at the feet of the other player. This player controls the ball with the first touch and passes it back with the second. This pair competes against 2 other pairs. These pairs stand a few yds away from the | Some players run slowly as they are worried about being hit by the ball. The run should be made as fast as possible but at an even pace. Some players do not take up the correct body position when attempting to curl the ball (they should approach the ball from the side). Some do not use the correct part of the foot to execute the skill. The correct points of contact are the little toe when using the outside of the foot and the start of the big toe when using the |

| No. | Objectives | Age | Developing the Games | Common Problems |
|-----|-----------|-----|----------------------|-----------------|
| 13 (cont) | | 19-30 | player doing the passing. As the passing starts one pair set off with a ball each, run to the poles, run around them and back to their starting point. The balls are handed over to the other pair who do the same. Once these pairs have completed this 5 times the players passing the ball have run out of time and swap with the fastest pairing. This pair now pass to each other as the others run back and forth to the poles 5 times and so on. The quicker the runs the less time the passers have to make lots of passes. Each accurate curled pass earns a point. The players running are not allowed to interfere with the passes. 3 points are deducted from the team's score if a player intercepts a pass as he runs to and from the poles. The pair with the most points at the end wins. A competition can be organized with 18 players. | inside of the foot. |

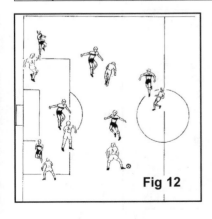

Fig 12

Fig 13

| No. | Objectives | Age | Developing the Games | Common Problems |
|-----|------------|-----|----------------------|-----------------|
| 14 | Perfecting 'the method'. Playing direct soccer. Mastering the '1 v 1' (goalkeepers and outfield players). Anticipation. Positioning. | 19-30 | Half the pitch playing from wing to wing. A game of '7 v 7' involving passing 'first-time' or 'two-touch'. The game involves 2 goalkeepers (no goals) and the players play 'the method'. A goal is scored when the ball is taken over the opposition's 'dead-ball line (in this case one of the wings). The goalkeepers have to concentrate and position themselves wherever necessary to confront the attacker (often in a '1 v 1' situation) to prevent a goal being scored. They play as the last defender and can only use their hands when saving a ball on or very near the 'dead-ball line'. In theory the goalkeeper can play anywhere on the pitch just like an outfield player but he has to get back in a hurry if the opposition mount a swift counterattack. The team that takes the ball across the opposition's line the most is the winner. | The game is maximum 'two-touch' unless playing '1 v 1' against the goalkeeper. This change in the number of touches confuses some players. Players forget to play 'the method'. The players do not change the direction of play very often and if they do it is done so slowly that the goalkeeper has time to get into position. |

**Fig 14**

| No. | Objectives | Age | Developing the Games | Common Problems |
|---|---|---|---|---|
| 15 | Long passes. Ball control. Peripheral vision. Concentration. Speed of execution. Aerobic stamina. | 19-30 | Pitch size 80 x 60yds. 18 players and 9 balls. The players run and pass to each other. The players must play 'three-touch' (control, move, lookup and pass). The goalkeepers are also involved as outfield players but they alternate between using hands and feet. The same type of pass should never be repeated and the ball should never be given straight back to the player who just made the pass. Each player calls for the ball or calls before passing it. As far as the passing is concerned, all the players should be conscious of this advice: 'Always look before passing.' | Not calling the player's name clearly and loudly before passing the ball to him. Making the call and passing without looking to see if the player as heard and is ready to receive the ball. Some players run too quickly and others move too slowly. Inaccurate passing. |

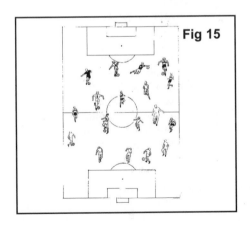

**Fig 15**

| No. | Objectives | Age | Developing the Games | Common Problems |
|---|---|---|---|---|
| 16 | Long passes. Ball control. Peripheral vision. Anticipation. Paying attention. Concentration. Stamina. | 19-30 | Pitch size 80 x 60yds. 20 players, 8 with a ball. The idea is to practice playing long passes (with or without swerve) in the following way: call name clearly (either for the ball or if passing it). However, the game is made all the more difficult because there are 4 other players (wearing bibs) who try to intercept the passes. This means that the passes have to be more accurate and the players receiving the ball have to make space effectively. The ball can be intercepted before it reaches its destination or as the ball is being controlled. Once the player on the ball makes a second touch the player trying to touch the ball has to look elsewhere. The fact that the players never stop jogging and change pace as required makes this a very tiring game. Every 5 minutes the 4 defenders are swapped so that all the players experience this role. Each player keeps a mental note of all the passes and ball control played correctly and the passes and balls intercepted because of poor control. | The player on the ball should spot a player running into space, call his name and pass the ball so that he can take it in his stride. However, the player does not usually make a run until the ball has been passed. The players should never stop moving and thinking. The defenders do not make enough effort. Some players produce more technical skills when controlling the ball. |

| No. | Objectives | Age | Developing the Games | Common Problems |
|-----|-----------|-----|---------------------|-----------------|
| 17 | Medium length passes. Ball control. Peripheral and focused vision. Paying attention. Multi-tasking. | 19-22 | Pitch size 25 x 25yds. 4 players (2 with a ball) run in this area. The idea of the game is to pass using 'two-touch' (control and pass) without stopping. The main emphasis of the exercise is concentration and getting into the habit of being aware of space | Passing to a player who is not expecting the ball. Only concentrating on one of the two balls. Passing the two balls to the same player at the same time. |
| 18 | Shooting from distance. Trying to shoot immediately. Judging time (both defenders and attackers). Concentration. | 19-30 | Pitch size stretches from the edge of one 18-yard box to the edge of the other. 2 goals marked with cones. This is a game of '9 v 9' (including a goalkeeper in each goal). The main objective is to shoot at goal as often as possible.The game has the following characteristics: 1.The goals are 10yds wide to encourage the players to shoot from distance. 2.As soon as a team gets possession of the ball they have 15 seconds to shoot. If they do not shoot within this time the ball passes to the opposition. If time is running out the defenders do everything possible to put the attackers under pressure. | The players do not judge how long 15 seconds is (defenders and attackers). They do not shoot from distance even if they can. On other occasions the shots are taken too quickly when there was time to develop the move further. 15 seconds is a long time for some and it is over in an instant for others. |

313

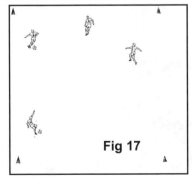

Fig 17

Fig 18

| No. | Objectives | Age | Developing the Games | Common Problems |
|-----|-----------|-----|---------------------|-----------------|
| 19 | Shooting from distance. Speed of execution. Judging time (both defenders and attackers). Playing the method. Concentration. | 19-30 | Pitch size 80 x 30yds. 2 goals with a goalkeeper in each. There are 12 outfield players on the pitch (4 teams of 3). There is a line marked 25 yds from each goal and the majority of the play takes place in the 30 yds in the middle. The team in possession has to shoot before 10 seconds are up or else a penalty is awarded. Shots can only be taken from within the 30 yard area. If a players goes over the 25 yard line he can pass the ball back so that a teammate can shoot from within the 30 yard area. The teams swap every 5 minutes when the two teams resting have a turn. The team that scores the most goals wins. | The players find it difficult to get used to the area restrictions and the time limit. Not enough shooting. Sometimes shooting too quickly when the move could have been developed. |
| 20 | Speed of execution. Judging time. Controlling the space around you. Shooting from distance. Bravery. Concentration. | 19-30 | Similar to the previous game but with one big difference: all 4 teams play at the same time. There are 2 games going on simultaneously. The fact that there are now 2 balls and 12 players in the limited space makes the game difficult and confusing. The goalkeepers have to concentrate on both balls. | Same as above. The goalkeepers only concentrate on one of the balls. The players do not make space effectively in order to give the player on the ball a target to aim at. |

Fig 21

| No. | Objectives | Age | Developing the Games | Common Problems |
|---|---|---|---|---|
| 21 | Speed of execution. Switching the play. Volleying. Heading. Playing in goal. | 19-30 | Pitch size 30 x 30y. A regulation size goal with a neutral goalkeeper is in the middle of the pitch. Goals can be scored from either side of the goal. The game is '3 v 3'. The attacking team is helped by 3 'neutral' players (2 play on the wings and 1 in the middle). The 'neutral' players are not allowed to shoot. Each time a team wins possession the ball has to be played to the other side of the pitch. The team can now shoot or move back to the other side and shoot if they wish. The game is 'two-touch'. Goals can only be scored with volleys and headers. The 3 teams rotate so that each team gets a chance to play as the 'neutrals'. | Shooting after winning the ball without moving to the other side of the pitch. Playing more than 'one-touch'. The players should not go from one side of the pitch to the other via the goal. Not scoring the specified way (volley or header). Forgetting the most important aspect of the game: goal-scoring passes and goals. |
| 22 | Mobility. Making space. Volleying and half volleying putting swerve on the ball. | 19-30 | Pitch size 25 x 12y. 2 regulation size goals. The game involves 3 teams of 3 players. Team 'C' rests as team 'A' (throwing the ball to each other) attacks team 'B'. Team 'B' defend with 1 player and the other 2 players stand on the goal-line. Shots should swerve and must be taken on the volley or half-volley. A player can shoot after throwing the ball up for himself or receiving it from a team-mate. Team 'B' the attacks team 'C' and then team 'C' attacks team 'A' and so on. The team that scores the most goals wins. | The players find the shooting technique very difficult. The coach may ask any player in the team that is resting to go to the 'suspended ball' to practice. The attacking team gets too close to goal. They should pass less and concentrate more on shooting. |

| No. | Objectives | Age | Developing the Games | Common Problems |
|-----|-----------|-----|---------------------|-----------------|
| 23 | Speed. Explosive power. Changing direction. Speed of execution. Shooting. Paying attention. Concentration. Playing in goal. | 19-30 | 2 players alternate in goal. 3 teams(Team 'A', 'B' and 'C') of 3 players take it in turns to play. Team 'A' stand on the edge of the 18-yard box with their backs to goal. There is a line of 3 cones each 1 yard apart ( 1 opposite each player) 5 yds from the 3 players. On the signal the players jog towards their cone and when they are approximately 2 yds away they do a forward roll. Then they run around their cone as quickly as possible and race back to their starting point. A ball is thrown in as soon as the first players arrives back and he can either shoot 'first-time' or control and shoot. Then another ball is thrown up for all 3 players and first to get to it shoots. Balls are thrown up until 3 goals have been scored (perhaps the players hit the woodwork or the shots are saved). Team 'B' and team 'C' do the same. A note is taken of all the shots and goals scored by each player. | The players take too long to shoot (too many touches). Lack of concentration. Lack of commitment which means some players never get to shoot. The teams are not evenly match and so the same player always shoots. |

Fig 23

Fig 25

| No. | Objectives | Age | Developing the Games | Common Problems |
|---|---|---|---|---|
| 24 | Speed. Explosive power. Speed of execution. Shooting. Acrobatics. Playing in goal. | 19-30 | An identical game to the previous one but with a different ending. Once the first player back has had his shot and all 3 players are together, they run back towards the cones where the last team to plays throws a ball to each of the players so that they can try a 'bicycle' kick or 'semi-scissors'. If a player fails to perform the required technique another ball is thrown up for him until he manages to shoot correctly. A note is taken of the players who shoot first and those who execute the correct techniques first-time. Any goals are also noted. | The players are not evenly matched and so 1 player always gets to the ball first. If the player has not mastered the techniques he could injure himself (especially on the landing). If this is the case the players should practice at the 'suspended ball'. |
| 25 | Speed. Explosive power. Speed of execution. The 'bicycle' kick. The diving header. Acquire the coordination and agility to produce these skills. Quick reflexes. Concentration. | 19-30 | 2 goalkeepers alternate in goal. 3 teams of 3 players. Team 'A' sit in a line (well spaced out) 3 yds from the 18-yard box. Each player is holding a ball. On the signal the players kick the balls up high towards the goal. They all stand up and run to try to volley the ball on goal before it bounces. Even if, for whatever reason the ball bounces, the player still shoots, but if a goal results it does not count. After shooting, the players position themselves (with their backs to goal) ready to try to perform the 'bicycle kick' or 'semi-scissors'. A note is taken of the legitimate goals scored, correct technique and who managed to shoot first. | This exercise is very physically demanding and so the coach must make sure it is performed at the beginning of the training session (after the warm up of course!) when the players are fresh. The coach should also make sure that all the players are in perfect shape before attempting this exercise. |

| No. | Objectives | Age | Developing the Games | Common Problems |
|-----|-----------|-----|---------------------|-----------------|
| 26 | Ball control. Speed of execution. The 'bicycle' kick. The diving header. Acquire the coordination and agility to produce these skills. Quick reflexes. Concentration. | 19-30 | 2 cones act as a goal and are placed 20 yds away, opposite a regulation size goal. The game is '5 v 5' playing a 'mobile round'. The players can catch the ball and then pass to each other on the volley, or control the ball and pass it on the volley or pass 'first-time'. Goals can only be scored with a 'bicycle kick', 'semi-scissors' diving header or header. There is no man-to-man marking until the game is fully mastered and the defending team cannot intercept with their hands. If the interception is made using the head, legs or body the player can pick it up and volley it to a teammate. If a mistake is made and the ball bounces at any time it goes to the opposition. The winner is established by multiplying the number of correctly executed attempts on goal by the number of goals scored. | Some players never shoot (after the game they need to practice at the 'suspended ball'). The attacker stops as soon as he loses the ball but he can still try to win the ball as long as it is not being held in the hand. Sometimes the ball is 'wrestled' from a player even though he is holding onto it. This is not allowed. If this happens a second time, the player goes and takes a penalty by executing a 'bicycle kick' from the penalty spot . A teammate throws the ball up for him from the edge of the 18-yard box. |

Fig 26

| No. | Objectives | Age | Developing the Games | Common Problems |
|-----|------------|-----|----------------------|-----------------|
| 27 | Speed. Explosive power. Changing direction. Running with the ball. Dribbling. Shooting. | 19-30 | 2 goalkeepers alternate in goal. There are 2 'false' walls 7 yds apart 5 yds beyond the 18-yard box. There are 2 teams of 4 players 5 yds from their respective walls. On the signal a player from each team heads towards the wall, and when they are close to it, they step on the ball (leave it behind) and run around the wall. They then run with the ball to the edge of the 18-yard box as quickly as possible. Once there, they turn with the ball and head back towards the wall, only touching the ball twice. The third touch is used to kick the ball against the wall in order to collect the rebound and shoot immediately. Then the rest of the players do the same. This game is very tiring and so the rest periods between the relays are very long. | Some players run around the wall with the ball when this is not necessary. The ball should be kicked against the wall in such a way so that the player can take it in his stride and shoot. |

**319**

Fig 27

| No. | Objectives | Age | Developing the Games | Common Problems |
|-----|-----------|-----|---------------------|-----------------|
| 28 | Marking. Making space. Speed of execution. Bravery. Concentration. Acceleration. Explosive power. The main emphasis is on shooting. Playing in goal. | 19-30 | 2 cones are positioned to form a goalmouth 20 yds opposite a regulation size goal. 4 goalkeepers take turns in goal. The game is '2 v 2' playing 'two-touch' (three touches are allowed if immediately followed by a strike at goal). The difficulty is that there are two games going on at the same time on the same pitch using the same goals. This an extremely exhausting game for the goalkeepers (physically and mentally) and this is why they are changed regularly. The goalkeeper has to be aware of both the balls because as soon as he saves one he has to be ready just in case the other is on its way. The game is also tiring for the 8 outfield players and these swap with the 8 idle players every 5 minutes. During the rest periods the players should perform light stretching activities. The pairings are always changed so that the same players do not play against each other. Make a note of the goals scored by each pair, which individual scored and against which goalkeeper. | Not shooting frequently enough (there are no restrictions on this pitch so the players can shoot from anywhere). Not playing the correct number of touches. Not passing or moving into 'the light'. Poor marking. Worried about getting hit by the other ball (the players need to be brave as it is likely that players will get hit by the other ball at some stage during the game). The goalkeepers only concentrate on one ball. |

| No. | Objectives | Age | Developing the Games | Common Problems |
|---|---|---|---|---|
| 29 | Marking. Making space. Speed of execution. Concentration. Peripheral and focused vision. Improvisation. Being astute. Playing in goal. | 19-30 | Similar to the previous game (4 goalkeepers and two games going on at once etc). Pitch size 40 x 30yds. Two games of '4 v 4' taking place at the same time. The game is 'two-touch' (three if immediately followed by a strike on goal). The game involves tight marking. The big variation from the previous game is that players can intervene in the other game. For example: if a player in the other game is not directly involved in the action and finds himself near a player with the ball in the other game who is being challenged by an opponent he shouts 'one-two', receives the ball and passes it back. Or the player on the ball can call for assistance by shouting 'one-two' only to play a dummy and move off in the other direction. If a player is in space and is running at goal a player from the other game is allowed to make one challenge to try to make his approach more difficult. Under these circumstances the attacking player has no restrictions on touches. | Not shooting enough (this is one of the main objectives of the game). Not playing with intelligence or imagination. Lack of improvisation. A player from the other game intervenes too often (the player should only be involved once in any move). |

321

Fig 28

| No. | Objectives | Age | Developing the Games | Common Problems |
|---|---|---|---|---|
| 30 | Marking. Making space. 'Pressing'. Improvisation. Shooting quickly. Concentration. | 22-30 | A goal (with cones as goalposts) is placed 20y opposite a regulation size goal. This is a game of '2 v 2' with a goalkeeper playing in each goal. There is no restriction on the number of touches. There is a 'neutral' player who always helps the defending team. This numerical advantage means that the defenders can play the 'pressing' game and harass the player in possession. This game is very intense and so after 5 minutes the 5 outfield players are swapped with 5 new players. The 'neutral' player is swapped because if the role is played properly it is very exhausting. | The players concentrate more on passing and dribbling when the main objective of the exercise is shooting. The defenders do not 'press' well. When one defender challenges for the ball the other looks on and waits for the outcome. He should challenge at the same time. |
| 31 | Speed of execution. Quick thinking. 'Pressing'. Bravery. Explosive power. Dribbling. Shooting. Concentration. Acceleration. Playing in goal. | 22-30 | This is a similar game to the previous one but this time two games are being played at the same time and there is a 'neutral' player in each. This game is so physically demanding that the players (including the goalkeepers) should be swapped every 5 minutes. | Not 'pressing' with enough determination. Not shooting at goal. Not producing moves involving quality dribbling. The goalkeepers do not concentrate on both balls. |

Fig 30

Fig 31

| No. | Objectives | Age | Developing the Games | Common Problems |
|---|---|---|---|---|
| 32 | Perfecting the 'overlap'. Attacking play. Shooting. 'Pressing'. Defensive discipline. Coordinated attacks. | 19-30 | 18 players. A game where 9 players (3 trios) attack a single goal (there is a goalkeeper). This is how the game develops: 3 players ('A', 'B' and 'C') with 1 ball running in a line in the middle of the playing area. The player in the middle ('A') has the ball and he passes it diagonally into the path of the player to his right ('B') and runs round him so that now ('B') is in the middle. Player 'B' passes to 'C' and runs round him. So now the lineup is 'B', 'C' and 'A' (from left to right). After they run 10-12 yds they are faced by 2 players whom they try to beat by playing the 'overlap'. If successful they are faced by 2 other defenders 10 yds further on whom they try to beat in the same way. If successful they are faced by 5 defenders on the edge of the 18-yard box playing the 'pressing' game. Once the attack ends (the ball can be lost at any stage but especially at the edge of the 18-yard box or with a shot on goal) the next 3 players set off. Once all 3 trios have attacked they become the defenders and the defenders the attackers (the goalkeeper is also changed at this stage). At the end the shots on goal are multiplied by the number of goals scored to establish a winning team. | The attackers do not play the 'overlap' correctly. When there are only 2 defenders they make little efforts as they take it for granted that they will be beaten. The 5 defenders also make little effort because they think they will win the ball easily. The 'pressing' game is not played properly. There is very little quality attacking play. |

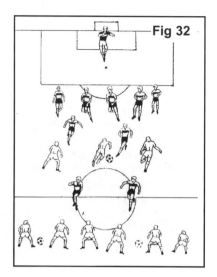
Fig 32

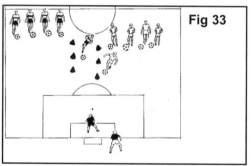
Fig 33

Fig 34

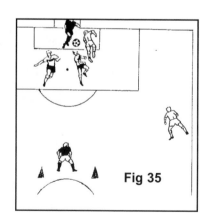
Fig 35

| No. | Objectives | Age | Developing the Games | Common Problems |
|-----|-----------|-----|---------------------|-----------------|
| 33 | Skill. Coordination. Peripheral vision. The 'bicycle' kick. The 'semi-scissors'. | 22-30 | Pitch size is half the pitch. 2 goalkeepers alternate in goal. 5 yds from the edge of the 18-yard box there is a line of 6 cones (each cone 3 yds apart) in a zigzag formation stretching towards the half-way line. There is a team of 5 players with a ball each waiting to the left of the cone closest to the half-way line. There is another team of 5 players with a ball each waiting to the right of the penultimate cone. On the signal the first player in each team runs around the cone-course as quickly as possible keeping the ball up. If the ball drops the player has to pick it up with his left hand, do a forward role and then continue keeping the ball up around the cones. Once beyond the last cone the players get sideways on or with their back to goal (still keeping the ball up) ready to play the 'bicycle kick' or 'semi-scissors'. The points system is as follows: 2 points if a shot is taken and the ball did not bounce at any stage. If the ball was dropped but the shot is on target or hits the woodwork 1 point is awarded. 3 points for a goal. Once each team has completed the course once they swap roles (start from the other cone). The team with the most points wins. | Some players focus so much on the ball that they hit the cones. The player who starts from the penultimate cone is sometimes so worried about the player behind him that he makes 'unforced' errors. This is similar to when players perform far better in training than in matches - the pressure. Some players do not perform the required shooting techniques correctly. The ball is often just kicked on the volley. These players are asked to practice at the 'suspended ball'. |

| No. | Objectives | Age | Developing the Games | Common Problems |
|-----|-----------|-----|---------------------|-----------------|
| 34 | Long and short passes. Dribbling. Shooting. 'Pressing. Concentration. Speed. | 22-30 | 2 goalkeepers alternate in goal. The game involves 4 teams of 3 players. Team 'A' and 'B' start off either side of the 6-yard box with a few balls. Team 'C' and 'D' are positioned near the wings 40 yds up the pitch. On the signal a player in team 'A' passes a ball to a player in team 'C' ( a player in 'B' passes to 'D' at the same time) and then he chases after it with another player in his team. The player in team 'C' returns the ball 'first-time' using the inside of the foot and chases after it. One of the players in team 'A' plays a short pass to the oncoming player in team 'C'. There is now a '2 v 1' situation as the players in team 'A' try to win the ball. If the player in team 'C' successfully gets beyond the 2 players he goes on and shoots at goal. If the two players win the ball then this particular move ends and a new one starts from the beginning. Team 'A' plays against team 'C' and team 'B' plays against team 'D' simultaneously. Once all the players have had a turn the teams swap roles 'C' passes to 'A' and 'D' passes to 'B'. When this is finished the scores are tallied as follows: goals scored multiplied by shots taken. Then the two high scorers play against each other and the other two teams meet. | Some players have very poor concentration levels. They 'daydream' and forget what they are supposed to do. Playing the 'pressing' game poorly. The players do not use creativity and improvisation to overcome the 'pressing'. Not shooting when given the opportunity (it is better to shoot from distance than to lose the ball near the goal). The players do not react quickly enough and continue the move if the ball rebounds off the woodwork or is parried by the goalkeeper. |

| No. | Objectives | Age | Developing the Games | Common Problems |
|-----|-----------|-----|---------------------|-----------------|
| 35 | Strategy. Speed. Positioning. Judging time. Shooting. The counterattack. Making space (using feints and dummies). | 19-25 | Pitch size 30 x 30y. Regulation size goals. This is a game of '3 v 3' (1 goalkeeper and 2 outfield players per team). The game starts with a 'throw-in' taken by one of the teams halfway up the pitch (standing on the touchline). The other player in the team must make space as he runs close to the opposition's goal. From this point everything depends on the intelligence of the players: the throw is well-directed towards the players making the run and he heads the ball or shoots at goal. The player receiving the pass plays the 'one-two' with the thrower (the 'give and support') and he makes an attempt on goal. No matter what the chosen move, the attacking team has a maximum of 5 seconds after the throw is taken to make an attempt on goal. Once the move is over the other team has a turn. This continues from alternate wings until each team has between 12-15 'throw-ins'. It is a good idea to take the throw as quickly as possible before the opposition has a chance to organize (of course this move will not surprise the opposition indefinitely). | Incredibly there is always someone who takes the 'throw-in' incorrectly (this is unforgivable at this level). The players need to realize that a good attacking strategy is to take the 'throw-in' quickly. Some players do not make space effectively near the opposition's goal. The players judge time poorly. |

| No. | Objectives | Age | Developing the Games | Common Problems |
|-----|-----------|-----|---------------------|-----------------|
| 36 | Strategy. Speed. Positioning. Judging time. The counterattack. Shooting. | 19-25 | Pitch is now 40 x 30y. Regulation size goals. This is a game of '3 v 3' (1 goalkeeper and 2 outfield players per team). As in the previous game the teams alternate and take between 12-15 'throw-ins' but this time from the middle of the pitch. A goal can be scored directly from the 'throw-in' and the players need to be ready to collect any rebound off the woodwork or clearance from the goalkeeper. The movements and ideas depend on the players but the attacks last a maximum of 5 seconds. Once an attack is over the other team should take the throw from the middle of the pitch as quickly as possible, sometimes throwing directly at goal and at other times throwing to the other attacking player. As soon as the ball stops moving the throw can be taken as long as the player is in his own half. | Taking the throw quickly when the ball is moving. This is not allowed and should be taken again. Not making an attempt at goal within the allotted time. Not playing creative moves to get near the opposition's goal. Not judging how long 5 seconds lasts. |

Fig 37

Fig 38

| No. | Objectives | Age | Developing the Games | Common Problems |
|---|---|---|---|---|
| 37 | Skill. Ball-juggling skills. Teamwork. Acceleration. Changing direction. Peripheral vision. | 19-30 | A ball-juggling competition where all the players in the team are split into pairs. The 2 players in the pairing stand 5 yds apart. One player has a ball in his hands. On the signal he starts to juggle with it using feet, thighs, chest and head etc. Meanwhile, the other player runs towards his partner, runs around him and back to his starting point. Now the player doing the ball-juggling plays a high ball to his partner so that he can continue juggling it. The player without the ball runs up to and around his partner and back to his starting point and so on. Once each player has done this 3 times without letting the ball bounce, they win a point. The team with the most points at the end wins. | This exercise causes few problems for the players. If the coach does not monitor the situation the players stand closer and closer together, sometimes ending up only 2 or 3 yds apart. Some players forget how many 'runs' they have completed. |
| 38 | Skill. Ball-juggling skills. Coordination. Agility. | 19-30 | 16 players standing in a circle. All the players are ball-juggling. Any player, at any time suddenly kicks the ball up high, sits down, stands up again and continues to juggle with the ball before it bounces. 1 point is awarded each time this is successfully achieved. After the allotted time the player with the most points wins. The players and coach make a note of the score to see what improvements have been made the next time the exercise is performed. | Some players only bend their knees and never actually sit down. When standing up some players fail to control the ball on their chest or thigh when the most important thing is to keep it from bouncing no matter what the contact area. |

**329**

| No. | Objectives | Age | Developing the Games | Common Problems |
|-----|-----------|-----|---------------------|-----------------|
| 39 | Skill. Ball-juggling skills. Coordination. Agility. Balance. Controlling the space around you. | 19-30 | This is a similar game to the previous one with the same number of players and points system etc. The only difference is that instead of sitting the player kicks the ball up high and does a forward roll and stands up again to control the ball before it bounces. Whether successful or not the player spends a while ball-juggling. If he attempts this exercise repeatedly he will probably feel sick. | The ball has to be kicked up very high and the forward roll has to be done as quickly as possible. Few players do both correctly. Some players are so competitive that they do not take a 'rest' in between forward rolls and end up feeling sick. |
| 40 | Skill. Ball-juggling skills. Coordination. Agility. | 19-30 | 16 players sitting in a circle are holding a ball each. On the signal they each kick their ball up high and stand up quickly to control the ball before it has a chance to bounce. If a ball bounces the player concerned sits down to try again. Those who were successful try to sit down while keeping the ball up (without holding onto it with their hands). When the player is ready he kicks the ball up high, stands up and continues the ball-juggling skills. After 4-5 touches the player catches the ball and is awarded a point for completing the routine successfully. He then sits down and starts from the beginning again. | This is very difficult but the quality players are able to perform the routine with great success. Any player who finds this too difficult should concentrate on simpler ball-juggling skills and attempt this exercise again when he is ready. |

| No. | Objectives | Age | Developing the Games | Common Problems |
|-----|-----------|-----|---------------------|-----------------|
| 41 | Skill. Ball-juggling skills. Coordination. Balance. Peripheral vision. Paying attention. Concentration. Craft. Being astute. | 19-30 | Pitch size 30 x 30y. 18 players. 9 players are ball-juggling and the other 9 try to win the ball. The latter can only win the ball by heading it. If a player ball-juggling sees a player coming towards him to try to win the ball he turns his back to him in order to shield it with his body. Both players should use feints and dummies in order to 'trick' the other player into turning the wrong way. If at any time the ball bounces and the 'challenger' heads it then the 2 players swap roles and the new 'challenger' has to look for a different ball. If the player being challenged is able to successfully keep his ball for 3 seconds then the 'challenger' has to look elsewhere. | Some players use their hands or feet to win the ball. Sometimes personal duels develop. This should be avoided. |

Fig 40

| No. | Objectives | Age | Developing the Games | Common Problems |
|-----|-----------|-----|---------------------|-----------------|
| 42 | Skill. Ball-juggling skills. Teamwork. Running backwards. Peripheral vision. Controlling the space around you. | 19-30 | 18 players (with a ball each) are put into pairs and they are 5 yds apart. They are both performing ball-juggling skills. On the signal one of the players has to turn and move backwards as fast as he can (still keeping the ball up in the air), go around his partner and then go back to his starting point running forwards. He should have his back to his partner at all times. Then the other player does the same. 3 points are awarded if both players are successful. 1 point if only one of the players is successful. In either case the players continue to do this 12-14 times (6 or 7 each). A note is made of the total number of points achieved by the pair and this score is compared against the score achieved when the players are in subsequent pairings. | It is difficult enough to run forward while juggling the ball, let alone run backwards. A good tip is to tell the players to kick the ball up towards the navel as they run backwards. Sometimes a player who has no difficulty controlling the ball loses control as he watches what his partner is doing. |

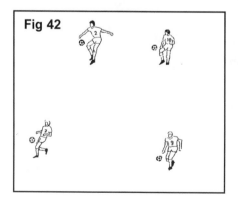

Fig 42

Fig 44

| No. | Objectives | Age | Developing the Games | Common Problems |
|-----|-----------|-----|---------------------|-----------------|
| 43 | Skill. Ball-juggling skills. Teamwork. Peripheral vision. Controlling the space around you. Speed off the mark. Changing pace. | 19-30 | The players are in pairs facing each other 5 yds apart juggling a ball each. Both players kick their ball up high and sprint across to continue juggling their partner's ball before it bounces. If the ball is kicked up too high it is difficult to control and if it is too low there is no chance of getting to it before it bounces. The players run and focus on the ball and often collide. 1 point is awarded each time the pair successfully swap balls. After the allotted time the pair with the most points wins. | The ball is not kicked up at the correct height. The biggest problem is that the players collide as they concentrate on the ball. If they run slowly in order to avoid a collision they do not get to the balls in time. The players have to get used to not solely focusing on the ball (after all, this is what they have to do in a match). |
| 44 | Skill. Ball-juggling skills. Coordination. Balance. Spatial awareness. | 19-30 | 12 players stand in a circle a reasonable distance apart and keep the ball up using their head. After a few touches the player attempts to kneel down and stand up again without letting the ball bounce. Each time this is achieved the player earns 1 point. Any player who has problems tries again. The players who manage this move onto the following: The player continues to control the ball with his head as he sits down. From the sitting position he continues to control the ball with his head as he stands up again. 2 points are awarded for this move if successful. The player keeps his score so that he can compare it to the score he achieves the next time he does the exercise. | Standing up is relatively easy for the players. Lowering the body is the difficult part. The players need to control the ball accordingly as they attempt to lower their center of gravity and not always kick the ball up the same distance irrespective of the body movements. |

| No. | Objectives | Age | Developing the Games | Common Problems |
|-----|-----------|-----|---------------------|-----------------|
| 45 | Skill. Ball-juggling skills. Coordination. Balance. Agility. Heading. | 22-30 | 12 players are keeping the ball up in the air in the following way: right foot, left foot, then head. Then 2 with right foot, 2 with left foot and 2 with head and so on up to 10 with each. If the ball bounces at any time the player starts from the beginning. Once the player has completed the sequence he sits down while controlling the ball with his feet. He kicks the ball up high, stands up and has to control the ball once or twice with his head. Any player able to complete all of the above is definitely a 'master' of ball-juggling skills. | Not taking the right number of touches in sequence. Sitting down without lowering the center of gravity. Kicking the ball too high when standing up. As the ball is to be controlled with the head it is better to kick it up just above head-height. |
| 46 | Skill. Ball-juggling skills. Coordination. Balance. Passing using the head. Agility. Teamwork. | 22-30 | The heading ball-juggling skills continue as the 12 players are put into pairs, 'A' and 'B'. The players are 5 yds apart. Player 'A' heads the ball to player 'B'. Player 'B' keeps heading the ball as he opens his legs as wide as possible. Meanwhile player 'A' runs towards his partner and goes on hands and knees between his legs and then runs back to his starting position. 'B' heads the ball to 'A' and the same sequence occurs. Make sure that the players know that this exercise is very difficult and anyone who is able to achieve it successfully gets more points. | This exercise is so difficult that it is unlikely that all the players will complete it successfully. The players who are unsuccessful should not be demoralized as they will improve with practice. |

| No. | Objectives | Age | Developing the Games | Common Problems |
|-----|------------|-----|----------------------|-----------------|
| 47 | Skill. Ball-juggling skills. Teamwork. Acceleration. Changing direction. Speed off the mark. Peripheral vision. Heading. | 19-30 | Another ball-juggling skills game using the head. The 12 players are put into pairs. They stand 5 yds apart. 1 player keeps the ball up using his head and then heads the ball up high to his partner. He immediately runs towards his partner, goes around him and returns to his starting point. Meanwhile the other player continues to keep the ball up using his head. Once his partner is back in position he heads the ball up high to him and runs around him etc. A point is awarded each time the players run around each other twice without the ball bouncing. When the allotted time is up the pair with the most points wins. | When the player returns from the run he calls for the ball. This is not allowed as the player doing the ball-juggling should know he is back by using his peripheral vision. If the coach is not careful the players get closer and closer together. He should make sure that the distance between them is 5 yds at all times. |

Fig 46

| No. | Objectives | Age | Developing the Games | Common Problems |
|---|---|---|---|---|
| 48 | Collocation (positioning on the pitch). Bravery. Skill. Heading. Quick reflexes. Concentration. | 19-30 | A 'round' 18 x 18y. 7 players, 4 attackers outside and 1 attacker and 2 defenders inside the area. This is a heading game where the attackers pass to each other and the defenders try to intercept the ball. At first the ball is allowed to bounce once but as the players get better at playing the game no bounces are allowed. The defenders can only intercept by heading the ball and if it bounces they swap with the attacker at fault. The attackers are allowed to head the ball more than once before passing and all the players are encouraged to produce 'diving' headers to reach difficult balls. All the players take turns playing as the attacker in the middle as this is a demanding role both physically and mentally. | The attacker in the middle is not involved in the game either because the ball is not passed to him or he does not get into space to receive it. The attackers outside do not position themselves correctly. The headed passes are too high which gives the defenders time to intercept the ball. The players do not understand that the game is about heading and this involves: jumping, stretching, diving and bending the knees to reach the low balls. |

Fig 48

| No. | Objectives | Age | Developing the Games | Common Problems |
|---|---|---|---|---|
| 49 | Heading (passes, clearances and attempts on goal). Practicing 'the method'. Marking. Making space. Jumping. Agility. Stamina. Concentration. Playing in goal. | 19-30 | Pitch size 35 x 20y. This is a 7-a-side heading game. The formation and movements are as per 'the method'. The players should make every effort to get to the ball. If the ball is high he should jump for it and if it arrives low he should dive for it. When the goalkeepers have the ball they throw it up high and head it back in play. There is man-for-man marking and so the players should be of similar ability as far as their heading ability is concerned. The game also focuses on physical fitness and playing as a unit. There are 2 points for a goal if all the players in the team (including the goalkeeper) are in the opposition's half of the pitch and 3 points if a player in the team defending is not in his own half. If the latter occurs and a goal does not result from the strike then a penalty is awarded (as long as all the attacker's are in the opposition's half of course). The 'penalty' kick is as follows: the ball is kicked from next to one of the posts to an on-coming player who shoots 'first-time'. | The players do not anticipate well. Some players still position themselves behind their opponent when jumping for the ball (as we all know by now, this is dangerous). Poor marking. The goalkeepers forget to head the ball back in play. The goalkeepers forget to run over the halfway line when their team is attacking. |

| No. | Objectives | Age | Developing the Games | Common Problems |
|---|---|---|---|---|
| 50 | Heading (competing for the ball, clearances, passes and attempts on goal). Perfecting crossing on the run. Shooting. Anticipation. | 19-30 | 12 players. A goalkeeper in a regulation size goal. The goal is defended by 4 defenders (a 'sweeper' and 3 markers). There is a player and 5 or 6 balls lined up on each wing slightly beyond the 18-yard box ready to cross balls towards 5 attacking players: 2 on the edge of the 18-yard box and 3 between this line and the 6-yard box. The players on the wing take turns running down the wing and crossing the ball into the box. The players in the area compete for the ball in the air to head at goal or clear it. The 2 players on the edge of the 18-yard box do not compete for the ball but wait for a rebound, clearance or deflection and shoot if the ball comes in their direction. The defenders run out to impede the shot if the ball reaches these 2 attackers. All the players rotate positions so that they all get a chance to experience each role. | The marking is poor. The clearances are directed towards the middle of the pitch. The defenders do not run to challenge the players on the edge of the 18-yard box. The attackers do not make the necessary effort to make a strike on goal. Poor body position and crossing technique. |

| No. | Objectives | Age | Developing the Games | Common Problems |
|---|---|---|---|---|
| 51 | Heading (competing for the ball, acrobatic attempts, passes, clearances and attempts on goal). Peripheral and focused vision. Paying attention. Concentration. Marking. Making space. Playing in goal under difficult circumstances. | 19-30 | Pitch size 20 x 12y. Two heading games being played simultaneously. There is a goalkeeper in each goal and 12 outfield players ('3 v 3') on the pitch. The heading ability of all the players should be evenly matched. When the ball drops to the ground the nearest player to it immediately picks it up and kicks it back up in the air for the heading game to continue. As soon as a goalkeeper gets the ball he has to put it back in play as quickly as possible whichever way he prefers. At first the players from the different games may get in each other's way but they soon adapt and pay more attention and use their peripheral vision to better effect. This is a very demanding game on the goalkeepers and so they should be changed regularly. | The players make little effort to jump or dive for the ball unless the coach reminds them repeatedly. If a player fails to mark his opponent the two are never put together in the future (or else the situation is ideal for both of them). |

339

Fig 51

| No. | Objectives | Age | Developing the Games | Common Problems |
|---|---|---|---|---|
| 52 | Heading (Competing for the ball, acrobatic attempts, headed passes, clearances and attempts on goal). Peripheral and focused vision. Paying attention. Concentration. Marking. Making space. Playing in goal under difficult circumstances. | 19-30 | Pitch size 15 x 12y. This is a 7 a-side heading game. The line up is the same for both teams: goalkeeper, 3 markers and 3 attackers in a 'v' formation (one playing deep and two out wide). The game is made more difficult as two balls are used. This increases the number of headers made and makes the players concentrate and encourages them to use focused and peripheral vision. The defenders concentrate exclusively on defending and the attackers on attacking. If one of the balls goes out of play the coach throws another one in play without telling the players. | The defenders attack because they find it more enjoyable and rewarding. This is not allowed as it defeats the object of the game. The goalkeepers keep hold of the ball a long time as they look who to give it to and meanwhile a goal is scored with the other ball. |

Fig 52

| No. | Objectives | Age | Developing the Games | Common Problems |
|---|---|---|---|---|
| 53 | Anticipation. Quick thinking. Control on the turn. Adopting correct body position (always side-on). Feints and dummies. Passes. Winning the ball. Concentration. | 19-23 | A 'round'. Pitch size 18 x 18y. 5 players on the outside compete against 2 in the middle. Apart from making space, passing into the 'light' and using all the available space effectively the game involves: always 'looking' for the ball, receiving a pass and controlling it on the turn. Then immediately dummy to play a pass by passing the foot over the ball or stepping on it only to play a disguised and 'unpredictable' pass in another direction. The player then makes space and gets into the 'light', ready to receive the ball at any time. All the players do the same. The players in the middle have to work hard and anticipate well in order to win the ball and swap with an attacker. Once this game has been mastered the players move on to playing '4 v 2'. | The players take it easy and make little effort unless the coach is there to make sure that the game is being played properly. The attackers do not adopt the correct body position (always side-on). The players in the middle dictate the pace of the game and if they make little effort (which is usually the case) the game is easy for the attackers. |

341

| No. | Objectives | Age | Developing the Games | Common Problems |
|---|---|---|---|---|
| 54 | Running with the ball. Paying attention. Concentration. Visual memory. Visually controlling the space around you. Aerobic stamina. | 19-30 | Pitch size 30 x 20y. 18 players each with a ball run around in this area. The players are asked not to run across each other and to avoid always running in the same direction. The players have to concentrate and make sure they know where all their teammates are located on the pitch. The coach calls the name of one of the players and after a short pause he calls out another name. The idea is that the player who was named first has 4 seconds to run up to the player who was named second. However, once the second player has been named all the players (apart from the first named) continue running, raising their arms, shouting and generally trying to disorient the first player named so that he does not get to his intended target in time. Then two other names are called out etc. | Some players stop running in order to locate all the players on the pitch. The second player named often spoils the game: he runs towards the first player, the others raise their arms and he does nothing or he even shouts "here I am." Strangely enough, the first player finds it most difficult to locate the second player named when he is virtually running alongside him. |

**Fig 55**

| No. | Objectives | Age | Developing the Games | Common Problems |
|---|---|---|---|---|
| 55 | Running with the ball. Paying attention. Concentration. Visual memory. Visually controlling the space around you. Aerobic stamina. | 19-30 | 15 players run with a ball each forming a large circle. 3 other players are inside the circle with a ball each watching them. The coach suddenly calls out the name of one of the players on the outside of the circle and the 3 in the middle have to locate him and run (with the ball) to touch him as quickly as possible. The other players make strange noises and movements and try to disorient the 3 players in the middle. The first 2 players to touch the named player are free and join the circle. The last player to arrive remains in the middle and is joined by the player named and another player nominated by the coach. The game continues with the coach calling out another name etc. The players find this game so enjoyable that they do not even realize that they are doing a physically and mentally demanding exercise. | The players in the middle stop to locate the player who has been named. They should always keep moving with the ball. Sometimes one of the players confidently runs in one direction and the other two players follow 'blindly' when the named player might be in the opposite direction. The named player often gives himself away by not shouting and making strange movements and so is easily spotted. |
| 56 | Paying attention. Concentration. Visual memory. Visually controlling the space around you. Aerobic stamina. Acceleration. Changing pace. | 19-30 | The same as the previous game but the players are not running with a ball. The game is all about acceleration and changing pace which are vital to any soccer player. | The players in the middle stop to locate the player who has been named. Sometimes one of the players confidently runs in one direction and the other two players follow 'blindly' when the named player might be in the opposite direction. The named player often gives himself away by not communicating. |

343

| No. | Objectives | Age | Developing the Games | Common Problems |
|---|---|---|---|---|
| 57 | Explosive power. Speed of execution. Performing skills at pace. Playing at a good pace. Taking shots quickly. | 19-30 | 2 goalkeepers alternate in goal. 3 cones are placed 2 yds apart to form a triangle 5 yds beyond the 18-yard box. 8 players are split into 4 teams of 2. The 2 players in team 'A' (each with a ball) stand at different cones. On the coach's signal the players chase each other around the cones. If the 'chaser' manages to catch the other player and touch him then the 2 players swap roles and the game continues in the opposite direction. The players also change direction on the coach's signal. When the coach shouts 'goal!', the 2 players leave the cones and head for the 18-yard box and once inside they shoot immediately. The players in 'B', 'C' and 'D' do the same. This is a very physically demanding exercise so it is important for the players to take an appropriate rest period in between runs. | Some players make little effort. The rest periods should be long so that the players are 'fresh' and ready to play the game. Often these recuperation periods are too short. |

| No. | Objectives | Age | Developing the Games | Common Problems |
|-----|-----------|-----|---------------------|-----------------|
| 58 | Playing with 2 balls at the same time has great psychological, technical and tactical benefits. | 19-20 | A 'round' 18 x 18y 6 players on the outside and 1 player inside. The game is played with 2 balls simultaneously and the idea is for the player in the middle to touch one of the balls as the players on the outside pass them to each other. If this happens, the player that made the pass swaps with the player in the middle. This game is played with 2 balls for the following reasons:<br>1.To improve concentration.<br>2.To improve coordination and timing.<br>3. To practice getting into space.<br>4. To improve decision making, reaction time and the ability to think quickly.<br>5.To practice performing technical skills correctly when playing as quickly as possible. | At first all the players, including the one in the middle, only concentrate on one ball. The players have to think so quickly that some panic and make unexpected mistakes. On the face of it, this game looks easy and straightforward but it is very difficult. |
| 59 | Peripheral and focused vision. Paying attention. Concentration. Thinking. Emphasis on technique. | 19-20 | 16 players are put into pairs and are 6 yds apart. 2 balls are used and they are passed at the same time, one along the ground using the inside of the foot and one in the air (headed). The players have to constantly change from peripheral to focused vision to deal with the 2 balls. The game is brief because it is very mentally exhausting. | At first some players do poorly both with the head and feet. This improves as the game goes on. The most difficult thing to do is to avoid concentrating solely on the ball in the air. |

345

| No. | Objectives | Age | Developing the Games | Common Problems |
|---|---|---|---|---|
| 60 | Technique. Speed of execution. Quick thinking. Peripheral and focused vision. Paying attention. Concentration. Multi-tasking (concentrating on more than one thing at once). | 19-30 | Pitch size 18 x 9y with a net 1.5 yds high across the middle. This is a game of soccer-tennis. There are 2 teams of 3 players. The game is always started with a volley and it is allowed to bounce once and then each player touches it (first-time) before sending it over the net to the other side. This game is made more difficult because 2 balls are used at the same time. When 1 ball has been successfully passed between the players they continue to control the other. The players have to play at speed and use their anticipation skills to the full. A point is earned each time the ball is sent over the net successfully. A competition can be organized between the players. | Trying to concentrate on several things at the same time is very difficult for the players. The fact that the player is multi-tasking means that he makes unexpected errors. |
| 61 | Paying attention. Concentration. Timing. Quick thinking and decision making. Speed of execution. | 20-30 | Pitch size 22 x 22y. 8 players form a 'round'. 6 players around the outside act as attackers (near the edge of the playing area) and 2 players in the central area act as defenders. The game involves 2 balls at the same time and is a passing game played 'first-time' in order to develop mobility and concentration levels. If a defender intercepts the ball he swaps with the player who made the mistake. | The fact that there are 2 balls makes it difficult for the players. Poor concentration causes the players to make 'silly' mistakes that they would not usually make under normal circumstances |

| No. | Objectives | Age | Developing the Games | Common Problems |
|-----|-----------|-----|---------------------|-----------------|
| 62 | Paying attention. Concentration. Timing. Quick thinking and decision making. Speed of execution. | 20-30 | This is a natural progression from the previous game involving 3 defenders instead of 2. It cannot be practiced until or unless the players master the previous game. Pitch size 22 x 22y. 8 players form a 'round'. 5 players around the outside act as attackers and 3 players in the central area act as defenders. The game involves 2 balls at the same time and is a passing game played 'first-time' in order to develop mobility and concentration levels. If a defender intercepts the ball then he swaps with the player who made the mistake. | The fact that there are 2 balls means that it is difficult for the players to concentrate on several things at once. This lack of concentration causes the players to make 'silly' mistakes that they would not usually make under normal circumstances. |

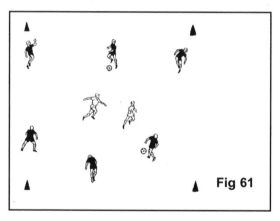

Fig 61

| No. | Objectives | Age | Developing the Games | Common Problems |
|---|---|---|---|---|
| 63 | Paying attention. Concentration. Timing. Quick thinking and decision making. Speed of execution. | 22-30 | Pitch size 25 x 25y. 3 teams of 3 players wearing different color bibs. There are 2 balls in the game. Two of the teams pass the ball to each other while the third team is in between them trying to intercept the passes. The teams passing the ball have a player at each corner and the 2 remaining in the central area of the pitch. Every 10 minutes the 'defending' team swaps with one of the other two teams. All the players should get a chance to play as the 2 attackers in the central area. The team that intercepts most balls and concedes the least is the winner. | The ability to concentrate on several things at the same time is difficult for the players and they lose concentration. This loss of concentration causes the player to make 'silly' mistakes that he would not make under normal circumstances. |

348

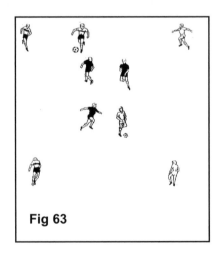

**Fig 63**

| No. | Objectives | Age | Developing the Games | Common Problems |
|-----|-----------|-----|----------------------|-----------------|
| 64 | Jumping ability. Explosive power. Acceleration. Agility. Shooting. Mastering bending the rules of the game (use of arms etc.) Balance. | 19-30 | Regulation size goal and goalkeeper. Various teams of 3 players are standing outside the 18-yard box. The game is as follows: 1 of the players is holding the ball facing the goal, the other 2 are standing next to each other 5 yds away with their backs to goal. The players try 'holding' each other off using their arms and hands. The ball is thrown up and the 2 players (still using their arms to gain advantage) try to head it towards the goal. When the ball bounces the players sprint after it using the body and arms as much as possible until they are almost 'wrestling'. The players then separate and do a forward roll before chasing after the ball again. The first player to reach the ball shoots and the other continues his run to take advantage of any mistake made by the goalkeeper or any rebound. The other teams of 3 players do the same. This is a very tiring game and so the players need an appropriate rest period. | Overdoing things during the first phase with arms and legs (almost wrestling, yes, but not elbowing and pushing each other over). Too cautious during the second phase when the player should defend his position as well as he can. Not doing the forward roll. Not jumping to get to the ball more easily. Contact can only be made using arms and hands but not feet. |

349

| No. | Objectives | Age | Developing the Games | Common Problems |
|---|---|---|---|---|
| 65 | Explosive power. Acceleration. Running backwards. Agility. Balance. Shooting. | 19-30 | A goalkeeper in a regulation size goal. 2 balls placed on the 18-yard line (10 yds apart). 8 players (4 pairs) are 12 yds from the goal. On the signal the first pair stand with their backs to goal, run backwards holding each other off with their hands. On the next signal from the coach the players do a forward roll (starting with their backs to goal), turn and run towards one of the balls. This is made more difficult because 2 other players are hassling and holding the players back. When they overcome the 'obstacles' and eventually get to a ball, they shoot at goal. Each pair takes a turn and then the players swap partners and have a go from the other side using their other foot. Players rotate and experience each role. The coach makes a note of the goals scored and who shoots first. | More worried about pushing than running at the start. Some players are worried about doing the forward roll. Some players show little fighting spirit and determination when being pushed and harried. Taking too long to shoot, especially with the weaker foot. Make sure none of the players get carried away and start kicking each other. |

**Fig 65**

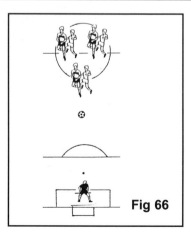

**Fig 66**

| No. | Objectives | Age | Developing the Games | Common Problems |
|---|---|---|---|---|
| 66 | Strength. Explosive power. Acceleration. Agility. Balance. Shooting. | 19-30 | A goalkeeper in a regulation size goal and a ball 8 yds away. A group of players in pairs inside the center circle. On the signal the first pair jog in the direction of the ball. When they are 5 yds from it they do a forward roll and then a backward roll. They then hold onto each other's wrists trying to gain advantage and get the other player off balance. When this is achieved the successful player sprints with explosive acceleration to the ball and runs towards goal, making sure he shoots before entering the 18-yard box. The player who was 'pushed aside' tries to stop him by giving chase and holding onto whatever he can: arm, waist, shirt or shorts. If the player on the ball is not resilient enough he may even lose the ball and the opportunity to shoot goes to the other player. Then the other pairs take their turn. After the rest period the pairs are changed so that the same 2 players do not compete against each other. | The emphasis in this game is to change from relaxed jogging to suddenly produce explosive power and acceleration. Some players never produce this sudden change. If a player gets to the ball but is pushed off it he does not react in time and loses it and ends up being the 'chaser'. Please note: legs and feet are only used to kick the ball. |

| No. | Objectives | Age | Developing the Games | Common Problems |
|---|---|---|---|---|
| 67 | Explosive power. Acceleration. Agility. Balance. Shooting. | 19-30 | A goalkeeper in a regulation size goal. Various groups of 3 players waiting to take part. The first trio perform ball-juggling skills on the edge of the 18-yard box with their backs to goal. The coach is facing them holding a ball. Suddenly the coach throws the ball up and the players stop what they are doing immediately and try to get to the ball first in order to shoot at goal. The players should use their arms to hold onto and unbalance their rivals. This exercise gets the players used to the illegal tricks and techniques used in the game but only allows for hands and arms to be used (not legs and feet). The next 3 players then have a go and so on. After the rest period the trios are swapped and changed so that the same players do not compete against each other. The coach makes a note of the goals scored, the number of shots taken and if the ball was dropped during the ball-juggling. | The players concentrate on the coach and consequently lose control of their ball when ball-juggling. This is remedied by imposing a 'penalty' if this happens. Some players are too 'polite' and 'well-mannered' when it comes to the pushing and pulling. |

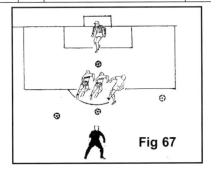

**Fig 67**

| No. | Objectives | Age | Developing the Games | Common Problems |
|---|---|---|---|---|
| 68 | Playing in defense. Playing as a unit. Knowing how to defend with numerical inferiority. Learning to react quickly to simultaneous attacks. Adapting (physically and mentally) to concentrating on more than one thing at once. | 19-30 | This is a 'special' game of '13 v 13'. Each team plays with a goalkeeper, 4 defenders (zonal marking), 1 midfield player and 7 attackers. Two balls are used at the same time and so the midfield player and the defenders play 'deep' and as soon as they win possession the ball is kicked long to the forwards just in case the other team is attacking or about to attack with the other ball. They play 'the method' and so the midfield player always challenges for the ball first. He rarely ventures into the 18-yard box and if he does a defender covers his position. The attackers always stay in the opposition's half and play with total freedom. The game lasts 20 minutes. The team that scores the most goals and the defense that concedes the least are the winners. | Sometimes players with or without the ball (in attack and defense) do not 'see' a move because they are concentrating on the other ball. Some defenders get the ball and start attacking. The coach needs to stop this from happening as the idea is to release the ball to the attackers as quickly as possible. |

353

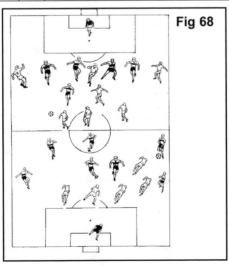

**Fig 68**

| No. | Objectives | Age | Developing the Games | Common Problems |
|-----|-----------|-----|----------------------|-----------------|
| 69 | Defensive discipline (Dropping back, playing zone, covering and swapping for each other). | 19-30 | A goalkeeper and 4 defenders (zonal marking). Their opponents are 8-9 attackers (split into 2 groups) who take turns. All the players get a chance to play in defense (even if they are attackers). The game starts with the defenders going into the opposition's half to get the ball. Apart from being very demanding physically this also leaves gaps for the attackers to exploit. Then the coach gives the signal, 'back' and the defenders drop back to the edge of their 18-yard box. This retreat now makes things very difficult for the attackers. If the defense plays to 'the method' then they win most balls. This game demonstrates the need for the defense to play as a disciplined and collective unit. | When the defenders are asked to go looking for the ball without worrying about staying back at the start, ironically the players that spoil the defensive discipline during matches stay back and play conservatively. There are so many attackers that if a defender makes a mistake it is usually punished with a goal (this is a lesson for everyone). |

Fig 69

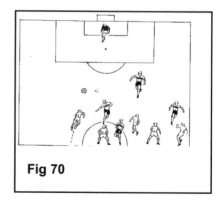

Fig 70

| No. | Objectives | Age | Developing the Games | Common Problems |
|-----|-----------|-----|---------------------|-----------------|
| 70 | The role of the 'sweeper'. Dropping back. Associated play. The attackers want to vary the pace of the game (fast then slow) but the defenders try to prevent this from happening. | 19-30 | This is a game of '4 v5'. There is a goalkeeper in goal, a 'sweeper', 2 defenders and a midfield player in between the 18-yard box and the half way line towards the right side of the pitch. The left side is left empty as the 4 players in the opposition are also on the other side of the pitch. The attackers kick the ball to one another without trying to make an advance. Suddenly a fifth player joins the game. He is given the ball on the run and sprints down the left side of the pitch (this is a wide open space). The 'sweeper' moves across to challenge this attacker and if he is unsuccessful a goal results. Suddenly the coach changes things. The 'sweeper' and the rest of the defenders drop back to the edge of the 18-yard box. The 5 attackers advance with the ball as a unit. The 'sweeper' comes out to challenge for the ball and the other defenders position themselves in a diagonal formation. Normally this is an advantage for the defense and the attacks end in failure. Each team attacks down both wings. All the players swap roles and teams and have a chance to play as the 'sweeper'. | Sometimes the attacker does not notice the arrival of a teammate on the other flank. Even though the coach is present and calling instructions the players find it difficult to position themselves correctly after the change in play. The tactic of dropping back and restricting the space is clearly demonstrated in this game. |

355

| No. | Objectives | Age | Developing the Games | Common Problems |
|-----|-----------|-----|---------------------|-----------------|
| 71 | Marking. Dropping back. Covering. Swapping positions. Playing 'offside'. Switching from a resolute defense into all out attack. | 19-30 | The main objective in this game is defensive play (marking, covering, dropping back and swapping positions). The other objective is to perfect playing the counterattack by turning defense into attack. The team defending always stay back and do not attack. As soon as they win the ball they start a counterattack by passing to 3 attackers waiting to receive the ball. As soon as a pass is made the coach gives the ball back to the attacking team and the process starts over. The counterattack is only valid under these circumstances: when the ball is cleared the attackers start running towards it. It is vital that the players start to run after the kick has been made as when the ball is in the air the defense cannot do anything. As soon as the ball is received the defenders must pressure with 2 or 3 players for the following reasons: 1.provoke the 'offside' trap. 2.stop any individual runs. 3.Mount a counterattack. The goalkeeper plays as a 'sweeper' as the players rush out and the opposition are caught completely out of position. If this happens the move is allowed to continue to see if it ends in a goal. There is no restriction on the number of touches. The coach makes a note of all of the counterattacks played. | There are always players who find it difficult to position themselves correctly as per 'the method'. This is particularly the case when the players are too late running out of defense. This is because not all the players run as fast as possible. The 'pressing' game not performed properly as the players stops 2 or 3 yds from the ball. Some players run to the central zone of the pitch and leave wide open spaces for the player on the ball to exploit. The goalkeeper forgets he has to 'cover' all the space left behind his defenders. |

| No. | Objectives | Age | Developing the Games | Common Problems |
|---|---|---|---|---|
| 72 | Marking. Dropping back. 'Pressing'. Playing 'off-side'. The counterattack. | 19-30 | Similar to the previous game as the objectives concern the defense and the counterattack. The 4 defenders play in a line 4-5 yds from the 18-yard box. The goalkeeper plays as the 'sweeper' covering the wide open spaces behind his defenders when the opposition has the ball. When the opposition has the ball on the wings the idea is to try to make them play the ball 'inside'. When this happens the defense practice this move: they all run up in a line to pressure the player on the ball. If he passes, his teammate is 'offside' and if he goes alone there is a strong possibility that he will lose the ball and the defense can mount a counterattack (these counterattacks are allowed to continue). If the ball is lost the defense reverts back to its original starting position. | The midfield players do not play close to the defenders which gives the opposition too much space to play in. A player challenging on the wing should stand on the 'touchline' to force the player on the ball inside. When a player is successfully forced inside the defense does not play as a unit |

357

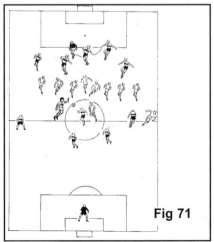

**Fig 71**

**Fig 72**

| No. | Objectives | Age | Developing the Games | Common Problems |
|-----|-----------|-----|---------------------|-----------------|
| 73 | Discipline in defense. Taking the pressure out of the game. The varied role of the goalkeeper. The main emphasis is perfecting playing 'offside'. | 19-30 | 1 goalkeeper in a regulation size goal, 5 defenders in a line 5 yds from the edge of the 18-yard box and 2 midfield players ahead of them. The opposition is made up of 8-9 attackers. The defense plays the 'offside' trap. They play across the whole width of the pitch. The midfield players always challenge the attacker on the ball. If the midfield players are beaten, one of the defenders comes out to try to win the ball. At the same time a defender stands behind him as cover and the rest of the defenders stand in line with this player in front of goal. This move is known as a 'line defense with cover'. The goalkeeper has to stay alert in order to shout instructions to his defense and to intercept any balls played deep that go beyond his teammates. If the defending team wins the ball they try to keep it for 30 seconds. If successful the game starts again, if not the attack continues. | The defenders make too many mistakes. These need to be corrected with constant repetition. The defenders 'panic' when they get the ball and so quickly lose possession again. The goalkeeper is not comfortable with his varied role. He struggles to anticipate and intercept the long balls. |

**Fig 73**

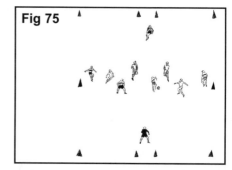

**Fig 75**

358

| No. | Objectives | Age | Developing the Games | Common Problems |
|-----|-----------|-----|---------------------|-----------------|
| 74 | Discipline in defense. Taking the pressure out of the game. The varied role of the goalkeeper. The main emphasis is perfecting playing 'off-side'. | 19-30 | The same numbers and objectives as the previous game. The only difference is that if an attacker gets free and runs into a defender's zone, the latter has to make a challenge for the ball. The other 3 defenders move up with him in a line and restrict the available space the attacker has to play in by playing the 'pressing 'game. The defense moves up as a unit to apply the 'offside' trap. If the defenders win the ball they try to keep it for 30 seconds. | The defense finds it difficult to play as a disciplined unit when trying to win the ball. The players need to time and coordinate their movements. The rest is similar to the previous game. |
| 75 | Playing the moves in 'the method'. Perfecting playing 'off-side' and using it to stop counterattacks The varied role of the goalkeeper. | 19-22 | This is a game of '5 v 5' using half the pitch. Each team has 2 goals side by side marked by cones. A cone on each wing denotes where the halfway line is situated. Both teams play 'offside'. The game starts with one of the teams attacking and the defending team plays in a line as far as possible up the pitch. The goalkeeper is allowed to play as an outfield player when necessary. If the team attacking loses the ball, they immediately move their defense as far forward as possible in a line. The teams have to anticipate and intercept any long passes while at the same time learn to defend 2 goals. Each time a goal is scored the outfield players swap halves. The goalkeepers stay in their own goals. | The defenders find it difficult to 'hold' the line (the coach must correct this). As both teams move forward the playing area becomes very constricted. |

| No. | Objectives | Age | Developing the Games | Common Problems |
|-----|-----------|-----|---------------------|-----------------|
| 76 | Overcoming the 'offside' trap. Teamwork. Rehearsing set plays. Inspiration. | 19-30 | This game involves practicing beating the' offside' trap. If possible the attacking team trying to perfect the technique should always be less gifted on an individual basis than the defenders. The attackers do the following: **1.**They play the 'one-two'. Players come from deep positions to play the 'one-two' with the strikers (the players running forward play the 'give and support'). They continue their run and the ball is passed behind the defenders. **2.**They exploit the space down the wings and play out-swinging crosses behind the 'flat' defense. A midfield player (not the strikers) makes a penetrative run anticipating the cross. **3.**They try individual runs. Of course, in reality this is a collective move: The player on the ball looks to play a pass. One or two teammates move into an 'offside' position on purpose and shout for the ball. The defense relax, confident that the attack is about to end. The player on the ball feints to pass it but suddenly changes pace and accelerates past the surprised defenders. Once the player has run forward he can pass to his teammates who are no longer in an 'offside' position. | The players do not combine effectively. Eg. the player on the ball spots his teammate making a run and he plays the ball behind the defenders but his teammate is caught 'offside'. The coach has to make sure the players practice beating the 'offside' trap time after time or else the players will never overcome it effectively. |

| No. | Objectives | Age | Developing the Games | Common Problems |
|-----|-----------|-----|---------------------|-----------------|
| 77 | Marking. Dropping back. Covering. Swapping positions. 'Pressing'. The counter-attack. | 19-30 | This game is all about the defense playing as a unit. It involves a 'sweeper' and zonal marking. The defenders play the 'pressing' game and of course do not play 'flat'. When the attack is made down the right wing the 'pressing' is done by the left back and the left-sided midfield player (if on the left, right back and right-sided midfield player). However, the 'sweeper' and the central midfield player are also involved either indirectly (covering) or directly ('pressing') depending on how the attack develops. If the defense wins the ball and a clear counterattack results then the coach lets the move develop. If this is not the case then each time the attack ends the ball is returned to the offensive team to have another go. | Once the ball is lost the players have to run back but some choose to stay in the opposition's half. Some players try to play the 'pressing' game in the central zone of the pitch. It is not easy to get all the players to play the 'pressing' game at the same time. |

**361**

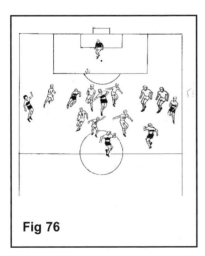

Fig 76

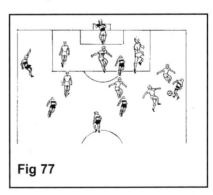

Fig 77

| No. | Objectives | Age | Developing the Games | Common Problems |
|---|---|---|---|---|
| 78 | Marking. 'Pressing'. Dealing with counterattacks. Surprising the opposition. Offensive play. | 19-30 | This is an exercise involving playing the 'pressing' game in the opposition's half. The marking and positions are as per the explanation earlier in the book in the section on the 'pressing game'. The only thing to point out is that the winger on the opposite side to where the 'pressing' is taking place (assuming the opposition's wing back or midfield player has the ball) should come across to mark the closest central defender to him. The defense plays in a line and comes up as far as possible to limit the available space and put pressure on the opposition. The goalkeeper needs to be vigilant and play as a 'sweeper' in order to intercept any balls played into the space behind the defenders. Despite what people think, if the system is played properly it is not very physically demanding. On the other hand, if it is played poorly the players run all around the pitch 'chasing their tails' and end up exhausted. | This system has to be played well or not at all. The 'pressing' game should not be played throughout the whole match. The player on the ball is at a great advantage if he is not challenged by 2 or 3 players and is free to run on goal. Very little physical effort is needed as long as the 'play' is confined to the opposition's half. But if an opponent breaks free then a lot of energy is expended. |

362

**Fig 78**

| No. | Objectives | Age | Developing the Games | Common Problems |
|---|---|---|---|---|
| 79 | Perfecting 'the method'. 'Pressing'. | 19-22 | Pitch size half the pitch playing from wing to wing. '7 v 7'. The exercise involves practicing the moves in 'the method' and playing the 'pressing' game. To help the players fully understand where they need to be at any given time, 2 parallel lines are marked along the length of the pitch to separate it into 3 equal areas. This helps the players understand where they should play the 'pressing game and when they should play normally. | The players are so concerned about playing the 'pressing' game that they forget to play 'the method'. Even though the players are thinking about 'pressing' they rarely do it and if they do they do, it is poorly executed. |
| 80 | Using anticipation to help thwart the opponent's attacks. Paying attention. Concentration. Mastering the '1 v 1' (in defense and attack). | 19-29 | A goalkeeper in goal and a 'sweeper' on the edge of the 18-yard box. In front of the 'sweeper' there are 3 pairs of players (3 defenders and 3 attackers) with each pair 8 yds apart with 1 ball between them. Each pair plays '1 v 1' in a different way. The first pair play conventionally with the ball at the attacker's feet. The attacker in the second pairing has the ball in his hands, volleys it and chases after it with the defender in hot pursuit. The third pairing compete for the ball in the air (which a third player throws up for them). The 'sweeper' has to concentrate on all three balls and anticipate and intervene as best he can. If a striker manages to get past the defender and the 'sweeper' he shoots immediately. The players swap roles on a regular basis. | As soon as a player plays as 'sweeper' his vision, anticipation and knowledge of the game is clear for all to see. If the 'sweeper' makes a challenge he often forgets the defender is on his side. |

| No. | Objectives | Age | Developing the Games | Common Problems |
|-----|-----------|-----|---------------------|-----------------|
| 81 | Taking advantage of numerical superiority. Passing. Shooting. Playing 'offside'. | 19-29 | A goalkeeper in goal. 14 players. There are 5 defenders: A 'sweeper' on the edge of the 18-yard box, 2 teammates 10 yds further up the pitch and 2 more 10 yds beyond these. 9 attackers wait near the halfway line and these are split into 3 groups of 3. On the signal the first 3 attackers run towards the goal with a ball. As they approach the first 2 defenders and try to get past them, the central attacker should always have the ball. If successful they continue towards the next 2 defenders. If they get past these then the 'sweeper' has to try to leave the attackers in an 'offside' position. If the 'sweeper' is also beaten the move ends with a shot on goal. Then the other attackers have a turn. This game should not go on too long or else the defenders become familiar with the attacking moves and the offensive players lose their advantage. | From the outset the attackers do not take advantage of the numerical superiority. Some very gifted players are continuously caught offside. |

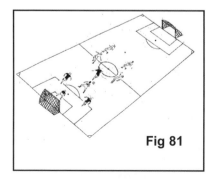

**Fig 81**

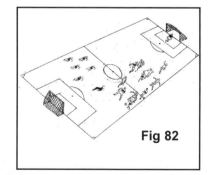

**Fig 82**

| No. | Objectives | Age | Developing the Games | Common Problems |
|---|---|---|---|---|
| 82 | Defensive play involving the 'sweeper'. Teamwork. 'Pressing'. Dropping back. Swapping positions. Covering. Controlling the pace of the game in attack and 'pressing' to recover the ball. | 19-25 | A goalkeeper, 'sweeper', 3 defenders and 3 midfield players play against 4 attackers ( 2 up front and 2 in midfield). At the start the attacking team has the ball on one of the wings. They try to keep possession for 10 seconds as the defense tries to win the ball by using their numerical superiority and by playing the 'pressing' game. If the attacking team successfully keeps the ball for 10 seconds, 5 other attackers join the game. As this happens the defending team shouts 'back' and drops back as fast as possible to the edge of the 18-yard box. From this position the midfield players challenge for the ball and the defenders cover and mark as best they can. If the midfield players are beaten the 'sweeper' comes out to challenge for the ball before the attackers reach the 18-yard box. If the defending team wins the ball they try to keep possession for 15 seconds. The attacking team now play the 'pressing' game using their numerical superiority to try to regain possession. If the defending team is successful the coach starts the game again from the other wing. | At first the defenders do not try hard enough and so never win the ball. Some players drop back too slowly. The attackers do not respond immediately once they lose the ball. When the defenders lose the ball before the 15 seconds is up they find it difficult to revert quickly from attack into defense. In other words it is difficult trying to perfect 'the method'. |

| No. | Objectives | Age | Developing the Games | Common Problems |
|---|---|---|---|---|
| 83 | Perfecting 'the method'. 'Pressing'. How to combat 'pressing'. | 20-30 | Pitch size half the pitch. The game is played width-ways (from wing to wing) with regulation size goals (marked by cones). The pitch is divided up into thirds marked by 2 dotted lines running length-ways to help the players know when the 'pressing' game is allowed (only on the two outside thirds and not in the central third). This is a game of '7 v 7'. The idea is to play 'the method' and overcome the 'pressing' game. Apart from inspirational individual moves the 'pressing' game is overcome by a team playing the ball back to the defense and the latter changing the direction of the play by passing the ball to a player making a run on the other wing. Of course, there is plenty of space there as the opposition is 'pressing' on the other side leaving this area largely unguarded. However, if this move is repeated over and over the opposition prepares for it, so alternative moves have to be invented such as making a penetrative run and passing the ball down the same wing as a surprise. | The 'pressing' game is only successful if the players play as a unit. The same is true when trying to combat the tactic. |

| No. | Objectives | Age | Developing the Games | Common Problems |
|-----|-----------|-----|----------------------|-----------------|
| 84 | Perfecting the offensive ideas of 'the method'. 'Pressing'. How to combat 'pressing'. | 20-30 | This game involves one team dropping back playing the 'pressing' game to stop the opposition's attacks. The attacking team plays 'the method' in order to advance through the congested area. If the ball is lost the coach stops the game and restarts it from the halfway line. From time to time a player in the attacking team playing on the wing will suddenly turn with the ball and head away from the goal (usually the coach provokes this move at first until the players get used to playing it). As this happens the rest of the attacking team start (or not) to move intelligently: the full back and central defender on the same side as the player with the ball make space to receive the ball in order to pass it first time over to the other wing where that winger makes an intelligent run to receive it. As this happens the central midfield player and the midfield player from the other side move across to cover for the advancing defenders. | As with the previous exercise, the 'pressing' game is only successful if the players play as a unit. The same is true when trying to combat the tactic. |

| No. | Objectives | Age | Developing the Games | Common Problems |
|-----|-----------|-----|---------------------|-----------------|
| 85 | 'Pressing' in defense and in attack. 'Zonal pressing'. Positioning. Covering. Swapping positions. Quick thinking. Concentration. | 19-30 | A goalkeeper in the regulation size goal. 4 defenders take on 5 attackers close to the 18-yard box. The 4 in defense play aggressively and occupy the whole width of the pitch. However, there is no 'sweeper' and they do not play 'flat'. Instead 2 'press' the player on the ball and the other 2 cover. To help make the 'pressing' game easier each player must touch the ball three times before passing it to a teammate. If a defender is beaten he immediately runs back to cover for the next defender trying to win possession. If the defense win the ball they try to keep possession for 30 seconds. There is no restriction on the number of touches they can take. Once they have the ball the attackers play the 'pressing' game to try to regain possession. | The defenders find it difficult to hassle the attackers with enough intensity and conviction. Some defenders forget to cover. The defenders play the 'pressing' game a lot better than the attackers. |

Fig 85

| No. | Objectives | Age | Developing the Games | Common Problems |
|-----|-----------|-----|---------------------|-----------------|
| 86 | 'Pressing'. The ability to quickly change defense into attack and vice versa. Playing at a fast pace. | 19-30 | This game is played in the 18-yard box. There is a goalkeeper in the regulation size goal and 4 attackers (team 'A') and 4 defenders (team 'B'). Meanwhile the 4 players in team 'C' await their turn outside the area. Team 'A' tries to score while team 'B' plays the 'pressing' game to try to prevent this from happening. If the defense successfully wins the ball they try to run out of the area with it (going to either side of the 18-yard box does not count). Team 'A' tries to regain possession. If team 'B' successfully leaves the 18-yard box then team 'C' plays as the defense and team 'B' as the attack (team 'A' rest). Later team 'A' defends against team 'C'. The team that scores the most goals wins. | The 'pressing' game is poorly executed. The coach needs to know exactly what he wants and how to relay this message to the players. Once the ball is lost the players do not try to regain possession immediately (they 'freeze and do not react at all). It is also true that the team that wins the ball does not take advantage of this momentary confusion. |

**369**

Fig 86

Fig 88

| No. | Objectives | Age | Developing the Games | Common Problems |
|---|---|---|---|---|
| 87 | Running with the ball. Dribbling. 'Pressing'. How to combat 'pressing'. Controlling the space around you. Peripheral and focused vision. Paying attention. Concentration. | 19-30 | Pitch size 40 x 40y. 18 players and 6 balls. On the signal each player tries to claim a ball and starts to run with it. Those players who were unsuccessful play the 'pressing' game in pairs to try to win possession. The player on the ball tries to keep possession. If he manages to dribble past the 2 players they cannot continue to hassle him and have to look for another player with a ball. If a player successfully wins a ball he cannot be challenged by either of the 2 other players involved in the previous confrontation. This ensures that no personal duels take place. The players should never stop moving. The 'pressing' game can only be played with 2 players (1 player alone cannot challenge for the ball). | The player on the ball is totally nullified by the 'pressing'. Sometimes 2 or 3 players harass the player on the ball and other times only 1 player makes a challenge. The coach needs to correct these mistakes or else the 'pressing' will not work. Be careful to avoid personal battles. |
| 88 | The same as above plus: Shooting. This is an extraordinarily demanding activity for goalkeepers. They need to concentrate totally and intervene constantly. | 19-30 | Pitch size 40 x 40y. 18 players and 6 balls. 3 goals with a goalkeeper in each. The same as the previous game but this time the player on the ball tries to score. After overcoming the 'pressing' the player on the ball is about to shoot at one goal but notices a goalkeeper is busy in another and so turns to shoot at that goal instead. The coach needs to make sure that there are always 6 balls or else the game loses intensity. | The player on the ball makes little progress against the 'pressing'. Sometimes 2 or 3 players harass the player on the ball (this is correct) and other times only 1 player makes a challenge. The coach needs to correct this mistake or else the 'pressing' will not work. Careful with the personal duels. |

| No. | Objectives | Age | Developing the Games | Common Problems |
|---|---|---|---|---|
| 89 | Running with the ball. Dribbling. Shielding the ball. The use of arms. Peripheral vision. Paying attention. Concentration. Stamina. Playing in goal. | 19-30 | Pitch size half the pitch. 4 goals, a regulation size goal, one on each wing and one in the center circle on the halfway line (the latter marked using cones). There is a goalkeeper in each goal. The game involves 22 outfield players and 11 balls. A player with a ball has to try to score in the goal furthest away from him while being challenged by a player. The player on the ball should: use feints and dummies, shield the ball with his body and use his arms to keep the challenger as far from the ball as possible. As soon as the player gets in sight of goal he shoots. The goalkeepers need to be very alert as shots come thick and fast from all angles. | The ball is picked up and thrown back in play immediately. Not shielding using body, shoulders and arms. Players without a ball make little effort to win one. This game is even more physically demanding on the goalkeepers than the previous one. |
| 90 | Marking. Making space. Personal duels. Unpredictable passing. 'Pressing'. Anticipation. Concentration. No time to think. | 19-30 | Pitch size the whole pitch. '10 v 10'. The game involves passing the ball trying to get from one end of the pitch to the other. There is tight marking and the 'pressing' game is played whenever the ball is near the wings. Passes can be made in any direction (unpredictable passes have more merit) and the game is maximum 'three-touch'. Each pass is worth 1 point for the team. A point is taken away from a team that wins the ball and does not start an attack within 2 seconds (there is no time to think). | Some players do not mark and this defeats the object of the game. The 'pressing' game is performed poorly. The 'pressing' game is played in central areas of the pitch. Too many touches are played because few feints and dummies are used. Monotonous play with little variety and imagination. |

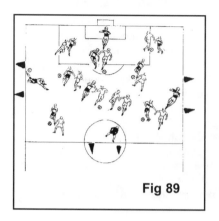

**Fig 89**

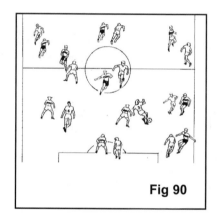

**Fig 90**

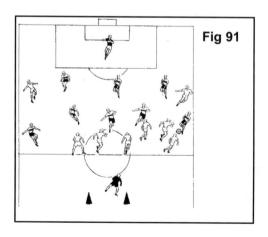

**Fig 91**

| No. | Objectives | Age | Developing the Games | Common Problems |
|-----|-----------|-----|---------------------|-----------------|
| 91 | Perfecting 'the method'. Defensive play. Dropping back. 'Pressing' in defense. The counterattack. Teamwork. | 19-30 | Pitch size half the pitch plus 18 yds where another goal is positioned. '9 v 9'. The formation is 3-3-2 and both teams play 'the method'. Once the team attacking the regulation size goal loses the ball they drop back to the halfway line to limit the space and stop the counterattack. They try to win the ball by playing the 'pressing' game from this deep position. The coach decides when the teams swap ends. | Mistakes when playing 'the method'. The players drop back too slowly. Too many wide open spaces when playing the 'pressing' game. |
| 92 | Adapting to either playing with numerical superiority or numerical inferiority. Trying to slow the pace of the game. 'Pressing' in attack. Developing the 'soccer brain'. Concentration. | 19-30 | '11 v 11' using the whole pitch. The game is maximum 'three-touch' and both teams play 'the method'. The only change is that in this game when the attacking team loses the ball 2 players have to 'stand still' and stay up front which gives the other team numerical advantage when playing the counterattack. The team that has just lost the ball has to play the 'pressing' game to try to regain possession. The 2 attackers up front cannot move until their team wins the ball. Once their team has possession they run to position themselves correctly. If they are passed the ball before this happens and they are in an 'offside' position a penalty is awarded to the other team. | Not 'slowing' the pace of the game effectively until strikers get back into position. Some players do not take part and 'press' the opposition. More than 3 touches. Some attackers do not play the 'pressing' game. Some attackers do not wait until their side wins the ball before moving. |

| No. | Objectives | Age | Developing the Games | Common Problems |
|-----|-----------|-----|----------------------|-----------------|
| 93 | 'Kill' the pace of the game. Timing. Changing pace. Speed. Shooting. Long passes. | 19-29 | Pitch size 75 x 30y. The game is one or maximum 'two-touch'. '4 v 4' (teams 'A' and 'B'). The pitch is split into 3 20-yd zones (1, 2 and 3) starting 7.5 yds from each goal. 2 regulation size goals with a goalkeeper in each. A 'neutral player in zone 1 helps team 'A' and a 'neutral' player in zone 3 helps team 'B' (there is no 'neutral' player in the middle zone and the aforementioned are not allowed to enter it). The game starts in zone 1 where team 'A', helped by the 'neutral' player, tries to keep possession as long as possible by passing it to each other. If team 'B' manages to win the ball they immediately pass it to the 'neutral' player in zone 3. Both teams run across zone 2 and enter zone 3 where a player in team 'B' shoots as soon as possible (the 'neutral' player is not allowed to shoot). Team 'A' tries to win the ball and pass it back to zone 1 where they can shoot. After team 'B' shoots the game restarts in their territory, zone 3. This is a very intensive game and so I recommend that two new teams swap after every 5 minutes to allow them to recover from the exertion. The 'neutral' players are also changed at the same time. The 4 teams can play a tournament. | The key to this game is to run the 25yds as fast as possible and still have enough energy to produce a long shot. Many players do not do both. The players do not play as a unit when trying to win the ball. The coach should make it clear that a counterattack should end with a strike on goal. |

| No. | Objectives | Age | Developing the Games | Common Problems |
|-----|-----------|-----|---------------------|-----------------|
| 94 | Changing pace (Playing at a fast or slow pace). Knowing how to attack (play the 'give and support' or give or feint to give but in either case support. Taking advantage of numerical superiority. | 19-30 | Identical pitch size and zones as the previous game. '9 v 9' (teams 'A' and 'B') with 3 players from each team in each zone. 2 regulation size goals and a goalkeeper in each. The game starts with team 'A' with the ball in the defense. The 3 defenders try to make a minimum of 5 passes (being harassed by the attackers in team 'B') before they can pass to the midfield players in zone 2. If successful the defender who made the pass moves to zone 2 to become an extra midfield player. Again a minimum of 5 passes have to be made before the ball is kicked to zone 3. If successful 2 players in team 'A' join the attack in zone 3 (the player who made the pass and another). Once in the final third team 'A' play the 'one-two', the 'overlap' the 'doblada' and the inside pass to try to work a position for a shot on goal. | The defenders should spread out across the pitch in a triangular formation but they do not. If one player fails to position himself correctly his teammates are also compromised. The idea is to play with accuracy in zones 1 and 2 and with speed in zone 3 but this is done in reverse. |

**375**

| No. | Objectives | Age | Developing the Games | Common Problems |
|-----|-----------|-----|---------------------|-----------------|
| 95 | Understand, assimilate and develop the attacking moves in 'the method'. Keeping the game 'simple' but surprising everybody with quality moves. 'Pressing' once the ball has been lost. | 19-30 | Pitch size is half the pitch. 10 players. A goalkeeper in a regulation size goal and 4 defenders in the defending team. The attacking team has 3 forwards and 2 midfield players. They have to try to develop and practice the attacking moves in 'the method' (the 'one-two', the 'doblada' etc) but without forgetting individual creativity. The 5 players make repeated attacks and each time they play in a different position (center forward, left and right wing and in midfield). The idea is to end each attack with a sudden shot made by a player who quickly and intelligently gets in the position for the strike. The moves should be fast and accurate and the game involves corners, throw-ins and 'offside' etc. If the defending team win the ball they try to pass it to the coach (this is not easy as he keeps changing his position). The attacking team play the 'pressing' game to try to regain possession before the pass is made. | The defense wins the ball frequently as the attackers fail to make space effectively (the latter have to learn to play without the ball). Once the ball is lost the attacking team does not 'press' as a unit. The players have so many tactical considerations to thinks about in this game (making space, marking, supporting etc) that they forget to shoot. |

Fig 95

376

| No. | Objectives | Age | Developing the Games | Common Problems |
|-----|-----------|-----|---------------------|-----------------|
| 96 | Understand, assimilate and develop the attacking moves in the method. Ball-juggling skills. Peripheral and focused vision. Analyzing the game. Being a 'real' soccer player. 'Pressing' once the ball has been lost. Concentration. | 19-30 | 10 players. A goalkeeper in a regulation size goal and 4 defenders in the defending team. 5 players in the attacking team as in the previous game. But this time there are also players in the other half of the pitch performing ball-juggling skills. They try to concentrate on the ball, observe what is happening in the game and watch the coach. He signals with his fingers which players should join in as extra attackers (the players are given a number before the game starts). The players join the game as quickly as possible and run to the most 'logical' position where they can help the attack and surprise the defenders. The coach monitors where the players join the game as this indicates the tactical awareness and intelligence of the players. The players doing the ball-juggling join in on a repeated basis. If the defenders win the ball the attacking team play the 'pressing' game. All the players swap regularly to experience each role. | This game clearly shows that even professional players are far from perfect. The most negative point is that the players lack concentration. On the positive side the 'pressing' game is played well and the numerical advantage is used to good advantage to regain the ball. |

**Fig 96**

**Fig 97**

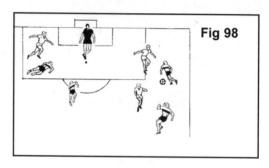

**Fig 98**

378

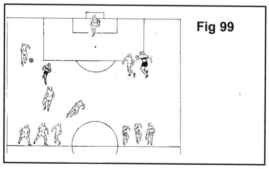

**Fig 99**

| No. | Objectives | Age | Developing the Games | Common Problems |
|---|---|---|---|---|
| 97 | Playing attacking moves 'auto-matically'. Playing direct soccer. Teamwork. Improvisation. | 19-30 | In order to get the players to play the attacking moves in 'the method' without thinking, they have to be practiced over and over. Pitch size half the pitch. A goalkeeper in a regulation size goal. '4 v 4' (4 defenders and 4 attackers). The attackers try different moves and options to beat the defense. For example, the inside right has the ball and the right winger runs inside towards him (shad-owed by his marker), takes possession of the ball and immediately changes the pace of the move. The defenders are now being 'dragged' out of position and the winger plays a pass behind them (down the wing where there is space as he has taken the defender with him) for the inside right (who has continued run-ning) to collect. He runs towards the 18-yard box and is confronted by a central defender. The left winger runs inside and the inside left runs down the wing to the far post. Depending on what the defenders do the player on the ball can play a high cross to the far post or a 'slide-rule' pass to the winger cutting inside. This move and a variety of oth-ers are practiced on both wings. | At first the defenders are always surprised. Later the attackers should improvise moves in 'the method'. The movements and moves are good but technically the play is poor. |

| No. | Objectives | Age | Developing the Games | Common Problems |
|---|---|---|---|---|
| 98 | Play attacking moves 'automatically'. Playing direct soccer. Teamwork. Improvisation. | 19-30 | Half the pitch. A goal-keeper in a regulation size goal. A 'sweeper' and 3 markers take on 5 attackers (2 in midfield, 2 on the wing and 1 up front). The game starts with one of the wingers with the ball. The center forward runs towards him as if to play the 'one-two' but turns suddenly to make space for the 'doblada'. If his marker is unable to stay with him, the winger plays the ball into his path so that he can take it on the run. The center forward runs down the wing as he observes and analyzes the movements of the other players. Before being challenged by the 'sweeper' he crosses the ball for the winger on the opposite flank who has run inside (shadowed by his marker). The winger may choose to play a dummy and let the ball go through his legs for one of the midfield players behind him. The midfield player now has a shot at goal. Another option is the following: the center forward 'drags' his marker and the 'sweeper' across to the wing leaving a clear space in front of goal for one of the midfield players to exploit. When the 'sweeper' comes across to cut out the danger the midfield player switches the direction of play. These moves are practiced down both wings time after time. | At first the players do not play direct soccer and position themselves poorly: if playing the 'one-two' the player runs towards the wing. The winger does not run diagonally inside but chooses to run sideways towards the other wing. The midfield player should run forward in line with the far post to get a better shooting angle. These errors can be corrected with constant repetition and practice. |

| No. | Objectives | Age | Developing the Games | Common Problems |
|-----|-----------|-----|---------------------|-----------------|
| 99 | Play attacking moves 'automatically'. Playing direct soccer. Teamwork. | 19-30 | Pitch size half the pitch. A goalkeeper in a regulation size goal. 3 players near the edge of the area (2 markers and 1 attacker waiting to shoot). 3 sets of attackers stand on the wing near the halfway line ( 2 on one wing and the third on the opposite wing). One of the trios (on the wing where there are 2 groups) sets off with the ball and plays the 'overlap' (the player in the middle passes to the player on the right and then runs round the outside. The player now in the middle passes to the player on the left and runs round the outside etc.). As the trio is about to be confronted by a defender, one of the players runs across to the other flank waiting for a cross. The other two players try to play the 'overlap' to beat the defender. If successful they cross the ball immediately towards the goal where 2 attackers and 1 defender are waiting to compete for it. The attacker who has been waiting runs to the near post and the other attacker who was playing the 'overlaps' runs to the far post. Then the next trio sets off form the other wing and does the same. The teams always attack from alternate wings. All the outfield players swap in order to experience each role. | All the players find it difficult to understand that the goalkeeper and the defenders have to play for 'real'. Poor crossing. The team that has just attacked should wait near the halfway line on the opposite wing once the attack has finished. |

381

| No. | Objectives | Age | Developing the Games | Common Problems |
|-----|-----------|-----|---------------------|-----------------|
| 100 | Perfecting quickly turning defense into attack and vice versa. Speed of execution (physical and mental). Teamwork. 'Pressing'. Switching the play. '1 v 1' with the goalkeeper. Concentration. | 19-30 | This is a '7 v 7' game on half the pitch. A regulation size goal and a goalkeeper at one end and 2 cones on the halfway line (a cone is positioned 10 yds from each wing). The goalkeeper at this end stands in the middle and runs form side to side to try to prevent the ball being 'walked' over the line. The game is a maximum of 'three-touch'. If the defending team win the ball they attack and try to 'walk' the ball between a cone and the touchline (either side of the pitch). The other team tries to prevent this from happening and the goalkeeper runs from one wing to the other, but if a goal is scored the teams swap ends and kick in the opposite direction and the game starts again (the goalkeepers swap halfway through the game). The game is made more intense because both teams play the 'pressing' game. If a player with the ball is not pressurized within 2 seconds of receiving it his team earns a point. The points system is: 3 points for a goal and 2 points for crossing the halfway line. The team with the most points at the end wins. The teams always attack from alternate wings. All the outfield players swap in order to experience each role. | It takes the players too long to change defense into attack. Lack of concentration. If all the players except one work hard to recover the ball, their efforts are in vain. The goalkeeper in the middle has to anticipate and run to one wing or the other. The goalkeepers do not like this physically demanding role. |

| No. | Objectives | Age | Developing the Games | Common Problems |
|-----|-----------|-----|---------------------|-----------------|
| 101 | Playing the game at pace but with quality. Speed. Anaerobic stamina. Concentration. | 19-30 | A triangular '5 v 5' tournament. The game is played width-ways using half the pitch with regulation size goals at each end marked by cones. The game is 'three-touch', involves tight marking and should be played at a good pace. The scoring system is as follows: 1 point for playing a move in 'the method' correctly, 1 point for knowledge of the rules, 1 point for a goal. 2 points if a goal is scored and the 4 outfield players are all in the opposition's half. Each game lasts 4 minutes and each team plays 16 games (total playing time 48 minutes). The team with the most points at the end wins. | There are always problems when changing from defense into attack. The players do not make every effort to play at a good pace. |
| 102 | Stamina. Changing pace. Shooting. Quick reflexes. Paying attention. Concentration. | 19-30 | '11 v 11' played on a full-size pitch. The game involves practicing 'the method', playing a maximum of 'three-touch'. The game ends when a team is winning by two goals (2-0, 3-1 or 4-2 etc). The players are expected to show total commitment and play at pace. The game is very physically demanding, especially when one team goes a goal down. | The game is only played with pace after a team has scored. In general, the more physically and mentally demanding a game is the more the following occurs: the standard drops, rules are ignored and 'the method' is not followed. |

Fig 100

| No. | Objectives | Age | Developing the Games | Common Problems |
|-----|-----------|-----|---------------------|-----------------|
| 103 | Playing the game at pace but with quality.<br>Being a 'real' soccer player.<br>Valuing quality.<br>Creating a good team spirit.<br>Improving concentration. | 19-30 | Pitch size half the pitch playing width-ways with the goals (marked by cones) on what are normally the wings. '7 v 7'. The usual formation and 'the method'. There is no limit on the number of touches. The coach holds a black and a yellow bib representing 'novice' and 'maestro' respectively. If a player plays an exceptional move he is a candidate for 'maestro' status. If he performs another exceptional move he wears the yellow bib. If a player makes a bad mistake he is one step away from being the 'novice'. Another error and he wears the black bib. The players wear the bibs until another player earns them. | Normally the players are enthusiastic when playing using these bibs but sometimes the player with the black bib is unhappy.<br>Some players make this situation worse by making 'cruel' jokes. The coach needs to stop this immediately. |
| 104 | Perfecting the team system.<br>Knowledge of how the opposition plays.<br>Adapting to combat the opposition's way of playing.<br>Understanding and knowing how to exploit the weaknesses in the opposition's system. | 19-30 | '11 v 11' is played using the whole pitch and regulation size goals. There is no limit on the number of touches. The 'first' team play 'the method' and practice the game-plan they will use in the next match. The rest of the players in the squad play in a similar style to the next opponent. The coach interrupts the play in order to correct any move until it works properly. The teams swap roles for the last 15-20 minutes so that the team likely to play in the next match gains a real understanding of how their next opponents play. | The so-called 'reserves' do not play their role well (perhaps it is better to use the 'B' team). Any coach who plays this system will soon realize that there is a tremendous difference between theory (talking and planning a strategy) and practice (playing it). |

| No. | Objectives | Age | Developing the Games | Common Problems |
|---|---|---|---|---|
| 105 | Paying attention. Concentration. Peripheral vision. Changing pace. Acceleration. Quick reflexes. | 19-30 | 16 players (8 pairs of similar ability) jog around the pitch. 1 player is in front (with no ball) and the other chases him running with a ball. At any given moment (the individual pairs do this when ready) the player with the ball kicks it past the other player and chases after it. The other player is waiting for this and as soon as he sees the ball he accelerates to try to get to it first. No matter what the outcome the players swap roles and jog for a while to recuperate from the effort and then do the same. The sprints should be about 8-12 yds. The coach makes sure the players have the necessary breaks so that they are fully rested. Any player who takes longer to recover from the exertion can have a longer break (with his partner of course). Any player who is exhausted should stop doing the exercise. | The players do not make maximum effort (better not to play at all if this is the case). The ball is kicked a long way so the amount of time spent on actually playing is greatly reduced. The rest periods are either too long or too short. |

Fig 103

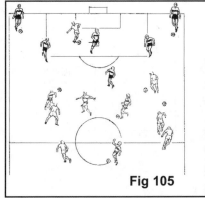

Fig 105

| No. | Objectives | Age | Developing the Games | Common Problems |
|---|---|---|---|---|
| 106 | Paying attention. Concentration. Peripheral vision. Changing pace. Acceleration. Quick reflexes. | 19-30 | 16 players (8 pairs of similar ability) jog around the pitch. 1 player is 2 yds behind the other and the player in front is carrying a ball concealing it from the chaser. Suddenly the player with the ball turns and kicks it over the chaser's head and sprints after it. As soon as the chaser sees the ball he turns and runs to try to get to the ball first. The players should run 8-12 yds. They swap roles and jog to recuperate before sprinting again. The coach makes sure the players get enough rest in between the sprints. | The players do not make maximum effort (better not to play at all if this is the case). The ball is kicked a long way so the amount of time spent on actually playing is greatly reduced. The rest periods are either too long or too short. |
| 107 | Paying attention. Concentration. Peripheral vision. Changing pace. Acceleration. Quick reflexes. Unpredictable passing. Shooting. | 19-30 | 16 players (8 pairs of similar ability). 2 goalkeepers, 1 in each regulation size goal. There is a 'wall' on the edge of the area in each half. The players jog (1 with the ball). The player with the ball kicks it against the wall (he uses feints and dummies to fool his partner) and runs to get the rebound in order to shoot. The other player reacts and sprints as fast as he can to try to get the chance to shoot. The players swap roles and jog to recuperate before trying again. The coach makes sure they get enough rest in between the runs. | The players do not make maximum effort (better not to play at all if this is the case). The ball is kicked a long way so the amount of time spent on actually playing is greatly reduced. The rest periods are either too long or too short. |

| No. | Objectives | Age | Developing the Games | Common Problems |
|-----|-----------|-----|---------------------|-----------------|
| 108 | Acceleration. Speed. Speed off the mark. Changing pace. Changing direction. Feints and dummies. Twists and turns. | 19-30 | Pitch size 30 x 20y. Maximum of 12 players. No balls involved. The players are in pairs, one is 'odd' and one is 'even'. The coach calls out either 'odd' or 'even' and the players chase each other. The player being chased does everything he can to avoid being 'tagged' (changes of direction, pace and feints). If he is 'tagged' the players swap roles and continue running. The exercise lasts for a period of 5-8 minutes. It is important that the players are fresh and fully warmed up before doing this exercise. There are 6-12 repetitions and rest periods in between where the players do stretching exercises. | Some coaches put players together who do not recover from the activity at the same rate. The game should be played with maximum effort but some players fail to do this. The player touched just stops running. |

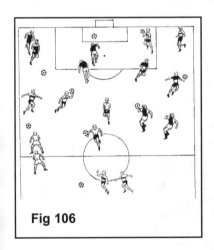

Fig 106

Fig 108

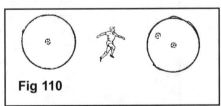

Fig 110

| No. | Objectives | Age | Developing the Games | Common Problems |
|-----|-----------|-----|---------------------|-----------------|
| 109 | Intelligent running and movements. Changing direction. Twists and turns. Anaerobic stamina. | 19-30 | Pitch size 30 x 20m. 12 players (put into pairs of similar ability. If this is not possible use 18 players so that if some take longer to recover the game can continue with enough players taking part). The players being chased need to run in between the other pairs as a strategy for not being 'tagged'. The chase should last between 1-3 minutes. The rest periods depend on the players as they should only continue once the pulse rate is at 140. There are 2-3 sets with 3-6 repetitions in each. | Some players do not make maximum effort. Feints and dummies are not played. Not taking advantage of the runs made by other players to help elude the 'chaser'. |
| 110 | Acceleration. Explosive power. Coordination. Twists and turns. | 19-30 | It is very important for soccer players to have explosive speed and acceleration. The coach needs to know the capabilities of his players and so should make them run short distances at maximum speed. For example: the player is standing in a circle with 3 balls and 3 yds away is a similar circle (no balls). On the signal the player sets off with the first ball and when inside the circles he steps on it and turns and heads back for the next ball. He does this until he moves all 3 balls from one circle to the other. Each players has two attempts. The player who does this in the shortest time wins. | Some players just turn and run once the ball enters the circle (they should step on it and leave it in the circle). Some players demonstrate poor control when running with the ball and sometimes even go beyond the circle. |

| No. | Objectives | Age | Developing the Games | Common Problems |
|-----|-----------|-----|---------------------|-----------------|
| 111 | Acceleration. Explosive power. Coordination. Twists and turns. | 19-30 | If the coach wants to find out which of his players is able to produce repeated short bursts of acceleration (essential in matches) then he can use the previous exercise or the following one: the players do 3 sets of 5 sprints with a 3-minute break between the runs. The break between each set is 6 minutes. This test should be carried out 2-3 times per year and the results compared. | There is usually a great improvement when this test is repeated a few months later. If there is no improvement it is up to the coach to find out why. |
| 112 | Acceleration. Explosive power. Twists and turns. Shooting. | 19-30 | A goalkeeper in a regulation size goal. 4 balls are lined up 1 yard apart on the edge of the 18-yard box. There is a player standing at a cone 2 yds away from the central balls. On the signal he sprints to the ball furthest to his right and shoots at goal. He returns, runs around the cone and heads for the next ball to his right and so on until the last ball is kicked. The player has to shoot twice (2 out of 4) using his weaker foot. The coach is looking for speed and shooting technique. In order for the rest periods to be correct only a maximum of 10 players should take part in this exercise. The whole squad can be split into 2 groups of similar ability. The players stretch during the breaks. | Some players do not make maximum effort. Nearly all the players stand and watch the ball after they have shot which affects their time considerably and slows the pace of the game. Some players forget to shoot with their weaker foot. |

389

| No. | Objectives | Age | Developing the Games | Common Problems |
|-----|-----------|-----|---------------------|-----------------|
| 113 | Acceleration. Explosive power. Changing direction. Peripheral vision. Controlling and changing speed. | 19-30 | 3 cones positioned in a triangle 3 yds apart. There is a player standing at each cone (no balls involved). On the signal the players start to run around the outside of the cones as fast as they can. As soon as a player changes direction the other 2 have to change as well. If a player is caught by another they all turn and start to run in the opposite direction. This is a very physically demanding game and so it only lasts between 5 and 8 minutes. The players should be of similar ability. They rest until the pulse rate is down to a comfortable 120 beats per minute before doing the exercise again. | The 3 players in the team do not recover at the same rate (the coach needs to make sure the players are similar in this respect). Sometimes this exercise is done at the end of the training session when the players are tired and injuries may result. Some players make little effort and so the object of the game is lost. |

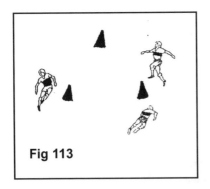

**Fig 113**

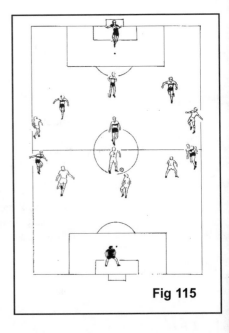

**Fig 115**

| No. | Objectives | Age | Developing the Games | Common Problems |
|---|---|---|---|---|
| 114 | Acceleration. Explosive power. Changing direction. Peripheral vision. Controlling and changing speed Shooting. | 19-30 | 3 cones are positioned in a triangular shape 1 yard apart. 2 players, one at each cone with a cone free. On the signal the players start chasing each other around the outside of the cones. On the coach's signal the players swap roles and change direction. Suddenly the coach shouts "ball" and the players sprint to 2 balls nearby and shoot at goal. The coach looks for a quality shooting technique and makes a note of who manages to shoot first. This is a very physically demanding game and so it only lasts between 5 and 8 minutes. The players should be of similar ability. They rest until the pulse rate is down to a comfortable 120 beats per minute before doing the exercise again | The 2 players do not recover at the same rate (the coach needs to make sure the players are similar in this respect). Sometimes this exercise is done at the end of the training session when the players are tired and injuries may result. In my experience the players make more effort in this game than in the previous one. |
| 115 | Perfecting 'the method'. The ability to beat a man. Anaerobic stamina. Occupying the space. | 19-30 | '7 v 7' played on a full-size pitch. The players play 'the method' but the main emphasis is on anaerobic stamina. The players who do well in '11 v 11' games do not do as well in this exercise. Players like Maradona, Jokanovic, Ivan de la Peña or Pantic would not excel at this game. However, less gifted players with plenty of stamina such as Poyet, Hierro, Mutiu, Arteaga, Soler or Aranzabal would surely do very well. | The players leave huge gaps (the coach needs to establish whether this is due to the physical exertion or lack of effort). This exercise is only valid if the players try their best. |

| No. | Objectives | Age | Developing the Games | Common Problems |
|-----|-----------|-----|----------------------|-----------------|
| 116 | Feints and dummies. A 'feel' for the game. Anticipation. Peripheral and focused vision. Body positioning. Intercepting. Paying attention. Concentration. Changing pace. Acceleration. Quick reflexes. Speed. | 19-30 | 18 players. 3 'rounds' of '4 v 2'. The game involves the following: 'one-touch', positioning, running backwards, passing into the 'light' etc. This game is both physically and mentally demanding. The 'rounds' are played in an area 18 x 18y with a gap of 20 yds between each. The coach observes the games and he holds 3 cards in his hands numbered 1, 2 and 3. If he shows the number 1 then the players continue playing as normal (the coach makes a note of the reactions and who notices the number first). If he raises the number 2 then the players run as fast as they can in a clockwise direction and change playing areas. If the number 3 is shown the players change playing areas but run in a counter-clockwise direction. The first 2 players in each group who arrive at the new destination get 2 points and the next 2 get a point each. The last 2 players to arrive have to play in the middle as defenders. This is done several times before the players have a rest and tally the points scored. The 2 players from each group with the most points form a new 'round' and the next 2 players from each group form another and so on. | This is a very difficult game for the players to grasp. Some lack concentration and/or peripheral vision. Some players set off too late and/or run in the wrong direction. Some coaches show the cards too often. This is not recommended as the players should play in the 'round' for a while before having to change again. |

| No. | Objectives | Age | Developing the Games | Common Problems |
|-----|-----------|-----|---------------------|-----------------|
| 117 | Stamina. Changing pace. Shooting. Quick reflexes. Paying attention. Concentration. | 19-30 | A goalkeeper in a regulation size goal. 10-12 players (in pairs of similar ability) jogging, one pair behind the other along the halfway line from wing to wing. The coach is standing near the edge of the 18-yard box with various balls and he holds 5-6 different colored bibs behind his back. Each pair is given a color before the start and when the coach raises the relevant bib the 2 players sprint towards him. The coach uses feints and dummies before kicking the ball in a certain direction. The players chase after it and the first to get to it shoots at goal. The player has to control the ball and take up the correct body position before shooting so he cannot shoot 'first-time'. The other player knows this and so if he is smart he can anticipate the control, win possession and shoot. The pair then run back to the line and continue jogging. The players jog next to each other with the player who did not manage to shoot now goal-side. Then another colored-bib is raised etc. | Instead of trotting some players walk and even stop and watch. Lack of concentration. Some players shoot 'first-time' even though this is not allowed. Players use their arms to 'hold' others off when the sprint starts (perfectly correct). Some players do not do this and get angry with the ones who do (with this attitude, these players will never make it in the game). |

393

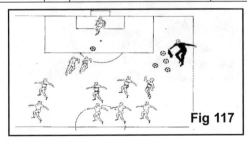

**Fig 117**

| No. | Objectives | Age | Developing the Games | Common Problems |
|-----|-----------|-----|---------------------|-----------------|
| 118 | Becoming more perceptive. Perfecting technique. Controlling the situation. Controlling body movements. Controlling the space around you. Spatial awareness. Paying attention. Concentration. | 19-30 | The players (in pairs and well spaced out) run up and down the pitch. 1 of the players is wearing a blindfold. The other player guides/supports him and helps him avoid any obstacles. The players swap every 5 minutes. The good thing about this game is that it makes the player concentrate totally on what he is doing (on the present moment and nothing else). The player tries to cope and adapt to the new situation and sensation and all his other thoughts and concerns are temporarily suspended. The player is able to 'read' and sense things that he is unable to perceive under normal circumstances. Once the player adapts to the run he does it on his own without any help. As the player progresses with this type of exercise he does the same over a different course but still for 5 minutes. The player is getting ready for a specific exercise at a later date. | At first some players take a while to get used to the new situation. Later they surprise themselves with the progress they make. The players are also conscious that concentration has improved. Some players do not accept criticism very well especially from teammates. The latter should always offer praise where appropriate as well. |

Fig 118

| No. | Objectives | Age | Developing the Games | Common Problems |
|-----|-----------|-----|---------------------|-----------------|
| 119 | Orientation. Spatial awareness. Spatial differentiation. Concentration. Imagination. | 19-30 | Three players are in the penalty box with 2 minutes to observe and memorize the situation. There are 3 balls near the penalty spot and 3 cones to the right and 3 to the left of these. Once the 2 minutes is over the players put on a blindfold and they have to walk to each of the objects and touch them. At first it is best to extend the arms for greater security. Then 3 other players have a go. Before trying a second time the players talk about their feelings and sensations. | It is very important for the players to extend their arms but some do not. Some players have a very poor sense of direction and end up going way-off course (the coach needs to encourage them by pointing out that they have more to gain than others from doing this type of exercise). |
| 120 | Orientation. Hearing. Doing things at pace. Concentration. Mental stress. Manual sensitivity. | 21-30 | The players are in threes. 1 player is wearing a blindfold. The other 2 players are 3 yds apart and 4 yds from the player with the blindfold. These 2 players take turns making a noise. The noise can be made with the mouth, hands or feet. The player wearing the blindfold has to locate where the sound is coming from and head towards the appropriate player. If successful, he touches the player, calls out his name and gives him the blindfold. | The different sounds coming from different areas of the pitch confuse the players and they lose concentration. This is precisely why this is a good exercise for the players (as long as the noise levels are within acceptable limits). |

Fig 119

Fig 120

| No. | Objectives | Age | Developing the Games | Common Problems |
|-----|-----------|-----|---------------------|-----------------|
| 121 | Orientation. Hearing. Dynamic differentiation. Honing skills. Controlling the situation. Concentration. Imagination. | 21-30 | A player (who will soon put on a blindfold) observes the situation from the regulation size goal: there are 3 players spread out across the midfield area of the pitch (left, middle and right). The coach stands on the edge of the 18-yard box holding a ball in his hands. The player in the middle puts on the blindfold and the coach throws the ball towards the goal making sure it bounces with as loud a noise as possible. The player wearing the blindfold has to control the ball and walk a few yards with it. Then one of the other players calls for the ball. The player wearing the blindfold has to perceive where the sound is coming from, position himself correctly and pass the ball in the right direction, making sure he puts enough pace on it. This player has three attempts and then another player has a turn. The players make observations or comments before trying again. | It is very difficult to do so many different things one after the other and expect quality. This is only achieved with hard work, determination and repetition. The player in the middle always passes poorly. Even when the coach stands further away from the action his mere presence puts some players off. |

| No. | Objectives | Age | Developing the Games | Common Problems |
|-----|-----------|-----|---------------------|-----------------|
| 122 | Dynamic differentiation. Balance. Improving the sense of 'touch'. Honing skills. Imagination. Concentration. | 21-30 | This exercise is done in pairs. 1 player is in goal and the other positions himself anywhere in the 18-yard box where he wants to shoot from. The shooter looks at the ball in his hands and the position of the goalkeeper and then he puts on a blindfold. Then he throws the ball up and shoots on the volley. His teammate in goal returns the ball and advises him on what went wrong or applauds the effort. The player has another two shots. The players swap roles. | The players tend to shoot at thin air if they do not concentrate and use their imagination. |
| 123 | Orientation. Action speed. Hearing. Controlling the space around you. Spatial awareness. Concentration. | 21-30 | The players continue to work in pairs and they are both in the 6-yard box. 1 player is wearing a blindfold as the other performs ball-juggling skills around him. The player wearing the blindfold has to listen carefully and touch the ball with his hands and if he does the players swap roles. A competition can be organized timing who manages to touch the ball the quickest. | There are always amusing moments when some players lose any sense of direction and head off towards the halfway line. At other times they walk straight into the other players. |

Fig 123

| No. | Objectives | Age | Developing the Games | Common Problems |
|-----|-----------|-----|---------------------|-----------------|
| 124 | Orientation. Hearing. Honing the skills. Controlling the space around you. Spatial awareness. Concentration. Imagination. | 21-30 | 3 players, 1 in goal, 1 on the halfway line and 1 wearing a blindfold on the edge of the 18-yard box with a ball at his feet. On the signal the player wearing the blindfold tries to beat the defender and shoot at goal (or at the very least keep possession). The defender plays at a slow pace. All the players swap positions to experience each of the three roles. | Even though the defender plays at half-pace this is still a difficult exercise. Nobody should expect perfection. The players make slow but sure progress with this type of exercise. |
| 125 | Orientation. Hearing. Action speed. Controlling the space around you. Spatial awareness. Concentration. Mental stress. | 21-30 | The players work in groups of five. 4 players each keep a ball up in the center circle. The other player is wearing a blindfold and listens for the sound of each ball in order to touch each of the players. He is told if he touches the same player twice. Once all 4 players have been touched one of them swaps with the player wearing the blindfold. Once all the players have had a go they make any comments and observations before starting again. The player who touches the other 4 the quickest (this is timed) wins. | The use of several balls at once causes confusion and even desperation in some players. The players need to concentrate totally. There is a danger that some players find this game too stressful. |

Fig 124

Fig 125

| No. | Objectives | Age | Developing the Games | Common Problems |
|-----|-----------|-----|---------------------|-----------------|
| 126 | Orientation. Hearing. Honing skills Spatial awareness. Controlling the space around you. Concentration. Imagination. | 21-30 | The players work in groups of three with two wearing a blindfold. 1 player stands on the goal-line (no blindfold), the second on the penalty spot and the third on the edge of the 18-yard box with a ball (these two wearing blindfolds). The idea is for the latter to dribble the ball past the player on the penalty spot (who tries to stop him) and shoot at goal. Then the player who shot goes in goal, the goalkeeper stands on the penalty spot and the other player on the edge of the 18-yard box. Comments and observations are made after each player has a turn. The goalkeeper is particularly important as he points out the mistakes (in the hope that when these are made clear they are corrected) and good moves (in order to motivate). | This is a very difficult game and often produces amusing situations. The coach should stress that this game is particularly beneficial for those players who make the most mistakes. |
| 127 | Pre-active 'transfer'. Retro-active 'transfer'. Dynamic differentiation. Balance. Honing skills A sense of 'touch'. Memorizing technical movements. Concentration. Imagination. | 21-30 | 3 players. 2 are standing in goal and the third takes a free kick faced by a plastic wall near the edge of the 18-yard box. The player takes the first free kick blindfolded and then it is removed and he takes a few more kicks from the same position. This situation can be done the other way round (first no visual restriction and then the blindfold). Then the other players have a go. Finally the players reflect on the experience and the sensations. | It is imperative that the player visualizes the trajectory of the ball in his mind before he strikes it. Very little progress is made and the object of the exercise is lost if this does not happen. |

| No. | Objectives | Age | Developing the Games | Common Problems |
|-----|-----------|-----|----------------------|-----------------|
| 128 | Analysis in the changing rooms. Orientation. Balance. Agility. Coordination. | 21-30 | It is impossible to stop a player from hearing so this game puts the player off-balance after which he is expected to perform technical skills. For example: 3 players form a triangle 8 yds apart. 1 of the players does a forward roll and then immediately the ball is passed to him. He jumps up to head it and as he does, he twists in mid-air in order to direct it towards the third player. All the players do the same. They repeat the exercise several times receiving the ball from different angles and directions. | If there are not enough rests at regular intervals some players start to feel sick. The game should be performed as fast as possible but some players ignore this and play too slowly. |
| 129 | Analysis in the changing rooms. Balance. Adapting. Concentration. | 21-30 | The player performs ball-juggling skills while balancing on a wooden cylinder. The player has to be flexible and adjust his body weight and position in order to stay on the cylinder, let alone keep the ball up in the air. The players take turns and each one is timed to see how long he is able to continue ball-juggling on the cylinder. | It is important for the players to get used to balancing freely on the wooden cylinder before a ball is introduced. |

Fig 126

Fig 128

| No. | Objectives | Age | Developing the Games | Common Problems |
|---|---|---|---|---|
| 130 | Breaking the tension. Fun. Getting on with team-mates. Concentration. Controlling the space around you. | 21-30 | The players form a circle. There are 2 players in the middle wearing a blindfold and carrying a scarf. One of these players says "Where are you?" And the other replies immediately, "I'm here". The players who form the circle remain quiet with their hands outstretched at chest-height. The players in the middle try to hit each other with their scarf. If one of the players moves away from the middle the players around the outside use their hands to push him back in the right direction. After a certain time two more players have a go in the middle. The players find this game very enjoyable and it also helps to relieve the tension. This is particularly true if at the end of the exercise the coach puts the smallest and the biggest player together. They are both given a scarf each and the smallest player puts on his blindfold first and then the tall player. The small player then takes off his blindfold and the game begins. You can imagine the laughter that follows as the tall player tries in vain to touch the other. | Players with poor concentration and spatial awareness are easily spotted during this exercise. Some players move the blindfold just enough so that they can see. The coach needs to be very conscious because the players will 'tamper' with the blindfold. |

Fig 130

| No. | Objectives | Age | Developing the Games | Common Problems |
|-----|-----------|-----|---------------------|-----------------|
| 131 | Skill. Ball-juggling skills. Concentration. A 'balanced' mind. Fun. | 21-30 | 3 players. 2 players are performing ball-juggling skills while the third is close by trying to put them off by clapping his hands, running around and shouting. If a player loses concentration and his ball bounces then he swaps roles with the player causing the distraction. The game continues in this way for no longer than 10 minutes. Lots of trios can be playing this game at the same time. | The players doing the ball-juggling skills are touched by the players trying to put them off. The distraction should only be audible and visual (no physical contact is allowed). |
| 132 | Perfecting 'the method'. Understanding the 'logic' of the game. Mental agility. Concentration. Imagination. | 19-30 | This is an '11 v 11' game. The idea is to perfect the playing system by practicing both the offensive and defensive movements in 'the method' The first 15 minutes are played without a ball. The coach gives an imaginary ball to a player and his teammates take up the correct positions on the pitch. The player in possession of the imaginary ball plays as normally as possible and shouts to a teammate and passes the 'ball' to him. Other players make runs and combine and pass and so on. If the coach is not happy with the pass or the movements he stops the game and corrects the problems. The game restarts with the other team in possession of the imaginary ball. After the 15 minutes is up, a real ball is introduced and the game continues as before. | Some players 'give up' or get annoyed but the game is all about having fun. Some players have poor positioning sense. |

| No. | Objectives | Age | Developing the Games | Common Problems |
|-----|-----------|-----|---------------------|-----------------|
| 133 | 'Blocking out' things in the mind. Concentration. Looking to execute moves precisely and effectively. | 19-30 | Top coaches prepare for every match during the week (tactically) in minute detail. They could also do psychological training during the week before an important away game. When playing the games and 'small-sided' games the loud speakers could transmit the sound of the hostile crowd with less than friendly chants and shouts. In this way the player is better prepared for what he is about to face and is not put off or surprised by what he hears when he plays away from home. The player is used to the competitive nature of the contest and he is able to 'block-out' the noise of the crowd and concentrate on performing the technical skills just as he does on the training ground. | Some players are naturally distracted by the noises. Others become noticeably irritated and frustrated. |

403

Fig 131

| No. | Objectives | Age | Developing the Games | Common Problems |
|---|---|---|---|---|
| 134 | Training the mind. Relaxation. Imagination. Concentration. | 19-30 | It is logical to correct mistakes after they have been made. Soccer players think about everything they should have done during the match. The same thing happens before the match as the players think about what they are going to do in advance. They think about how the opposition plays, focusing on their strengths and weaknesses. They think about ways to overcome their way of playing. The players think about their own system and how they are going to put the tactics into practice. Each player thinks about his opposite number and how to play against him. In other words the players go through the system of play and run through certain moves in their heads a few days before the match. This is made possible by developing the right side of the brain where all the visualizations take place. | Some players try to visualize the whole match (it is only realistic to visualize small 'snapshots'). The players do not try difficult moves that require creativity and imagination. The players do not find a quiet and relaxed place to do the exercise. |

| No. | Objectives | Age | Developing the Games | Common Problems |
|-----|-----------|-----|----------------------|-----------------|
| 135 | Relaxation. Imagination. Concentration. Breathe in deeply to supply the brain and muscles with plenty of oxygen. Breathe in slowly and lower the pulse rate. Strengthen stomach muscles. | 19-30 | It is essential to know how to fully relax and in order to do this effectively the player must know how to breathe properly. The first time this exercise is attempted the player should be lying down in a quiet area where he is unlikely to be disturbed. As time goes on, and the player is familiar with the exercise, the location and body position are less significant. Follow these steps in order to breathe correctly: **1.**Lower the diaphragm in order to empty the chest and send oxygen to the deepest regions of the lungs. **2.**The lungs start to fill and the abdomen expands (from below the ribcage to just above the navel). **3.**The chest expands as the lungs are fully inflated. Practice the technique every day. | Not concentrating totally on breathing technique. The players forget to do the exercise. To try to overcome this it is a good idea to associate the exercise with something done everyday (eg. Tie a small piece of ribbon to your watch so that this reminds you to do the deep breathing exercise every time you want to know the time). |

**405**

| No. | Objectives | Age | Developing the Games | Common Problems |
|-----|-----------|-----|---------------------|-----------------|
| 136 | Learn to 'disconnect' the left side of the brain and concentrate on the right side (this side controls the necessary movements for sporting activities) and think of sporting images. | 19-30 | The dominant part of the brain (the left side for right-footed players) controls thought processes, language and ideas. The less dominant side of the brain (the right side for right-footed players) has less to do with words and more to do with emotions and the imagination. So, if the left-side of the brain is temporarily suspended the right-side of the brain can be more fully developed. If the player reflects, analyzes, thinks what is likely to happen and talks too much (all using the left side of the brain) during matches he is likely to suffer an 'overload'. The player should not think about the past or the future if he wants to improve his performance. Instead, he should only focus on the present (using the right side of the brain). The following 4 steps (137 - 140) highlight a good technique for achieving this ability. | Some players are unrealistic as they want to master the four steps at the same time. These should be learned slowly until finally they can be done automatically once the mental technique has been perfected. |
| 137 | Use visualization techniques to help improve performance. | 19-30 | Visualize the match. Find a quiet spot one hour before the match and visualize the activity you are about to perform. Keep trying to repeat these images over and over. Sometimes other irrelevant images come to mind. If this happens forget the image you were trying to visualize and think of another one. | Too many thoughts, images, feelings and ideas are used that have no connection with soccer. |

| No. | Objectives | Age | Developing the Games | Common Problems |
|-----|-----------|-----|---------------------|-----------------|
| 138 | Total concentration on the physical activity helps to relax the mind. 'Block out' all irrelevant thoughts. | 19-30 | Relax the mind. The more the player concentrates and visualizes the physical activity involved the more his mind relaxes. If possible the player should close his eyes. Some players sit in the changing rooms with a towel over their heads. In this way they are telling their teammates that they want to be alone and they establish a routine, almost a 'ritual', making the exercise a lot easier to perform. Try not to think about anything. If irrelevant thoughts appear imagine yourself wrapping them up in paper and depositing them in the recycling bin in the mind. Relax the mind by emptying it of all irrelevant thoughts, sensations or ideas. | The player does not remove effectively (or at all) the thoughts, feelings and sensations that come to mind. |
| 139 | Use 'visualization' techniques before or during games to dispel any negative thoughts. | 19-30 | Dispel any negative thoughts. Disregard any negative thoughts. The player imagines he is a 'maestro' and that he can eradicate negative thoughts as easily as rubbing chalk off a blackboard. He practices this visualization over and over and uses it before and/or during games. | The player does not fight to ignore the undesired images. |

| No. | Objectives | Age | Developing the Games | Common Problems |
|-----|-----------|-----|---------------------|-----------------|
| 140 | Only focus on the present moment. Concentrate on the senses. | 19-30 | Focus on the present. The player uses his senses to concentrate totally on what is going around him. He concentrates on any noise he hears, but on the quality of the sound and not the meaning. He focuses on the volume, the rhythm or if the sound is pleasant or unpleasant. The mind focuses on the visual elements as well. The player does not try to catalogue what he sees but instead he concentrates on the colors, the light and the shadows. The player also concentrates on his sense of smell and especially his sense of touch. Lastly he should pick up a ball and focus on it's weight and texture. He should study the grooves and the pattern and he should notice how it reflects the light. The key to being able to focus on the present is to use the senses to concentrate on quality, making no attempt to try to interpret meaning or significance. | The player focuses on the meaning of the sound, not its quality. Not concentrating on the senses of touch, taste and smell. |
| 141 | Improve concentration. Expand your 'conscious' mind. Learn to increase and decrease attention span. | 19-30 | In order to improve concentration it is necessary to learn how to ignore irrelevant stimuli and focus totally on the job at hand. To help him with this the professional soccer player can use the technique discovered by Sauron to expand the mind. The soccer player has to be fully relaxed and comfortable to gain the full benefit from these exercises. | Sometimes the exercises are not done under the best circumstances. Some players are never able to dominate this technique. |

| No. | Objectives | Age | Developing the Games | Common Problems |
|-----|-----------|-----|---------------------|-----------------|
| 142 | Focus on breathing. Learn to control it. | 19-30 | 1.The player should concentrate totally on his breathing. He should breathe in slowly and deeply expanding the chest with the neck and shoulders relaxed. Then take 3-4 normal breaths and inhale deeply again and so on until the technique comes more naturally. | If a player is tense or in a bad mood he finds it difficult to control his breathing. |
| 143 | Only focus on the present moment. Say whatever you are thinking. | 19-30 | 2.Next concentrate on what you can hear. Separate the sounds, identify each one and categorize them (step, cough or voices etc). Then listen to all the sounds at once without trying to identify or categorize any of them. Think of the sounds as music and let your mind roam freely as you listen. | The identification and classification requires total concentration. |
| 144 | Catalogue perceptions. Be aware of what is happening inside your body. | 19-30 | 3.The next step is to be conscious of the sensations your body is experiencing. Be aware of and catalogue everything that is around your body (the carpet, the chair you are sitting on etc). Then think of all these things again at the same time without attempting to identify them or catalogue them. In order to do this effectively the player needs to be aware of what is happening, not only outside, but also inside his body. | The players are conscious of their feelings but on a superficial level only. |

| No. | Objectives | Age | Developing the Games | Common Problems |
|-----|-----------|-----|---------------------|-----------------|
| 145 | Concentrate on emotions or feelings. Keep totally calm and relaxed. | 19-30 | 4.From now on the player only concentrates on feelings and emotions. However, these sensations should never be forced. Instead, they should come naturally and smoothly. The player gets in touch with his inner self and stays totally relaxed and calm. Next, the player empties his mind of all these thoughts and sensations. If this is not achieved the player tries again, but this time he only focuses on one feeling or sensation. | The inability to relax and stay calm. Some players cannot 'empty' their mind. |
| 146 | Reduce and increase your field of vision. Total concentration. Peripheral and focused vision. | 19-30 | 5.The player opens his eyes and concentrates on any object directly in front of him. He keeps concentrating on this object as he uses his peripheral vision to see what other objects are in the room. In order to get a clearer idea of what 'Sauron' means: imagine the mind is in a funnel and the player has to concentrate on the object in the center. The player imagines that the contents of the funnel (the mind) are gradually being squeezed until only this object is left clearly visible. Then use the peripheral vision to widen the funnel again so that the other objects become clearly recognizable. Another way to imagine this is to think about what happens when binoculars are used and objects are magnified or out of focus depending on the desired effect. | The players find it difficult to change their field of vision. |

| No. | Objectives | Age | Developing the Games | Common Problems |
|-----|-----------|-----|---------------------|-----------------|
| 147 | Imagination. Concentration. Improve your memory. Improve your will-power. | 19-30 | 'Will power' can be improved and strength-ened in various ways. The player can do this by remembering what gave him the strength to over-come difficult situations in the past. If this is done repeatedly it becomes automatic and these feel-ings and sensations can be called upon during dif-ficult times in the future. The player remembers a game when he played particularly well or achieved a personal objective (could be both). The player should make himself comfortable in a chair, close his eyes, and remember the positive experience. He should remember with as much detail as possible: the ground the game was played on, the crowd, his teammates, opponents and even what the weath-er was like. How did he feel? He should re-live the emotions and sensations. Was he proud? Nervous? Optimistic? Was he aware he had such ability? Once the player has relived the experience he should write a few notes high-lighting the positive words. He should repeat this exercise often and re-read the positive words constantly. | The player must have total confidence in the technique for it to be of any benefit. He should be totally isolated so that he has no distractions. Some players are inhibit-ed when they write. They should use their imagination and write freely. |

# Also available from Reedswain:

#185 **Conditioning for Soccer**
by Raymond Verheijen
$19.95

#188 **300 Innovative Soccer Drills**
by Roger Wilkinson and Mick Critchell
$14.95

#290 **Practice Plans for Effective
     Training**
by Ken Sherry
$14.95

#787 **Attacking Schemes and
     Training Exercises**
by Eugenio Fascetti and Romedio Scaia
$14.95

**415**

#788 **Zone Play**
by Angelo Pereni and Michele di Cesare
$14.95

#792 **120 Competitive Games and
     Exercises**
by Nicola Pica
$14.95

#793 **Coaching the 5-3-2**
by Eugenio Fascetti and Romedio Scaia
$14.95

# www.reedswain.com
# 800.331.5191

# Also available from Reedswain:

# Also available from Reedswain:

#783 **Eriksson on Soccer**
by Sven Goran Eriksson
$14.95

#781 **Team Building**
by Rinus Michels
$16.95

#180 **Soccer Coaching Handbook**
by Martin Bidzinski
$14.95

#790 **Maximizing Soccer Practice**
by Stephen Faulkner
$14.95

**417**

#190 **The Weekend Warrior : A Comprehensive Guide to Coaching 8 to 10 Year Olds**
by David Griffiths
$14.95

#796 **Recognizing the Moment to Play**
by Wayne Harrison
$14.95

#171 **Attacking Soccer**
by Massimo Lucchesi
$14.95

418